PHYSICAL EDUCATION UNIT PLANS FOR GRADES 5-6

Second Edition

**Bette J. Logsdon, PhD / Luann M. Alleman, MEd
Sue Ann Straits, PhD / David E. Belka, PhD
Dawn Clark, EdD**

Human Kinetics

Library of Congress Cataloging-in-Publication Data

Physical education unit plans for grades 5-6 / Bette J. Logsdon ...
    [et al.].--2nd. ed.
        p.   cm.
    Rev. ed. of: Physical education teaching units for program
development, grades 4-6. c1994.
    Includes bibliographical references (p.   ).
    ISBN 0-87322-784-0
    1. Physical education for children--Curricula.   2. Curriculum
planning. I. Logsdon, Bette J. II. Physical education teaching
units for program development, grades 4-6.
    GV443.P473   1997
    372.8'6--dc20
                                                    96-43908
                                                    CIP
ISBN: 0-87322-784-0
ISBN: 0-88011-697-8 (set)

This book is a revised edition of *Physical Education Teaching Units for Program Development: Grades 4-6,* published in 1986 by Lea & Febiger.

Acquisitions Editors: Rick Frey and Scott Wikgren
Developmental Editors: Christine Drews and Julia Anderson
Assistant Editors: John Wentworth and Alesha G. Thompson
Editorial Assistant: Jennifer Hemphill
Copyeditor: Bonnie Pettifor
Proofreader: Erin Cler
Graphic Designer: Judy Henderson
Graphic Artists: Angela K. Snyder and Yvonne Winsor
Cover Designer: Jack Davis
Photographer (cover): Wil Zehr
Photographers (interior): Terry Fell and Jim Kirby
Illustrator: Craig Ronto
Printer: United Graphics

Printed in the United States of America   10 9 8 7 6 5 4 3 2

Human Kinetics
Web site: http://www.humankinetics.com/

United States: Human Kinetics, P.O. Box 5076, Champaign, IL 61825-5076
1-800-747-4457

Canada: Human Kinetics, 475 Devonshire Road, Unit 100, Windsor, ON N8Y 2L5
1-800-465-7301 (in Canada only)

Europe: Human Kinetics, P.O. Box IW14, Leeds LS16 6TR, United Kingdom
+44 (0)113-278 1708

Australia: Human Kinetics, 57A Price Avenue, Lower Mitcham, South Australia 5062
(08) 82771555

New Zealand: Human Kinetics, P.O. Box 105-231, Auckland Central
09-523-3462

Contents

Sixth Grade Gymnastics

Sixth Grade Dance

Preface

Over the years, we have met a host of caring, capable, and knowledgeable teachers who believed they needed to do more to fully challenge their students' movement potential. Many teachers were quick to point out that they felt their program lacked not only breadth and depth but also progression. Some of them were frustrated by the time required to plan, develop, and evaluate quality programs for children of many different grades and levels of development. Others were overwhelmed by the awesome task of planning for scope and sequence throughout the early childhood and elementary school curriculum.

We have shown many teachers our materials for teaching physical education, and invariably they have expressed appreciation and encouraged us to make the materials widely available. In 1986, we developed a two-book set with lesson plans for grades K through 6. These books have been used by teachers in both public and private schools in urban, suburban, and rural areas in the United States and abroad. Freed from the burden of long-range planning and some of the daily preparation, teachers who use the books have been able to focus more on enhancing their instruction methods to meet their students' individual movement needs. Spending less time on the question, *What am I going to do today, and how will it lead to what I want to do tomorrow?* allows them to spend more time answering the question, *How can I help each of my students benefit most from the time they spend in my class?*

The units in the two-book set served us well for ten years, but it's always the case that the more familiar you become with materials, the more ways you find to improve them. The most obvious changes are that this edition includes units for preschool children and that the set has grown from two books to four, each containing plans for two grade levels: Preschool & Kindergarten, 1 & 2, 3 & 4, and 5 & 6. We have redeveloped, re-edited, and revised the instructional units in three program areas—games, gymnastics, and dance. To help us establish models for quality teaching and program planning, we have developed and tested the units in real-life movement and physical education settings. Each of the four books features an introductory perspective on different aspects of physical education, addressing "Movement as Content" (Preschool & Kindergarten); "Developing the Program Overview" (Grades 1 & 2); "Developing Unit Plans and Lesson Plans" (Grades 3 & 4); and "Accommodating Individual Needs" (Grades 5 & 6).

Our objectives for each unit are consistent with the National Standards for Physical Education (NASPE Standards and Assessment Task Force 1995) and the National Standards for Arts Education (Consortium of National Arts Education Associations 1994). To help you determine whether or not children have met these objectives, we have added assessment tools that correspond to the national standards. These tools will help you collect evidence of student achievement and make judgments about student learning and teaching effectiveness—a process that is essential in order to develop *performance* standards that indicate the level of achievement required to meet *content* standards (NASPE Standards and Assessment Task Force 1995). Assessment can also help you identify content progression, for example, which parts of a unit have been well learned, which skills and concepts require more practice or need revisiting in a different way, or which children show control and variety in their movements and which do not (McGee 1984).

Of course the goal of this edition remains the same as it was for the first edition: To help children fulfill their movement potential in games, gymnastics, and dance and to further their abilities to think and interact effectively with others while promoting an active and healthy lifestyle. To achieve this goal, we have added some physical fitness concepts and assessment tools in many units.

We welcome this opportunity to help you teach. We hope our efforts help you provide your students with the kind of meaningful movement experiences that stimulate development.

ACKNOWLEDGMENTS

We would like to acknowledge the help so willingly given by the following teachers in sensitively critiquing the units in this book and the other three in this series and who also permitted us to interrupt their classes to photograph their students at work: Ann Black, Glendale-Feilbach; Sara Davison, Walbridge; Amy Kajca, Beverly; Karen Keener, McKinley; Jane Lyon, Harvard; Kay Siegel, Franklin; Becky Summersett, Reynolds from the Toledo, Ohio Public Schools and Janet Frederick, Liberty Center, Ohio. We would also like to acknowledge the cooperation of the principals, teachers, parents, and students in the above schools as well as Terry Fell, Director of Media at the University of Toledo for the photographs of children in games and gymnastics.

Our gratitude is extended to Kathleen Landfear, Director of Reston Montessori School, and to teachers and parents affiliated with this private school in Reston, Virginia, for allowing us to photograph the children during dance experiences. Our grateful thanks are given to Brian Ziegler, Theatre and Dance Specialist, Arts Focus Project–Lake Anne Elementary School in Reston, Virginia (and to the administrators, teachers, and parents of this Fairfax County School) for their enthusiasm and support during the dance photo shoots. A special thank you is given to Jim Kirby, photographer, who brought life to our dance units by providing us with a photographic record of learning experiences. Thanks are also due to Ann Erickson, Curriculum Leader, Art Program of Studies–Fairfax County Public Schools, and to Patty Koreski, Visual Arts Teacher, for their assistance in providing children's artwork from Armstrong Elementary School and Lake Anne Elementary School, Reston, Virginia.

We would also like to thank Human Kinetics and their publishing staff, especially Chris Drews, John Wentworth, Angie Snyder, Jennifer Hemphill, and Alesha Thompson, for their infinite patience and professional attitude and expertise during the completion of this instructional series.

Grateful acknowledgment is made to the following authors or publishers for the use of copyright material: Yolanda Danyi Szuch for "Haiku" from *Motion in Poetry*, copyright 1996 by Yolanda Danyi Szuch.

Finally, we are deeply grateful to family and friends for their moral support during the final stages of this project.

Introduction: Methodology— Accommodating Individual Needs

PLANNING FOR TEACHING

The quality of your physical education program should not be judged only on the appropriateness of its content. Teaching methods also play a highly significant role in the kind of learning atmosphere present in the classroom or gym and largely determine what students learn. In fact, it is important to recognize that teaching methods affect not only *what* your students learn but *how* they learn. Thus, to be an effective teacher, you must

- pursue a deeper concern for affective, cognitive, and motor development to understand the range of differences to be expected and the needs that must be addressed in the educational setting;
- know the purpose and characteristics of various teaching methods and understand the specific outcomes each method is intended to promote;
- commit to developing the ability to address student needs and to encourage improvement on individual levels of ability while retaining responsibility for progress of an entire class;
- be accountable for the methods you choose and be able to adjust your teaching style to help students in varying developmental stages achieve success commensurate with their ability; and
- recognize each role teachers play, the significance of the role, and the responsibilities you assume or share with the students when playing each role.

The more you learn about the teaching-learning process, why students respond differently, and how various methods specifically affect learning, the greater appreciation you'll have for the understanding, skill, and sensitivity required for effective teaching.

It's also important to be able to shift your focus smoothly from content goals to student needs, trying to match methodology with the needs of students in relation to existing conditions. Effective teachers realize that true gratification is realized more often both by their students and themselves when they are successful in sensitively orchestrating changes in focus to match the needs of the students with the purpose of the lesson.

You will learn that to be truly successful in teaching it's essential for you to

- know the content and the objectives of the unit;
- prepare lessons considering student strengths, weaknesses, and needs as well as concentrating on a plan for teaching that addresses cognitive, affective, and motor objectives commensurate with the abilities of the students;
- remain attuned to the needs of students and to your objectives as you teach, making adjustments based on perceived needs;
- observe carefully and respond thoughtfully to individual and class strengths, weaknesses, and needs; and
- be sensitive in the selection of appropriate teaching behavior, matching the requisites of the situation with your ability to respond professionally.

The learning experiences (tasks) in the unit plans in each of the four books in this instructional series have been prepared to help you focus on instructional content, the needs of your students, and the teaching-learning processes. The experiences have been based on the feedback of hundreds of students who participated in similar experiences. The tasks in each of the teaching units were written with two objectives in mind: (1) to help you select and develop appropriate content to assist you with what to teach and (2) to demonstrate methodology by stating tasks as they might be given to a class to give you verbatim examples of how to teach.

Important factors that distinguish your personal teaching style from others are your knowledge of the kinds of decisions you make when teaching and your sensitivity for and the value you place on the benefits derived through sharing the decision-making responsibility with your students. Expertise in teaching is determined largely by your knowledge of the content to be taught and your philosophy on teaching, which influences the decisions you choose to keep and which you allow the students to make. No matter what your philosophy, for your teaching to be effective, you'll need a variety of learning experiences (tasks) in each lesson that challenge all students to achieve at their level of ability. Sequencing tasks in meaningful progression to encourage each individual to achieve is a continuous challenge. Of course, the most effective teachers are always pursuing better ways to make learning more exciting for students.

A systematic model for clarifying types of learning experiences (tasks) can be extremely useful in helping you understand that the type of task you give should be closely aligned to the needs of your students. The closer your choices match these needs, the more likely it is that you and the students will have a gratifying experience. Let's examine the classification of tasks used in developing, sequencing, and categorizing those in this series. They are as follows:

Organizing task—adjusts or influences the arrangement of the class or individuals
Basic task—initial or introductory task used when introducing a new idea
Refining task—helps students improve some aspect of performance
Extending task—changes the degree of difficulty of a previous task
Applying task—provides opportunities to use previously learned movement skills

(Rink 1981 and Barrett 1984 provided the origins of this system for classifying tasks.)

To develop or improve your ability to differentiate the kinds of tasks, we suggest you keep a finger on this page and turn to one of the units in the book and practice classifying each of the tasks. Identify each task by type with the following letters: **B** for Basic, **R** for Refining, **E** for Extending, **A** for Applying, and **O** for Organizing.

It's important to remember that *extending* is used either in increasing or decreasing the degree of difficulty of a learning experience. As you plan your lessons and as you teach, you'll need to purposely plan ways and means to increase and decrease the complexity of the tasks to accommodate individual differences. For those students whose performance satisfies the requisites of a task, you need to consider devising an extending task that will challenge further achievement. For those not achieving satisfaction in their performance, you must decide whether giving them more time to spend with the same task or decreasing the requisites of the original task is best. While success in teaching and the achievement made by students are a result of many factors working in harmony, both are often reflective of your ability to classify tasks accurately and to match the selection of tasks with the needs of the students.

ACCOMMODATING INDIVIDUAL NEEDS

Teachers using the resource units in this set of four books for program development are encouraged to interpret the units in ways that are personally meaningful and with an approach to teaching that accommodates the needs of their students. Lessons need to be personally designed by each teacher to fit the time frame imposed by individual teaching schedules and make best use of available teaching facilities. Then select a unit from games, gymnastics, or dance, noting the content of the unit. Following the selection of the unit, familiarize yourself with its content and reflect on the capabilities of your class. Refer to the Movement Framework (pp. x–xi) and the guide to progression (p. xii); note where the content of the unit is categorized in the Movement Framework and how the focus of the unit relates to a specific theme or themes. Before sketching your plans for a series of lessons, take time to study the units, noticing especially these characteristics:

1. Each unit offers the potential for designing several learning experiences (tasks). The number of tasks will vary depending on the focus of the lesson, the nature of the task, and the ability and needs of the students.
2. The way tasks are phrased determines whether students are encouraged to seek a variety of responses or whether they're being directed toward developing the same response. It's important to realize that both are important and the objective for giving the task should determine the nature of the response.
3. Tasks may be focused on cognitive, affective, and/or motor development.
4. Tasks may be repeated within a lesson or from lesson to lesson.
5. Ultimately, the teaching progression is determined by the teacher to fit student needs and is likely to differ from class to class even when the classes are at the same grade level and taught by the same teacher.
6. Tasks taken verbatim from the book are marked with the number listed in the unit.
7. The classification of the task is listed following each task.

The Movement Framework

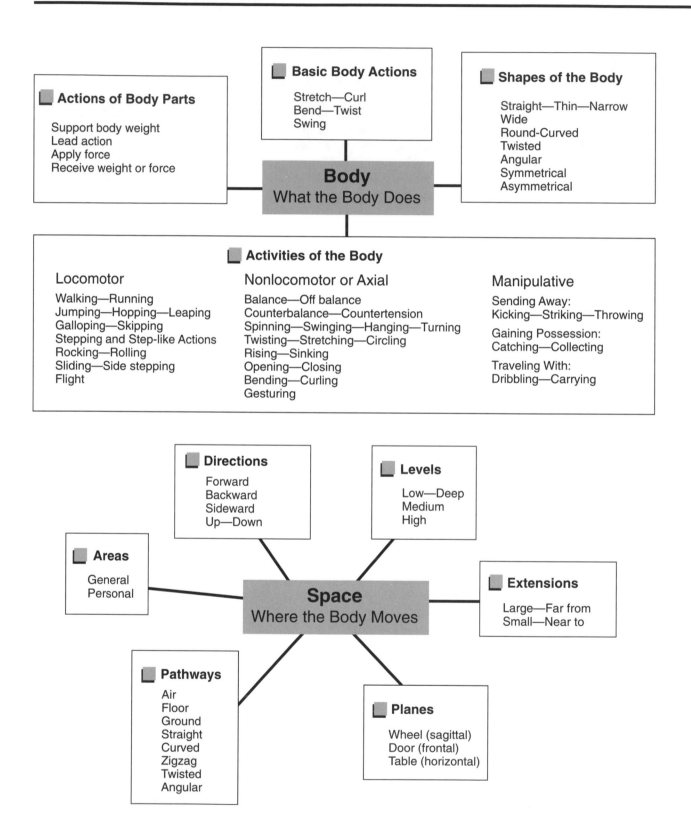

Actions of Body Parts

Support body weight
Lead action
Apply force
Receive weight or force

Basic Body Actions

Stretch—Curl
Bend—Twist
Swing

Shapes of the Body

Straight—Thin—Narrow
Wide
Round-Curved
Twisted
Angular
Symmetrical
Asymmetrical

Body
What the Body Does

Activities of the Body

Locomotor

Walking—Running
Jumping—Hopping—Leaping
Galloping—Skipping
Stepping and Step-like Actions
Rocking—Rolling
Sliding—Side stepping
Flight

Nonlocomotor or Axial

Balance—Off balance
Counterbalance—Countertension
Spinning—Swinging—Hanging—Turning
Twisting—Stretching—Circling
Rising—Sinking
Opening—Closing
Bending—Curling
Gesturing

Manipulative

Sending Away:
Kicking—Striking—Throwing

Gaining Possession:
Catching—Collecting

Traveling With:
Dribbling—Carrying

Directions

Forward
Backward
Sideward
Up—Down

Levels

Low—Deep
Medium
High

Areas

General
Personal

Space
Where the Body Moves

Extensions

Large—Far from
Small—Near to

Pathways

Air
Floor
Ground
Straight
Curved
Zigzag
Twisted
Angular

Planes

Wheel (sagittal)
Door (frontal)
Table (horizontal)

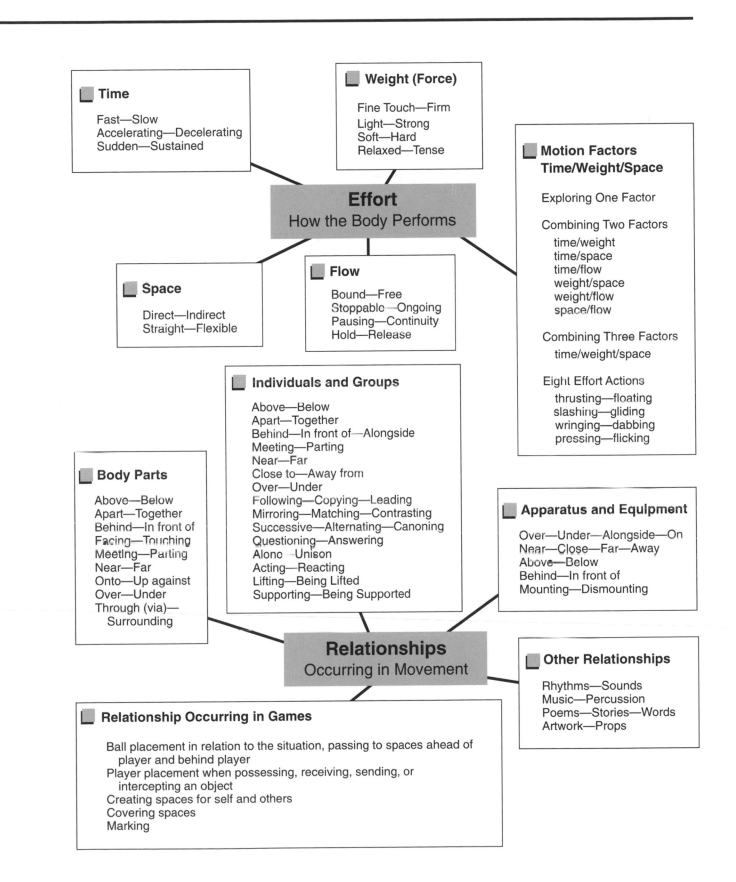

Time

Fast—Slow
Accelerating—Decelerating
Sudden—Sustained

Weight (Force)

Fine Touch—Firm
Light—Strong
Soft—Hard
Relaxed—Tense

Effort
How the Body Performs

Motion Factors
Time/Weight/Space

Exploring One Factor

Combining Two Factors
  time/weight
  time/space
  time/flow
  weight/space
  weight/flow
  space/flow

Combining Three Factors
  time/weight/space

Eight Effort Actions
  thrusting—floating
  slashing—gliding
  wringing—dabbing
  pressing—flicking

Space

Direct—Indirect
Straight—Flexible

Flow

Bound—Free
Stoppable—Ongoing
Pausing—Continuity
Hold—Release

Individuals and Groups

Above—Below
Apart—Together
Behind—In front of—Alongside
Meeting—Parting
Near—Far
Close to—Away from
Over—Under
Following—Copying—Leading
Mirroring—Matching—Contrasting
Successive—Alternating—Canoning
Questioning—Answering
Alone—Unison
Acting—Reacting
Lifting—Being Lifted
Supporting—Being Supported

Body Parts

Above—Below
Apart—Together
Behind—In front of
Facing—Touching
Meeting—Parting
Near—Far
Onto—Up against
Over—Under
Through (via)—
  Surrounding

Apparatus and Equipment

Over—Under—Alongside—On
Near—Close—Far—Away
Above—Below
Behind—In front of
Mounting—Dismounting

Relationships
Occurring in Movement

Other Relationships

Rhythms—Sounds
Music—Percussion
Poems—Stories—Words
Artwork—Props

Relationship Occurring in Games

Ball placement in relation to the situation, passing to spaces ahead of
  player and behind player
Player placement when possessing, receiving, sending, or
  intercepting an object
Creating spaces for self and others
Covering spaces
Marking

Movement Themes: A Guide for Planning Teaching Progression

	PK	K	1	2	3	4	5	6
Theme 1 Games Gymnastics Dance								
Theme 2 Games Gymnastics Dance								
Theme 3 Games Gymnastics Dance								
Theme 4 Games Gymnastics Dance								
Theme 5 Games Gymnastics Dance								
Theme 6 Games Gymnastics Dance								
Theme 7 Games Gymnastics Dance								
Theme 8 Gymnastics Dance								
Theme 9 Dance								
Theme 10 Dance								

Key for content selection: ·············· Introduced

━━━━━━━━ Emphasized

————▶ Continues

Creating a Series of Lessons

Each unit in this set of books is designed to be interpreted individually by teachers for their specific students. We recommend outlining the learning experiences for a progressive series of lessons as the first step in this process to help ensure that class time is used effectively and the teaching-learning progression is best served. *Following is a sample for projecting progression in a series of four lessons using Grade 6, Gymnastics Unit 2 on counterbalance and countertension.*

Planning for Progression

Lesson 1 Learning Experiences

Today to develop countertension, you place your base of support very close to you partner's base of support and lean away until your balance depends on your partner. Let's see how you can carefully hold on to someone, place your base of support close to each other, and gently, both at the same time, lean away until you are forming one balance, each dependent upon the other for support. Select someone about the same height and weight as you, a place where you can work safely, and begin. (Basic task 1.0.)

Don't let any part of your body sag. Make yourself feel like you are a block of wood. Let your whole body lean away from each other slowly and carefully. When you feel you are dependent upon each other for balance, slowly pull up toward your partner to regain your individual balance and lean away again, perhaps holding on to each other in a different way. (New refining task.)

Try a new base of support, moving your new base of support close to each other. Hold on to each other and start to lean away at the same time. See if you both can gently lean away until you achieve counterbalance. Then carefully regain your independent balance and select a new base and lean away again. (New applying task.)

First, try to feel the countertension developing as you lean away from your partner. When both of you sense you are mutually supported by your partner, carefully plan the body part which is going to receive your weight when you release your hold and begin to travel independently out of your partner balance. (Extending task 1.1.)

Communicate with your partner so you both know to leave your counterbalance safely at the same time. (New refining task.)

Each time as you and your partner travel out of your balance created by countertension, make your body lines sharp and clear by maintaining alertness in all parts of your body. Each of you arrive carefully into an independent balance and hold it for a moment. Then start over again and make a new countertension balance. (Refining task 1.3.)

Keep trying new bases of support. If you are feeling successful, try working with new partners. (New extending/organizing task.)

Lesson 2 Learning Experiences

Continue experimenting with countertension today. Some of you might like to begin your work by creating a balance showing countertension with you and your partner balanced on top of or holding onto a piece of apparatus. Take extra care as you release your partner because you both must be ready to travel on your own. You may need to be prepared to land on the mat or floor as you travel off the apparatus. (Extending task 1.5.)

To develop counterbalance, lean against your partner or apparatus. Together, gradually move your base of support away from each other until you become dependent upon the other for support and balance. Then move your base back close to your partner's. (New basic task 1.0, rephrased to focus on counterbalance.)

When you come out of your counterbalance, establish another relationship with your partner. Lean against each other with a different part or side of your body touching. Then again slowly edge your base of support away from your partner's returning to your own base of support again after you feel dependency on each other for balance. Carefully return to your own base of support. (New refining task [1.1 rephrased].)

Keep experimenting with counterbalances by changing bases of support and/or creating different partner relationships. (New applying task.)

Each time as you and your partner travel out of your balance created by counterbalance, make your body lines sharp and clear by maintaining alertness in all parts of your body. Each of you arrive carefully into an independent balance and hold it for a moment. Then start over again and create a different counterbalance. (Refining task 1.3.)

Create a counterbalance where both of you can lower your center of gravity. Then maybe adding another body part to your base, travel safely away from each other by performing a recognizable, gymnastic movement. (New extending task [1.2 rephrased].)

Each time as you travel away from each other, make your body lines sharp and clear by maintaining alertness in all body parts and arrive carefully into an independent balance and hold it for a moment. Then begin again creating a new counterbalance. (Refining task 1.3.)

Work with a different person and share your favorite counterbalance and way of traveling out of it. Remember to communicate carefully so your movements are synchronized. (New organizing/refining task.)

Lesson 3 Learning Experiences

Let's start today by paying closer attention to what you choose to do and how you perform as you come out of your partner balances. Try to make your individual movement represent your best gymnastic talent. Think "performance" all of the time. Decide with a partner whether you will start in counterbalance or countertension and begin. (Basic/refining task 3.0.)

Begin away from your partner (and apparatus). Plan how you are going to travel to your partner (or apparatus). Try to perfect your movement to look like a performer all of the time. (Extending/refining task 3.l.)

After you lean away from your partner to create countertension, you may want to carefully pull back so you are close to your partner instead of traveling immediately out of your balanced position. Returning close together creates stability over your own base which gives each of you more options in how you choose to travel apart. (New refining task.)

See if you can add a little variety in the way you are traveling away from and back to your partner. Some of you are doing all rolls. (Name the activity observed most; if necessary, suggest alternatives.) (Extending task 4.l.)

Work on maintaining your best performance posture and try to rid your sequence of all unplanned movements. (New refining task.)

Watch your partner as you perform your sequence. Constantly show each other a caring performance attitude. Try to remember the two of you are performing as a unit to create a skillful, smooth flowing, gymnastic sequence. (Refining task 3.3.)

For those who would like, we will give you a chance to share your work with the class. Polish your two balances a few more minutes and try to eliminate all unplanned movement, then have a seat. (New refining task.)

Those of you in this part of the room who care to share your work, stand up and take your starting position. I'll not start you. Just begin when you both are ready. Everyone make it a real show by holding your finishing position very still until all have stopped. (Call on those in other areas of the room to perform until all those who wish have shared.) (New organizing/applying task.)

Lesson 4 Learning Experiences

(This lesson format could be repeated in a variety of ways to create other lessons, i.e., selecting a different option; linking two options together into one longer sequence.)

Begin today by trying to repeat the partner sequence you polished in the last class. Remember you traveled into and out of two balances—one with countertension and one demonstrating counterbalance. Basic/organizing task (3.1 rephrased.)

You and your partner read and discuss the posted options and decide on one challenge for the two of you. After selecting your option, join with others, if that is your choice, find a space, and begin. (Basic/organizing task.)

Posted Options:

1. Select new partners and teach each other the balances created with your previous partner. Then combine all balances into one long sequence. (Organizing/extending task.)
2. You and your present partner work together to expand the sequence to include balances where you are either on top of the apparatus or use the apparatus in some way for support when counterbalancing. (Extending task 1.5.)
3. You and your present partner join with another pair or two and work up a sequence of balances involving countertension and counterbalance in which your group of 4 (or 6) interchange partners each time a different balance is created. (Organizing/extending task 5.0.)

Take care and watch the (space/speed) you use as you travel away from and toward your partner so you can duplicate your performance each time you repeat it. (Determine whether space, speed, or both need to be the focus. It is usually best to focus on one at a time at first.) (Refining task 4.2.)

If working with apparatus to create a balance, give special attention to where you locate your base in relation to the apparatus. Remember, your base of support will be close to the apparatus if leaning away in countertension and far from the apparatus if leaning toward the apparatus preparing to create counterbalance. (New refining task.)

See if you can add a little variety in the way you are traveling away from and back to your partner. Try to select a different gymnastic movement to perform each time you move out of a balance. (Extending task 4.1.)

Remember, move back close together after creating a counterbalance where you both have an independent, stable position. A stable position gives you more options to choose from when traveling apart. (New refining task.)

Have you tried to develop countertension or counterbalance with three or more people? Some of you might want to try it, and if successful, add it to your sequence. (Organizing/extending task 5.0.)

Take a moment to get the rough edges of your performance worked out of your routine. Concentrate on posture, focus, and synchronizing your departures and arrivals away from and back to each balance. (Note refining task 5.1.) You should be pleased with your performance. Let's enjoy the results of your dedicated work. (Give everyone an opportunity to share.) (Organizing task 5.2.)

Second Phase of Accommodating Individual Needs

The second phase in preparation for personalizing instruction is recalling and incorporating additional information you have or can garner from specific resources and past experiences. To expand your view of personalizing instruction, the planning format on page xvii draws attention to several concerns sensitive teachers consider in planning to accommodate student needs. These concerns focus on all three basic areas of development and instruction, cognitive, affective, and psychomotor, and provide a format designed to keep all three aspects of development constantly in focus in every step of the planning, teaching, and assessment process.

The first two aspects of development, cognitive and affective, are too frequently neglected in the early stages. Often these are the areas of development that receive the least attention both in planning the lesson and when actually teaching. When cognitive enrichment in physical education is neglected, student's lack of relevant knowledge often limits or deters skill acquisition. Growth in skill development when blocked for lack of knowledge and understanding of the content being taught often causes the student to withdraw and fall behind. When this happens, learning is slowed or stops and the lack of personal satisfaction experienced through success and accomplishment takes its toll. Students often unknowingly, even to themselves, develop avoidance behaviors that further compound efforts by teachers to reach them. Identifying behaviors during the planning process that need to be taught or modified in a lesson because of the content focus and/or the structure of the class can help teachers circumvent problems. This often can be accomplished by attending to all three areas of development through sensitive sequencing and phrasing of tasks so a foundation of knowledge, skill, and concern for themselves and others is developed by the students. Teachers who are sensitive to the cause and effect of a variety of conditions which can or should occur in the teaching environment often have developed teaching techniques to influence or improve appropriate behaviors. See if you can detect examples of foresight in the planning format on page xxi.

Once you have selected appropriate content and planned for divergent needs of students, you'll find yourself playing many different roles, purposely or subconsciously, as you teach each lesson. The following is the script taken from a multimedia program and the caricatures depict an artist's interpretation of fourteen important roles teachers need to play to positively affect the teaching-learning process.

TEACHERS ARE CHARACTERS

Teachers are characters. Good teachers play many highly varied roles. Each role requires a different kind of sensitivity and a specific set of skills. Learning the roles and knowing when each role is most appropriate is the basis for effective teaching.

Planning Format for Accommodating Individual Needs and Encouraging Affective, Cognitive, and Motor Development

Learning Experiences

Let's be very careful of one another when working on counterbalance or countertension. Remember to develop countertension, you place your base of support very close to your partner's base of support or to the apparatus and lean away until your balance depends on your partner or the apparatus. Be sure both people know when to move out of your balance to change your base of support.

(Task Type—BASIC [B])

Let's see how you can carefully hold on to someone, placing your bases of support close to each other, and gently lean away until you are forming one balance, each dependent upon the other for support and balance. Select someone about your height and weight, a place where you can work safely, and begin.

Accommodating Individual Needs

Observe partner selection—Help those having difficulty matching up with a partner.

- If the number of students is uneven, group three who appear to understand the concept of countertension.

EXTENDING TASKS

Decreasing challenge:

Look for those having difficulty. Provide verbal cues for leaning away from their base at the same time.

Increasing challenge:

Challenge those successful in creating and maintaining countertension to change their base of support.

Improving Cognitive and Affective Behavior

Affective: Responding to partner selection.

- You did a great job of matching your height and weight to your partner.
- Great! You got a partner quickly!

Affective: Developing mutual confidence.

- Trust each other as you lean away.
- Your balance depends on each other.

Cognitive: Observing proximity of bases of support.

- In countertension, is your base of support supposed to be close to your partner's or away? (Close)
- Why does your base have to be close to your partner? (Creating a small base makes it easier to develop tension between the two of you needed to develop and maintain countertension.)

Improving Motor Performance

Look at proximity of their bases of support.

- Make your base of support touch your partner's to create a single base for the two of you.

Observe movement away from base.

- Communicate with your partner as you lean away from your base.
- Lean slowly and gently so you don't pull your partner off balance.
- Keep all body parts in line with your base of support.
- Don't let your hips drop out of alignment.

One of the roles teachers play is the role of an *informer*. Teachers are called on to play the role of informer whenever ideas or concepts are being presented and teachers need to provide information. The role of an informer is used to verbalize information and to structure the learning experience. When playing the role of an informer, you will want to be accurate and sensitive to the needs of the students and select your words and the information you wish to convey carefully so students can understand quickly and respond appropriately.

Another role the teacher plays is the role of a *listener*. As a teacher, you play the role of a listener when students respond to questions, when they ask questions, during conversations between students, as well as when other sounds, such as music or working noise, are present in the lesson. The role of a listener is to receive verbal information and all other auditory stimuli which are present in the learning environment. The teacher must listen in order to stay tuned in to the level of student understanding and to keep abreast of the constant change of events.

The teacher is not only a listener, a teacher is a *responder*. As a teacher, you play the role of a responder anytime you react to a situation or when the students ask questions or request your reaction concerning their work. When asked, a responder is expected to show or to give a reaction. In responding, the teacher needs to be knowledgeable, accurate, sincere, fair, and consistent. Each response must fit the situation.

Another role a teacher sometimes plays is the role of a *performer*. The performer participates in physical activity. As a teacher, you become a performer when you demonstrate or when you join in actively with the students. When you change your role to play the role of a performer, you must remember you are being observed. Move skillfully, demonstrate accurately, and, if you join in an activity, don't neglect the other roles you may need to be playing also.

When giving tasks or instruction, you may play two different roles. You may be a commander or an elicitor. You play the role of a *commander* when you give instruction with the intent of having the students perform in a specific way. A commander expects all students to respond similarly with little or no variation. Teachers play the role of a commander to direct learning. You need to be aware that this teacher's role is selected intentionally when you wish to make little or no allowances for individual differences and when you want to require all students to respond in a preconceived way.

The second role a teacher may play in directing learning experiences is the role of an *elicitor*. You will play the role of an elicitor when you design a task which allows each learner to respond in a different way. An elicitor values different responses and frees students to move and to think independently. As an elicitor a teacher also directs learning; however, in the role of an elicitor the teacher must word tasks carefully to provide students opportunities to develop personal responses. This role allows the teacher to design experiences which promote creative responses or experiences that reassure students who are responding at different levels of ability.

A distinctively different role essential to teaching is the role of an *organizer*. An organizer is alert to the placement of experiences, students, and equipment in the available space and time. An organizer structures, reinforces, or directs the arrangement of students, experiences, and equipment in space and time to create or to change the learning conditions. When playing the role of an organizer, you must organize time, students, and equipment keeping in mind safety, best use of space and equipment, best teaching situation, and maximum opportunity for each student to participate fully and to learn.

A teacher is often called to perform the role of a *mediator*. You can be placed in the role of a mediator when students have conflicting opinions or when situations arise where alternative solutions need to be examined. A mediator initiates the examination of alternatives or arbitrates decisions. As a mediator, the teacher often needs to clarify the episode which created the conflict, examine alternatives, and, if necessary, arbitrate the solution.

Six different roles are played by teachers when developing tasks or providing meaningful feedback to students. To develop insight essential to creating appropriate tasks and in providing helpful feedback, teachers must play the role of an *observer*. As a teacher, you need to play the role of an observer constantly to make it possible for you to base your teaching on the current needs and accomplishments of your students. The observer observes with a purpose. When observing, teachers need to isolate the specifics to be observed. They need to know what they are looking for in order to obtain information essential to providing appropriate feedback. They also need to be alert for responses not anticipated in order to redesign tasks and to make other changes necessary to encourage learning.

Another role played by the teacher is the role of an *analyzer*. The role of an analyzer is played to examine information. This analysis can be used to develop content or develop student feedback. When you play the role of an analyzer, you must examine all information carefully. As an analyzer, you must learn to use learning processes to obtain information essential to providing appropriate feedback or to structure new learning experiences.

A role closely associated with the role of an analyzer is the role of the *appraiser*. You play the role of an appraiser whenever you make judgments about the work or responses of the students. The appraiser assesses the work of a student and acknowledges to the student or the class the progress made. The appraiser judges performances. As an appraiser, you will want to keep in mind the developmental levels of the learner, the desired requisites of the task, and provide feedback appropriate to the achievement of that individual.

Another teacher role is the role of an *extender*. As the students are working, a teacher playing the extender role, will change the challenge of the task to fit individual needs. An extender provides feedback to a student, group of students, or to the class to change content progression within a task. There are three ways you extend a task as the class works.

- You can increase the complexity of the task for students who are achieving.
- You can decrease the complexity for those who can benefit from a lesser challenge.
- You can direct students to seek greater variety in their responses to the task.

Another role played by the teacher is a *corrector*. Teachers play the role of the corrector anytime they respond to a situation and attempt to improve it. A corrector detects a need for improvement and reacts to help the student achieve a higher level of performance or understanding. As the corrector, you will need to be alerted to all behaviors—affective, cognitive, motor—because there will be times when each will benefit from your attention. The behavior needing your assistance for improvement changes from moment to moment as well as from student to student.

The last of these selected roles effective teachers play is the role of a *refiner*. A refiner provides information to improve performance. Essential to playing the role of a refiner a teacher must have in-depth knowledge of the content being taught, must know the developmental stages of the students, must know how people learn, and must have the ability to give pertinent cues to improve the response to help the student achieve a higher level of performance. The teacher will need to rely heavily on the skills of observation and the knowledge of skill analysis to provide appropriate cues essential to refining the responses of the student.

The purposes of these roles need to be examined and understood. The roles should be practiced often, and your teaching needs to be critiqued continually for expertise and sensitivity to these roles. Selecting and performing each of these roles effectively influences what students learn, how students learn, how students feel, and how students feel about what they are learning. Teaching is many things—but it is not easy.

"Teachers Are Characters," a multimedia program prepared by Logsdon and Rink (1980) to sensitize university students to the responsibilities of teachers, was adapted for inclusion in this book. If you're interested in accepting greater responsibility for how you teach, if this approach to teaching physical education seems new to you, or if you're interested in reflection on methodology in greater detail, we encourage you to examine writings by Barrett, Rink, Wall, and Murray, noting especially the references that have influenced their study.

REFLECTIONS ON TEACHING PHYSICAL EDUCATION

Motor skillfulness is essential if we are to achieve a nation of physically active people (Clark 1995). Yet, becoming skillful in movement doesn't just happen. We know that movement and motor development must be nurtured, encouraged, and given time to unfold. Children learn in different ways and at different rates. Each child in your class will demonstrate a unique time schedule of learning and development as he or she explores movement content and interacts with the environment. It is the teacher's job to identify where each child is in this developmental process and match the task (learning activity) to the learner's capabilities (Roberton 1989) so that all children may become skillful and experience the challenge, success, and joy of movement.

There are typically 25 or more students in a physical education class and numerous classes to teach daily. Where should you begin? Start by reflecting upon the teaching roles just described in "Teachers as Characters" and ask yourself the following questions.

- Do you clearly communicate goals and content to enhance student learning?
    Two critical components of effective teaching are setting clear goals and performance criteria, and being explicit as you present material (Rink 1996).

- Do you hold high expectations for all students?
    Remember, your job as a teacher is to increase the self-esteem, understanding, and performance level of each and every student. (See Danielson 1996).

- Do you use student demonstration effectively?
    When learning how to perform a movement or motor skill, students can benefit from a clear explanation accompanied by an expert "model of movement"; student demonstrations are especially useful because they promote cognitive processing of the skill, rather than simple imitation (Lee 1994).

- Do you provide adequate practice time when learners are asked to move in a specific way?
    Research suggests that a direct teaching approach is most useful when accompanied by full demonstration (teacher or student), summary cues, and student practice (Rink 1996).

- Do you design learning experiences so that different students can be working at different skill levels?

    This takes "preparation and a real commitment to the importance of student success rate in learning," explains Rink (1996, p. 177). Ask yourself: Are the students successful? Are they showing their best efforts at their own developmental levels? If you can answer "yes," then your role in eliciting skillful movement is effective and the learning experiences are probably appropriate.

- Do you accommodate the physical growth characteristics of children and provide maximum opportunity for learning?

    Provide equipment that differs in size, weight, texture, color, and sound. (See Herkowitz 1978; Roberton 1989; and Wahl 1994a). Keep in mind safety, the best uses of space and equipment, and maximize opportunity for each student to participate fully. The key to successful management is the teacher's ability to maximize the time students spend actively engaged in learning activity (see Danielson 1996).

- Are your students motivated to learn?

    It's important to focus on student actions and responses. Identify your students' needs and interests. Explore ways to increasingly challenge children to improve the amount and quality of their performance (Siedentop 1996). If movement tasks are both challenging and offer a high degree of success, then students will continue to work at improving their performance (see Graham, Holt-Hale, and Parker 1993).

- Do you practice the observation techniques of "scanning" and "focusing"?

    Techniques of scanning and focusing help teachers improve their abilities to (a) identify a safe environment for learning, (b) see and describe critical components of movement and motor skills, and (c) explain or interpret what they observe in order to make a judgment (Barrett 1984; Wahl 1994b). Use these observation techniques often. This process of "thinking out loud" as you teach can help you make thoughtful, appropriate instructional decisions, especially when combined with a depth and breadth of movement knowledge. See Fernandes-Balboa, Barrett, Solomon, and Silverman 1996 for further reading.

- Do you ask questions and give feedback at appropriate moments?

    Knowing when and how to intervene in a student's learning—to ask questions, to give feedback, to alter the physical space, to adjust equipment, to change (or not change) the movement task—are important considerations that affect learning and development (Roberton 1989; Roberton and Halverson 1984). Barrett and Collie (1996) describe teaching as "a highly creative process that takes thought, a commitment to helping children become increasingly skillful, and an understanding and respect for the nature of the subject matter and the time needed for developmental change to occur" (p. 307).

- Do you access student learning on an ongoing basis?

    "Effective teachers plan for the evaluation of student progress in relation to the stated learning goals," explains Danielson (1996, p. 123). Ask yourself: Are students meeting intended goals and objectives? Use assessment to provide feedback to your students and to involve them directly in self-evaluation and reflection on their performance. The primary reason for assessment is to enhance student learning (NASPE 1995).

Teaching was never meant to be easy. Our descriptions of the varied roles that teachers play are merely sketches of your completed portrait. *You* must decide what directions to take: What is important for students to learn? How can you best introduce this content? What works for you and your students—in what settings, under what conditions? What goals have been met? Where could you and your students improve?

We encourage you to explore the complex, exciting, and challenging activity of teaching from multiple dimensions: (1) planning and preparation; (2) the environment; (3) instructional practices; and (4) professional practices (see Danielson's "Framework of Teaching," 1996). (Also see perspectives by Barrett & Collie 1996; Fernandez-Balboa, Barrett, Solomon, Silverman 1996; and Ennis 1996). Read professional journals about teaching, including TEPE (Teaching Elementary Physical Education); the Journal of Teaching in Physical Education; Quest, JOPERD (The Journal of Physical Education, Recreation & Dance); Teaching Strategies, and the like. Most importantly, be willing to share your ideas and what you are doing with many people—students, other teachers in your school, administrators, parents, community groups, and legislators. We need to spread the good news that all children can become skillful in movement and that we, as a nation, are *on our way to becoming physically educated for life.*

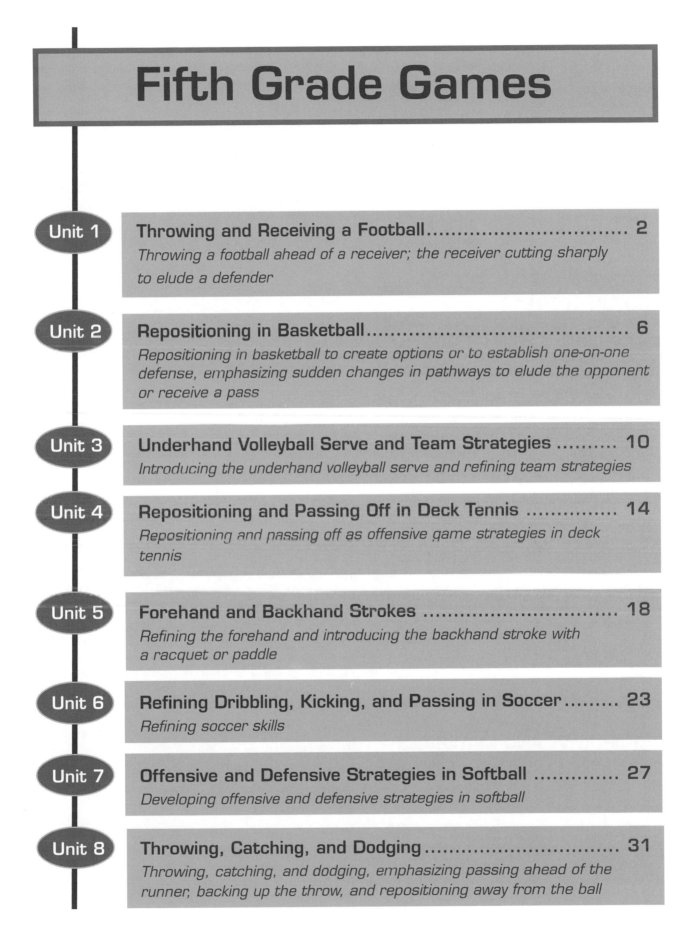

Fifth Grade Games

Throwing and Receiving a Football

4 or 5 lessons

FOCUS Throwing a football ahead of a receiver; the receiver cutting sharply to elude a defender

MOTOR CONTENT

Selected from Theme 2—Introduction to Space (with emphasis on pathways) and Theme 7—Introduction to Complex Relationships (cooperative and competitive in nature)

Relationships

Player placement—receiver running and cutting sharply to change pathway to elude a defender; one-on-one defense
Ball placement—passer throwing to a spot ahead of the receiver

OBJECTIVES

In this unit, students will (or should be willing to try to) meet these objectives:

- Catch passes by adjusting speed, stride, and pathway to break free of a defender.
- Adapt their speed and direction to changes made by the receiver to intercept or deflect a pass.
- Understand and demonstrate that they must, as receivers, travel far enough in one direction to get the defender traveling with them before a sudden change in pathway will be effective, and, as defenders, decide at the beginning of the pass play the length of lead to allow the player they are defending.
- Accept equalizing skill on opposing teams as a means for improving personal skills and increasing the challenge in the game situation.
- Play by the rules to avoid unsafe play and to settle differences of opinion.

EQUIPMENT AND MATERIALS

One junior-size football for every three students; two "flags" and one belt or two 20-inch strips of cloth about two inches wide for each player; four traffic cones for every 6 to 10 students.

LEARNING EXPERIENCES

1.0 Start passing and catching, taking pride in trying to complete each pass. Get in groups of three, get one football, find a space, and begin.

1.1 Passers, remember to point the little finger side of your throwing hand toward your receiver. Give the air a karate chop with the side of your hand as you pass the football overhand. [Many more refining tasks will be needed by individual students and the whole class. Select tasks and give relevant feedback based upon observed needs. Encourage the students to plant the rear foot and step out with the foot opposite the throwing arm; spread the fingers and grip the ball near one end with the whole hand; make the ball spin off their fingers by having the tips of their fingers leave the ball last; and throw ahead of the running receiver.]

1.2 Passers, give the receivers time to reposition to catch the ball. Make the ball travel in a high arc by releasing the ball upward, above and in front of your throwing shoulder.

1.3 Receivers, start your run before the passer throws. Try to catch on the run.

1.4 Passers, when throwing passes to a running receiver, aim your throw for a spot in front of your receiver. Don't aim at your receiver.

1.5 If you are completing your passes, throw a little farther ahead of your receivers to make them speed up to catch the pass. If your passes are going too far in front of the receiver, ease up slightly on your throw. Remember, a pass is not worth an inch in football if it is not caught.

2.0 Receivers, begin to test the ability of your passer to see changes in your pathway. Start running. Then suddenly make a sharp change in your pathway. Passers, watch for that sudden change. Pass the ball in front of your receivers the moment you see the change in pathway.

2.1 Passers, watch the hips of your receiver closely. The hips will often give you a clue when the change of direction will come because the hips usually start the shift in pathway.

2.2 Receivers, don't fake your passer. If you start to change direction, go for it. Your passer is going to throw when seeing your first change in pathway unless your fake was planned with your passer before you started running.

2.3 One person in each set of three be a defender and try to intercept the pass. Change roles after 10 passes.

2.4 Receivers, take several fast running steps in one direction before changing your pathway. Why is it important to run several steps in one direction before changing pathways? Right! They get your defender moving with you. Once your defender is committed to traveling fast in one direction, you have a better chance of losing the defender by suddenly changing your path.

2.5 Defenders, divide your attention between the ball and the receiver. Try to sense the relationship of your receiver. Decide how much lead you are going to give the receiver, staying aware of your passer and the ball. You will play receivers differently based on their ability to run and whether you think the pass is going to be short or long.

2.6 Receivers! Think about the path you make as you change pathways! Change your path drastically by making a sharp, sudden turn. This is difficult for the defender to anticipate and the quick change in pathway breaks you open to receive the pass.

2.7 Defenders, change your strategy based on personal experience. Were you unable to intercept or deflect the ball because the offensive lead was too great or did you decide too early in the play to stay close and the offense ran for the long pass?

MUSCLE CONCEPT

Muscles can adjust or adapt when you slowly and gradually use them longer with increasing force. This requires small increases over weeks and often months. As you practice passing, gradually increase the distance and force of your pass.

2.8 If you are completing your passes, tell your receivers to expect the pass farther ahead of them as they change pathway. This helps pick up more yardage by getting the receiver running faster.

2.9 Passers, as you step forward to throw, push off of your rear foot and plant your stepping foot firmly on the ground, pointing the toe of your stepping foot toward your target in front of your receiver. Pushing forcefully with your rear foot and planting the stepping foot firmly helps create power needed for distance. Pointing your toe as you step toward your target helps you throw more accurately. [Break task into two parts for students having difficulty focusing on both.]

3.0 [Select students ready for more complex relationships found in a game; have the others continue passing, cutting, and intercepting the ball. Sixth Grade Games Unit 1, 4.0 illustrates using these advanced teams to demonstrate the game to the class.] Get with someone whose football skills closely match yours. Then form groups of six or eight and divide into two equal teams. Sit in the middle of your field opposite the person whose skills match yours. This puts the two of you with similar skills opposing each other, equalizing the competition and making the game challenging for everyone. [Discuss the rules of "Modified Flag Football" found on page 5.] Keep one ball. Put all others in a ball bag on the side of your field. Remember, you may only use passing plays to advance the ball. Work to eliminate all body contact. Start your game.

3.1 [Demonstrate the primary options of one-on-one defense: deciding when to permit the receiver a lead and when to stay close and determining how long the lead should be when allowed. If a defender decides too early in the play to stay close, the receiver can keep running for the long pass. Following the discussion, have all teams practice these options on their parts of the field. Be sure to arrange teams so they're not running into each other.]

3.2 [Observe the various games and stop play on one field or reassemble the entire class, depending for whom your feedback is relevant. Design tasks based on your observations, select one of the remaining tasks, or review those given earlier that you feel the students are not demonstrating in game play.] Passers, throw the ball the moment your receiver changes pathway. Aim your throw in front of the receiver. A perfect pass is one that a receiver can catch without changing pathways or changing speed.

3.3 In your defensive huddle, everyone should make sure of their individual assignments. Some of you should defend the receivers while others may need to go for the passer's flag before the passer releases the ball.

3.4 Take time on your half of the field to practice long and short pass plays in which the receiver cuts sharply to elude the defense. Name each play so it can be called quickly in the huddle.

3.5 Sometimes on defense you need to play some receivers close, and other times you may intentionally let them get a short lead. Plan your strategy each time you are in the defensive huddle. Remember which strategies work best in a game setting for your team. Practice your least effective strategy the next time we stop for a practice session.

MODIFIED FLAG FOOTBALL

This game is played by two teams of no more than seven players each. Every player tucks a strip of cloth in at each side of the waist with about 15 inches of the cloth still hanging out. Instead of tagging the person with the ball, the defense stops play by pulling a 'flag' from the belt of the ball carrier. Pulling the flag eliminates the need for body contact and makes the game safer when playing without protective equipment. The offense [offensive team] is the team that has the ball. The defense [defensive team] is the team trying to get the ball. The offense has four chances (called *downs*) to advance the ball 10 yards toward the defender's goal line or to score a touchdown. When the ball is advanced 10 or more yards without scoring a touchdown, the offensive team keeps possession of the ball for four more downs. The defensive team gains possession of the ball in one of four ways:

1. By intercepting a pass
2. By recovering a fumble
3. When the offense does not gain 10 yards in four plays
4. Following a touchdown by opposing team

Your team can score a touchdown, which is worth six points, if one of you carries the ball across the defensive (the other team's) goal line or when one of you catches a pass behind the other team's goal. After your team scores a touchdown, place the ball on a line about 10 steps from the other team's goal. You can get two extra points if you can score in one play from this point. After the try for the extra points, your team lines up about 20 steps in front of your own goal line, and someone punts (dropkicks) the ball back to the other team.

ASSESSING LEARNING IN FLAG FOOTBALL

Class list	Knows that increasing speed, then cutting sharply in a new pathway causes a defender adjustment problems.	Knows that the defender must decide before the play how much space to give the receiver.	Wants teams that are matched in ability and appreciates reasons for doing this.	Accepts and abides by safety and fair play rules.	Shares responsibilities and communicates clearly with teammates.
Angie	5	5	3	3	3
Kendrick	3	3	1	1	3

Scale: 5 = Understands or does this well 3 = Satisfactory understanding or behavior 1 = Unsatisfactory understanding or behavior

Repositioning in Basketball

4 or 5 lessons

Repositioning in basketball to create options or to establish one-on-one defense, emphasizing sudden changes in pathways to elude the opponent or receive a pass

MOTOR CONTENT

Selected from Theme 3—Introduction to Movement Quality (Effort) and Theme 7—Introduction to Complex Relationships

Effort

Space—indirect, flexible
Time—sudden changes in direction and pathways

Space

Pathways—sudden changes

Relationships

Player placement—Offense: repositioning to create options for the teammate with the ball, changing from offense to defense; breaking toward or away from the ball or teammates; breaking away from the guard; or changing to defense. Defense: repositioning to block the passing lanes, staying near and between the opponent and the goal, keeping the ball and opponent in constant focus, or changing to offense.

OBJECTIVES

In this unit, students will (or should be willing to try to) meet these objectives:

- Reposition to create an open space between themselves and the ball, away from the opponent and teammates; give options to the teammate throwing the ball; get free from their guards; change offensive and defensive roles; and reestablish a position needed in their new role.
- Reposition by executing quick changes in direction; running toward the ball, open space, or goal in relation to how open the passer is and to the positions of teammates and opponents.
- Know that the break (a sudden change in pathway) to elude the guard comes after traveling far enough to get the guard moving in one pathway and that sudden changes in pathways that cover little space are easier to guard because changes that cover little space do not require guards to commit their movement to a definite pathway.

• Accept a variety of skill levels of both genders as team members by demonstrating a willingness to share the ball.

EQUIPMENT AND MATERIALS

One 8-inch playground ball or junior-size basketball for every four students; masking tape to create "goals" on the walls for groups not working at basketball hoops (see 3.6).

LEARNING EXPERIENCES

1.0 Pair up with another classmate who has developed about the same skill in basketball as you. The two of you join with another pair and stand facing them. The person facing you is your teammate. The person you chose with the same skill as you will be your guard. Why have I asked people with similar skill to guard each other? That's right—we all have to work harder when the person who is guarding us is closer to our own skill. This also helps to even up teams, making the competition more fair. Let's work on making short, completed passes while playing two versus two. Find a working space away from other groups, one person get a ball for the four of you, and begin to work on short passes.

1.1 [If the guards are overwhelming the offense, you may need to change a few players to equalize play or, more frequently, you may need to encourage guards to hold back a bit so the offense can practice moving the ball quickly without having it intercepted.]

1.2 You are being very considerate of others. Equalizing the skill between groups is making for some very close competition. Offense, return the ball as soon as you get it. Don't hold the ball. One of the best offensive strategies is to keep that ball moving so the guards can't really get set up. If the ball is intercepted or if the pass is incomplete, the other pair gets the ball.

1.3 These lead passes are similar to those we did in football. Make the passes go right to the shoulder area of your receiver to make it easier to catch on the run. A ball caught low is easier to guard.

2.0 Throwers, just as you throw the ball, dash to a new spot, keeping your eyes on the ball.

2.1 Some of you are jogging. Really run—don't jog. You have to move fast to get open.

2.2 When running to shake your guard, travel fast in one pathway, then suddenly change pathway and dart toward a new spot. [Usually you need to encourage students to take a few more steps since most do not travel far enough to get the opponent traveling with them before they cut in a different direction.]

2.3 Passers, stay alert. Lead your partners with that pass by throwing ahead of your receivers as they change their pathway. If you wait even a moment after your receiver suddenly changes pathway, you give the guard time to change, too, and the guard has a better chance to intercept your pass.

2.4 Think a moment: Is it easier to keep up with a running player when the runner makes curvy bends in their pathways or sharp, abrupt changes in their pathways? [Quietly get answers from a few.] Good. Sharp, sudden turns are more difficult to guard because the defense doesn't know when the change in direction is coming.

2.5 Play two versus two [or two versus one] and see how many completed passes you can make in 30 seconds. Then the other pair will see if they can beat the record. If the ball is intercepted or the pass is incomplete, the ball goes back to the same pair, but they must start counting all over. First pair, ready? Go! [Change roles.]

3.0 [Organize the class into groups of six.] Working three versus three, the two offensive teammates without the ball, begin to think as you travel where you need to reposition yourselves to always give your teammate with the ball two very different passing options. Think about your relationships to each other, your opponents, and the ball, always giving the teammate with the ball two very different choices of where to pass. [Note court markings for each group in 3.6.]

3.1 Offensive players without the ball, you need to keep your eyes on the ball as you break to open spaces. Don't turn your back to the ball. Be ready to receive the ball at any time.

3.2 Guards, each time the person you are guarding gets the ball, count one, two, three, four, five. Let's see if the offense can pass the ball before the guard counts to five! Discipline yourself not to run with the ball.

3.3 Passers, don't stand and hold the ball. Catch and throw the ball immediately into the free space ahead of an open receiver.

3.4 Receivers, if you get to the open spot you selected and have not received the pass, show you still want the ball by hustling to a new spot. Passers, pass only to running teammates.

3.5 The two receivers need to get a feel for each other in relation to the passer and work as a team trying to go to two very different spots, hoping one is free to receive a pass. Both need to keep looking at the teammate with the ball. The thrower might need one of you to break back toward the ball.

3.6 As you pass, count your completed passes. After the fourth completed pass, the team member who has the ball can shoot if they're free and near the basket. Don't dribble. Dribbling is illegal now because we are encouraging passing and moving the ball quickly. Do you notice the pieces of tape on the walls about the height of a basketball goal? [Number each group, pointing to each as you number them.] Groups [2, 3, 5, and 6] will start out shooting to see if the arc of their ball can brush the space on the wall inside their taped baskets on its way down. Groups [1 and 4] will shoot for the basket at their end. We will rotate courts so all will get a chance to practice at the real hoops. [Use all available hoops before substituting taped baskets on walls.]

3.7 Let's begin to show a great team effort by making sure everyone on a team has caught the ball at least once before you pop up a shot. After one team makes a basket or has a pass intercepted, the other team goes for the four completed passes before shooting. [Change teammates to help achieve the objective of learning to work with everyone. Encourage the same skill level to guard each other to equalize the teams.]

4.0 If your team loses the ball, you must quickly become a guard. Look for the player who was guarding you. Keep that player and the ball in your sight at all times, running quickly to get near that opponent and stay between them and the basket. [Drop the rule of four passes before shooting. Stress taking a shot only when they are free of the guard and close to the basket.]

4.1 Stay alert. Passes are going to be intercepted. The important thing you need to do is to switch from offense to defense or defense to offense quickly. Watch who has the ball.

4.2 When playing defense, make it difficult for the person you are guarding to get around you by moving quickly to position yourself so the person you are guarding must adjust their pathway.

4.3 Defense, keep your eyes, mind, and body in the game. Stay up on the balls of your feet in a ready position, with your knees bent or flexed so you can move quickly in any direction to stick near the person you are guarding or to change offensive and defensive roles.

5.0 [Organize class to work three versus three or four versus four, with two teams working at each basket playing half-court and two teams working across court shooting at paper targets, if needed. Group size may vary but keep the number on a team low, organizing the class so all are in a game situation. After a team that is playing half-court scores, have the other team put the ball in play with a throw in from out of bounds at a point near the free throw line. Rotate groups so all have an equal opportunity to shoot at a hoop.] Play starts with a player throwing the ball in from behind the free throw line or from under your opponent's basket. Begin to work the ball down the court with short passes—no dribbling permitted. Move the ball toward your basket with short passes, and when you are near the basket, shoot. Guards, try desperately to stay near your player and between him or her and the basket. Don't let your player be the one who makes the basket. The game we are playing is 'No-Dribble Basketball.' It requires short, completed passes and team members who can reposition often to receive passes.

5.1 Offense, you must keep repositioning in relation to your teammates, the opposing players, and the location of the ball. This is hard! Keep moving all the time! Find a clear path between you and the ball so the pass won't get intercepted. Don't stand and wave your arms or yell. Break free!

5.2 Let's put in a rule to help us improve our passing skills. Decide on how many passes must be completed before anyone can score. Count aloud each time a pass is completed. If the offense gets the rebound, they can shoot again immediately. If the defense gets the rebound, they must start counting their passes before taking a shot.

5.3 Think about how much more enjoyable the game is when you have the ball. Look for the person who hasn't had the ball lately and share the enjoyment with them. If you haven't been getting your share of passes, see if you can run faster and make your change in pathway really sharp to get free for a pass.

5.4 Offensive player with the ball, you have to try to see all your teammates all the time. Some of you are missing teammates who are free. Look for your players and throw that lead pass out into the spot where they are moving, just as they start to change direction.

5.5 Some of you need to discipline yourselves not to run with the ball. Decide on your court if traveling with the ball is going to be a violation. If so, the person who runs with the ball gives it to the other team who throws the ball in from out of bounds. [Regrouping students throughout the unit helps to foster the ability to accept everyone as a team member and, when done often, students learn that the groupings change frequently.]

SELF-ASSESSMENT: REPOSITIONING STRATEGIES AND PLAY

Individuals or small groups compare and contrast their game skills and strategies in this unit to those in fourth grade (see Fourth Grade Games Unit 1). Encourage them to use clear descriptive phrases. Have them record these either in writing or on audiotape. Summarize the class's or entire grade's assessments to determine improvements, strengths, and current needs.

Underhand Volleyball Serve and Team Strategies

5 or 6 lessons

FOCUS Introducing the underhand volleyball serve and refining team strategies

MOTOR CONTENT

Selected from Theme 6—Advanced Body and Manipulative Control and Theme 7—Introduction to Complex Relationships

Body

Manipulative activities—developing the underhand serve and refining the bump and set

Relationships

Player placement—backing up a teammate
Ball placement—passing the ball in front of a teammate, sending the ball away from opponents

OBJECTIVES

In this unit, students will (or should be willing to try to) meet these objectives:

- Improve the bump and set by working to control height and direction of the ball.
- Serve the ball underhand with a closed hand or with the heel of an open hand.
- Understand that "backing up" means to play or cover the space behind or near another player; the larger the hitting surface used in serving, the easier it is to control the direction of the ball; passing the ball to teammates keeps opponents off-guard.
- Improve teamwork by backing up teammates, playing balls coming into own area, and passing the ball to teammates.
- Reposition quickly to back up a teammate.

EQUIPMENT AND MATERIALS

Enough for class to work in partners: nets; standards; 8- to 10-inch vinyl balls.

LEARNING EXPERIENCES

1.0 See how long you can bump and set the ball back and forth over the net with a partner. Get a partner, one ball, find a place at a net, and begin.

1.1 Travel to get your forearms in front of and under the ball if it isn't coming directly to you.

1.2 Set the ball in a high arc to give the receiver time to move under the ball.

1.3 When setting the ball, make a triangle or window the size of the ball with your thumbs and index fingers. [Demonstrate.] Return the ball by holding this triangle out above your forehead and looking at the ball through your window. Remember to set with both hands.

1.4 Get in line with the oncoming ball with the front of your body facing your receiver. Look up through the triangle at the ball.

1.5 Set the ball with the pads of your fingers—not your palms. Extend your knees and elbows as you contact the ball to create more power.

1.6 Contact the ball with your fingertips, making your hit soft so you don't hear a sound. Create your power by bending and extending your knees and elbows—not by hitting with your hands or fists.

2.0 [To improve the bump, first review tasks 1.5 through 2.5 in Third Grade Games Unit 4 (if available), then go forward with the following experiences.]

2.1 Make your arms absorb some of the force by bending your knees. Let your arms move down from the shoulders, giving with the ball.

2.2 Bend your knees to make your arms absorb some of the force when they contact the ball.

3.0 [Have students work in pairs hitting over nets to practice the underhand serve.] To serve the ball, hold it out in front of you, letting the ball rest in the palm of your nonhitting hand. Keeping your elbow straight, swing your arm and hitting hand underhand and contact the ball near the bottom to send it over the net. Make your serving arm and hand reach out toward your partner. Partners, catch the ball and serve it back.

Make your serving arm and hand reach out toward your partner as you serve.

3.1 Extend your nonhitting arm diagonally across your body to hold the ball so it is below your waist and in line with your serving hand. [Demonstrate.] As you serve, make your serving arm and hand reach out toward your partner.

3.2 Face your partner with your feet side by side. As you swing your arm and hand to serve, step toward your partner on the foot opposite your hitting hand.

3.3 Try contacting the ball with different surfaces of your hand as you serve. See which surface feels the most comfortable to you. [Some may like the fist while others prefer the heel of the open hand.]

3.4 Don't toss the ball up. Hit it out of your hand. Contacting the bottom of the ball helps send the ball high over the net.

3.5 Check to see that your striking hand is pointing above the top of the net to the spot where you aimed the ball.

3.6 Remember to square your shoulders and point your forward foot to your target before you serve, bump, or set the ball.

3.7 Receivers, right before the ball is served, move to a new spot. Servers, adjust your feet to square your shoulders and point your forward foot toward your receiver before serving.

3.8 Stay to the back of the court when receiving the serve. Servers, to create more power, take your serving arm back farther, firm it up, and swing it faster, pointing your hand where you want the ball to land. [Evaluate the students on the underhand serve at least twice during the unit.]

ASSESSMENT FOR THE UNDERHAND SERVE IN VOLLEYBALL

1. Hits ball out of hand with closed fist or heel of hand.
2. Keeps serving arm straight.
3. Steps forward on foot opposite serving hand as ball is contacted.
4. Controls placement of serve.

Name	1	2	3	4
Brown, Sue	Oct. 10	—	Oct. 10	—
	Oct. 20	Oct. 20	Oct. 20	—
Baker, Dana	Oct. 10	—	—	Oct. 10
	—	—	Oct. 20	Oct. 20

4.0 Working two versus two, try to keep the ball going. If your partner is receiving the ball, run quickly behind or near your partner to get ready to return the ball in case the ball goes over your partner's head or spins off their fingers.

4.1 When receiving, stand side by side as you wait for the serve. The receiver nearest the ball should call for the ball. The other person repositions behind or near the receiver to get the ball if the receiver misses.

4.2 Don't send the ball to an opponent. Send it to an empty space. This makes both the receiver and the backup person practice repositioning.

4.3 Alternate positions. After you receive the ball, let your teammate receive the next serve while you play the backup person.

4.4 As you play the backup position, watch the fingers of the receiver you are backing up. Check to see if they are pointing forward or back toward you.

When pointing back toward you, you will probably have to play the ball because there is a good chance it will spin off the receiver's fingers.

4.5 After you play backup, run back quickly to cover your own space.

4.6 Send the ball to a different open space on the opponent's court every time you return the ball over the net.

4.7 Receivers, be quick to reposition to get in front of the ball. Stay in an alert, ready position, looking at the ball. Adjust your feet to face the ball each time the location of the ball changes.

4.8 Count how many times the four of you can send the ball back and forth, making each receiver reposition to return the ball.

5.0 Let's play with three on each side of the net. Two people play near the net and one play backup behind the other two. The player in the back row must reposition to receive every ball sent over the heads of the front row players. Front line players must be ready to receive a pass from the back row as well as from a serve.

5.1 Back line players, set the ball high in front of a player near the net to give the receiver time to reposition so they can control the direction of the ball.

5.2 Run to position yourself under the ball. Work to contact the ball high with all 10 finger pads.

5.3 Front row players, as you reposition to receive the pass, face the direction you plan to send the ball.

5.4 Servers, send the ball to the back row. This makes the receivers work hard to return the ball.

5.5 Let's see if your team can take two hits before sending the ball over the net. This makes volleyball a real team sport. All players must reposition to square their bodies to the ball each time someone passes the ball.

5.6 How many times can both teams take two hits before sending the ball over the net?

6.0 Let's play a game with four people on each team. Start your game with a serve. Decide whether you want a cooperative game, seeing how many times two teams can send the ball back and forth over the net, or a competitive game, scoring points against the other team. If you keep points, decide how many points it will take to win a game. Decide on your boundaries, the type of game you will play, and begin. [Teams playing a competitive game may need more court space.]

6.1 If you decided on the cooperative game, return the ball in a high arc to give the receiver time to reposition under the ball. If competing against the other team, try to send the ball to open spaces on the opponent's court to make it difficult for them to return the ball. In either game, pass the ball among your teammates before returning it over the net.

6.2 Always hustle to play the ball with two hands. [You may need to insert a rule that one-handed hits are the same as a miss.]

6.3 No matter which game you are playing, let's see everyone on every court adjusting their feet and squaring their bodies to the ball each time the location of the ball changes. [Evaluate on high sets, backing up teammates, and playing ball in own area at least twice before end of unit.]

6.4 See if your team can make two passes to teammates before sending the ball over the net. Help your teammates by making high passes, giving them time to get under the ball.

6.5 Work as a team. Back each other up. Remember to return to your own area so all parts of the court are covered. Don't be upset when someone misses the ball. Encourage each other while you all learn the skills of volleyball.

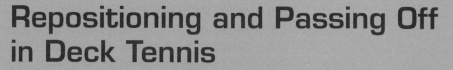

Unit 4

Repositioning and Passing Off in Deck Tennis

5 or 6 lessons

FOCUS Repositioning and passing off as offensive game strategies in deck tennis

MOTOR CONTENT

Selected from Theme 3—Introduction to Movement Quality (Effort) and Theme 7—Introduction to Complex Relationships

Effort

Flow—catching and throwing the ring with one continuous motion

Relationships

Player placement—squaring the body to the ring as you catch, positioning behind the receiver to back up the catch, and returning the ring into empty spaces. Ball placement—passing off to a teammate rather than returning the ring over the net

OBJECTIVES

In this unit, students will (or should be willing to try to) meet these objectives:

- Catch and throw in one continuous motion with either hand, returning the ring quickly to keep the defense from being able to anticipate the throw.
- Use offensive strategies by passing off to a teammate or sending the ring into empty spaces on the opponent's court.
- Reposition behind the receiver to back up the catch, resuming own position quickly.
- Allow each teammate the opportunity to remain fully involved by playing their own position.
- Understand that the placement of the ring and quickness are necessary to make deck tennis challenging and enjoyable.

EQUIPMENT AND MATERIALS

For every four students: One deck tennis ring; ropes or nets; standards.

LEARNING EXPERIENCES

1.0 Let's start our unit on deck tennis by showing how cleanly you can catch and throw the ring with the same hand. Each time you return the ring over the net, try to send it so that it spins parallel to the floor. You will have two people on each side of the net. Get one ring for the four of you and begin.

1.1 To toss the ring over the net, take the ring low across the front of your body beneath your waist in your backswing and release the ring high with your throwing hand pointing over the net.

1.2 Remember, prepare your whole body for throwing by turning your feet and hips so your throwing shoulder points toward your partner. Don't have the front of your body facing the net.

1.3 Remember to have your fingers on top of the ring when catching the ring high and your thumb on top of the ring when the ring is low.

1.4 Don't stop after you give in your catch. Toss it back immediately so you catch and throw in one motion. This keeps the defense alert.

1.5 Make each receiver travel a bit by sending the ring in the space close to the net or slightly over the receiver's head.

1.6 Everyone on this side of the net, move down one person to your right. The last person on the far right, come to the opposite end and work with the first group. Challenge the group of four next to you and see which group can toss and catch the ring the most times without missing. [Change groupings several times during the first lesson either by alternating the line that moves or by having everyone move one place to their left.]

2.0 Begin to practice backing up the receiver. When you are the teammate nearest the receiver, face the receiver and move quickly to be near them or in back of them to catch the ring if they miss.

2.1 If you move out of your position to back up a receiver, scoot back quickly to your own space as soon as the ring is returned so you don't leave your own space uncovered.

Point your shoulder toward your partner and prepare your whole body for throwing.

2.2 Every time the ring starts to come over to your side of the court, two people should reposition to catch the ring. One will be the likely receiver, the other will play the backup position. Remember to call for the ring.

2.3 The four of you may begin to play 'Deck Tennis Doubles.' Send the ring back to an open space as quickly as you catch it. Decide how many points it takes to win [maximum of 11]. [You may use ropes or cones to outline your court or put up nets about 6 feet high.]

2.4 Make your game a bit tougher offensively by sending the ring deep into your opponents' court or close to the net—never straight to an opponent. Toss to those open spaces.

2.5 When playing your doubles game, remember to back up and support each other.

3.0 [Quietly reorganize sets of partners who are going all-out in doubles and suggest they may play three versus three or four versus four rather than doubles. Do not be in a hurry to increase the size of all groups. Permit others who decide to or ask to regroup to do so when they wish. When increasing the size of the groups, have them figure out a rotation system for serving the ring to start each point and where the server should stand—either behind the back line or at a spot nearer the net. This spot may vary according to the skill of the players.]

3.1 Work hard in your larger teams to make all players feel they are important to your game. Give everybody a chance to share equally by trying to return the ring to a different person each time.

3.2 Analyze [think about] your relationship to the net, to the back line, and to each other. Front line players should stand no more than two small steps away from the net. Back line players should stand two big steps away from the back line. Each line spread out, making each person responsible for the same amount of space so that all important areas of the court are covered at all times.

3.3 Back line players, you must work twice as hard when it comes to backing up. This is because you back up the front line plus any other back line players. Let's really see the receiver and the backup player reposition every time the ring is tossed.

3.4 Blend your catch into your throw. Start your throw just the moment you finish your catch.

4.0 Except when you are the tosser, as you continue to play your game, make the toes on both of your feet and your shoulders turn to face the exact spot where the ring goes every time the location of the ring changes. Do this whether the ring is on your side of the net or your opponents' side. If you haven't been playing four versus four, join with another group to do so now. This will give you practice backing up and squaring yourself to the ring when you are not the receiver. [If the class is not divisible by four, we suggest putting five or six on a team—but no more than six. More on a side significantly reduces the actual practice time of each student. We also recommend that you improvise court markings; don't let permanent markings on the floor dictate the number of courts.]

4.1 All players on both sides of the net, reposition your feet and shoulders to face the ring every time the ring is about to be thrown. Your movement should be very quick and precise so that if a TV camera was overhead the picture would show each of you turning on a dime, almost like you were on a turntable. Everyone should be turning quickly and at the same time.

4.2 Work to send the ring to a different place on the court each time, forcing a different player to catch the ring every time.

4.3 Reposition your feet to turn your whole body to face the new location of the ring each time it is thrown. Develop that feeling of mental alertness needed to square the front of your body to the ring every time it is thrown.

4.4 Everyone stop what you are doing and begin a short game of seven points. Remember the serving team is the only team that can score a point. When the serving team fails to return the ring, the receiving team wins the [gets to] serve but not a point. Send the ring to open spaces—even try some faking.

4.5 Stop your games and have a seat for a moment. Let's sit and watch these two teams play their next three points. Notice how all players on both sides of the net are always repositioning their feet and turning their entire bodies to face the ring every time the ring changes location. Everyone, let's work harder on squaring your body to the ring.

4.6 The people in the back line on each court on this side of the net, move one court to your right. The back line players in the far right court, come all the way down to the first court. When your new opponents have arrived, play another short game of seven points.

4.7 Everyone have a seat, and let's watch these two teams hustle to back up the receiver. Let's all sharpen our backing up skills as we play another short game of seven points. Notice how the person backing up the receiver squares their body to the ring behind the receiver. To start play again, those players who did not move to a new court last time, move one court to your left.

5.0 [Still have students playing over a net with four to six on a side.] All teams of four to six players on a side will be playing a timed game five minutes long. [Time the game. Vary the length if you wish, keeping it between five and eight minutes.] You can only pass the ring twice on your own court before one of you must send the ring over the net. Make a definite attempt to fool your opponents by sometimes passing off to a teammate before sending the ring back over the net. We call this an *offensive strategy*.

5.1 Everyone on both sides of the net, square your whole body to the ring every time it is tossed because no one knows when the ring might be coming to you.

5.2 Keep that ring moving constantly. Catch and toss it quickly. The quicker you move the ring, the more difficult it is for the defensive team to anticipate when and where the ring is going to come.

5.3 It's great to see teamwork, but when you have repositioned to back up a teammate, be sure you return quickly to your own area.

5.4 Keep looking for open areas on your opponents' court. Look especially for those areas in the deep back corners and near the net. Aim for the empty spaces to make the ring harder to return.

Unit 5 — Forehand and Backhand Strokes

5 or 6 lessons

FOCUS Refining the forehand and introducing the backhand stroke with a racquet or paddle

MOTOR CONTENT

Selected from Theme 1—Introduction to Basic Body and Manipulative Control; Theme 5—Introduction to Basic Relationships; and Theme 6—Advanced Body and Manipulative Control

Body

Manipulative activities—introducing the backhand, refining the forehand

Effort

Force—introducing effective and efficient selection of force

Space

Levels—refining altering the level of the ball

Relationships

Ball placement—placing the ball to make it difficult for the receiver to return

OBJECTIVES

In this unit, students will (or should be willing to try to) meet these objectives:

- Refine the forehand and develop the backhand, giving special attention to changing the side of the body facing the net and bending the knees to contact low balls.
- Transfer weight from the rear to the front foot and straighten the knees when contacting the ball.
- Understand that one of the chief differences between the forehand and the backhand is that the backhand is performed with the racquet side of the body pointed toward the net instead of the nonracquet side.
- Understand that choosing and controlling the force and level of the ball are important offensive and defensive tennis skills because they can help make the ball difficult to return.
- Intentionally altering the level and force of the swing by changing the path and angle of the racquet as well as the speed and range of the stroke.
- Always seek to maintain a safe situation for themselves and others by stopping their strokes when someone comes into their space and by waiting for others to finish their rallies before retrieving or asking for a stray ball.

EQUIPMENT AND MATERIALS

For each student: One paddle or short-handled racquet; one ball. (You can use various kinds of racquets and balls. Take care to ensure the weight and size of the ball are consistent with the durability of the racquet. A strong plastic tennis racquet along with a soft, resilient foam tennis ball are useful when teaching this unit inside.)

LEARNING EXPERIENCES

1.0 Let's first review the tennis forehand. Discipline yourself to always get your nonracquet side facing the spot where you want the ball to go. See how many carefully executed forehand strokes you can make. Catch the ball instead of making a sloppy stroke so the ball doesn't disturb others. Remember to take responsibility for safety by being cautious about striking the ball when others come into your space and by waiting to retrieve a ball until players have finished their rally, making it safe for you to retrieve the ball.

1.1 Remember to let the ball bounce and, as you do, adjust your whole position so your body is far enough away from the ball so you can step into the ball.

1.2 Think about your knees, especially when the ball comes back a little low. Bend your knees to keep your racquet and stroke parallel with the floor, then straighten your knees as you complete your stroke.

1.3 Begin to feel yourself rocking back on your rear foot to start your swing. Feel yourself stepping onto the forward foot as you finish. Every stroke, feel yourself transferring your weight from your back foot to the forward foot.

1.4 Challenge yourself to see if you can increase the number of times you can stroke the ball with your forehand. [Some may want to challenge others to see who can keep the ball going longer.] Remember to step from your rear foot to your forward foot on each stroke.

2.0 How many of you can tell us what the stroke is called when we turn and have the racquet shoulder leading the action? Right! We call it a *backhand*. The backhand stroke is similar to throwing the deck tennis ring because both actions require you to have your throwing or striking shoulder pointed toward your target. Many tennis players have two-handed backhands. They place their least favorite [weaker] hand above their favorite hand. The receiver [stroker] decides whether to stroke with one or two hands on the racquet and stands with the racquet side of the body pointing toward the tosser. The tosser tosses the ball so it bounces about two steps in front of the stroker and goes up to about waist height. Each time you stroke the ball, try to keep the side edge of your racquet horizontal with the floor and the face of your racquet looking at your tosser. [Demonstrate. Have students change roles after about 10 tosses. Capable partners could hit back and forth over a net in any of the tasks in learning experiences 2.0 through 2.4.]

2.1 Remember to move your feet to position your body away from the ball so you can reach out as you stroke, keeping your arm fairly parallel with the floor as you swing. [Change roles.]

2.2 Tossers, toss the ball up in a low arc so it bounces about waist high. Be sure it lands on the stroker's nonracquet side.

2.3 Strokers, try to get that same stepping, rocking feeling each time you stroke the ball. Put most of your weight on your rear foot [nonracquet side] as

PARTICIPATION AND AEROBIC ACTIVITY

To improve your tennis skills requires much practice. At home, try to keep breaking your record of consecutive hits for backhands, forehands, or both. Work with a partner over a crack in a cement driveway or alone against a wall or door for 15 minutes or more.

you take your racquet back and then step forward on your front foot as you swing. [Demonstrate.]

2.4 Tossers, begin to toss the ball gently to either side of your partner or a little in front of them or let your stroker tell you which side. Strokers, be ready to adjust your feet and body position to play either a forehand or a backhand.

2.5 Stroking toward the wall, see how many times you can keep the ball going, making sure to get your feet and body fully turned to play either a forehand or a backhand.

3.0 Begin to alternate strokes from forehand to backhand. You need to stay alert and up on the balls of your feet so you are ready to reposition your feet and whole body to get the correct side to the net or wall.

3.1 After each stroke, quickly go back to your ready position. [You or a student demonstrate. Show the students how to hold the racquet out in front of them with two hands, making the head of the racquet point across the net.] In this ready position, you need to bend your knees slightly and keep your weight forward on the balls of your feet. This makes it easier for you to start to move in either direction.

What corrections would you make to help this student improve her "ready position"?

3.2 Hustle to move into your stroking position with your racquet back, ready to stroke the ball. See how many times you and your partner can alternate forehand and backhand strokes. Start over again any time one fails to alternate their strokes.

4.0 [Organization can vary: partners playing across a net, individuals striking a ball against the wall, or partners alternating hits against the wall.] Still concentrate on getting back to your ready position and getting your body fully turned to stroke either forehand or backhand. See how many times you can stroke the ball without missing. Make the ball bounce close enough to your partners so they can get to the ball.

4.1 To really hustle, stay up on the balls of your feet. Do not rest back on your heels.

4.2 Strokers, as you stroke that ball, feel the angle of the face of your racquet as you contact the ball. Notice how the angle of your racquet face determines the height of your return. Begin to take pride in knowing you and your racquet determine the placement of the ball.

4.3 Each time after you are pulled away to stroke the ball, see if you can return to the middle of your space and quickly resume that 'pouncy' ready position: knees easy, weight on the balls of your feet, racquet held out in front of your body pointing toward your partner, and head in the game!

4.4 As you return the ball, pay attention to the face of your racquet. Turn it slightly to place the ball in different spaces about your partner to make them run to get into position to play the ball. Work to make the ball playable.

5.0 [Place pieces of masking tape on the walls or on the floor on each side of the net.] See how close you can make your ball land to the tape. Tennis is a game of inches. Don't be happy just returning the ball. See if you can master *placing* the ball.

5.1 Hitting hard isn't always effective. See if you can reduce the speed of your stroke so the ball barely lands over the net. It takes many variations in the speed of your stroke to play a good game.

5.2 Now try to make each ball bounce back near your baseline. Watch the flight of the ball. Make it go near the net—not high up in the air.

5.3 Watch the level of your swing and the angle of your racquet. If you swing up or tilt your racquet face up, you will make the ball go higher.

5.4 Play a game to see how many times you and your partner can make the ball fall way into the back of the court.

6.0 Let's play either singles or doubles [on reduced size courts, depending on the space available]. Try playing tennis and keeping score. I have posted a brief set of rules. Read the rules, decide which ones you feel you can handle on your court, and begin. The recommended rules are (1) a server starts each point by standing behind the baseline, dropping the ball, letting the ball bounce, and stroking the ball with a forehand over the net into the court, (2) . . . . [List as many or as few tennis rules needed for the range of abilities in the class. The reason we did not introduce the regular serve is that dropping the ball puts the ball in play more quickly, providing more practice for all players. Base your decision about serving on your own preference and situation.]

6.1 As you are playing, concentrate on returning to the ready position to play the ball with a forehand or a backhand.

6.2 Let's see which court can keep their rally going the longest and beat their previous record.

6.3 Begin to take pride in seeing if you can place the ball to force the receivers to practice their backhand.

6.4 Some of you may like working on changing the force of your strokes. Hit the ball harder or softer to intentionally make your receiver move to the net or back to the baseline to stroke the ball.

SELF-ASSESSMENT FOR THE BACKHAND TENNIS STROKE

Six tips for assessing your tennis backhand:

1. Place the thumb of your gripping hand on the back of the racquet grip.
2. Prepare early by turning your shoulder on racquet side toward the ball.
3. Touch thumb of gripping hand to opposite hip.
4. Step forward on the foot on the same side as the racquet hand.
5. Keep wrist firm.
6. Swing low to high, taking racquet low in the backswing, swinging out and upward to contact the ball.

Unit 6 — Refining Dribbling, Kicking, and Passing in Soccer

5 to 8 lessons

MOTOR CONTENT

Selected from Theme 3—Introduction to Movement Quality (Effort) and Theme 7—Introduction to Complex Relationships

Body

Manipulative activities—dribbling, kicking, and passing a ball with either foot

Effort

Speed—accelerating and decelerating while dribbling

Relationships

Ball placement—kicking and passing for accuracy

OBJECTIVES

In this unit, students will (or should be willing to try to) meet these objectives:

- Accelerate and decelerate while dribbling to elude a defender.
- Kick and pass the ball to intended spaces or teammates accurately to move the ball down the field to score a goal.
- Understand that following through by extending the kicking leg and foot toward the target can improve passing and kicking accuracy.
- Show regard for others by working to maintain a safe play environment, by trying to avoid body contact, and by running or dribbling around defenders.

EQUIPMENT AND MATERIALS

One soccer ball for each student; cones, goalposts, or ropes.

LEARNING EXPERIENCES

1.0 [While still inside, give this task to the students so they will be ready to immediately begin working when outside. Explain the boundaries or mark them on the ground with cones or ropes. Be sure there is a ball for each student and cones for the tasks that require them. Change partners several times in every lesson.] When you get outside, start running and dribbling by pushing the ball with your feet on every step as you travel from one side of your area to the other. Work to develop a comfortable running rhythm with the ball. Watch and avoid others as you dribble back and forth. Take a ball out with you and be responsible for bringing it back in.

1.1 See if you can keep changing the speed of your dribble by speeding up and slowing down. Accelerate [speed up] and decelerate [slow down] often.

1.2 Focus on accelerating and decelerating. Make only a few touches on the ball traveling at one speed before you drastically change your speed.

1.3 Sometimes stop your ball abruptly, then accelerate your dribbling to a different spot a few steps away. Mastering this can help you elude opponents.

1.4 Now, change your pathway each time you accelerate or decelerate. Don't chase the ball! Control it! Pretend different players keep coming to take your ball. Show a change in speed and in pathway.

1.5 Now let's see if you can decelerate, accelerate, change pathways, and stop abruptly when a defender is trying to take the ball away from you. As you work, stay in a small space by agreeing to stop once the dribbler passes the defender. Don't just chase one another up and down the field. Find a partner, put one ball to the side, and start. [Make sure that unused balls are well out of the way of the playing area to prevent students from tripping over them. Have them change roles after three or four tries.]

1.6 Defenders, don't work too hard to get the ball at first. Hang back. Let your partners practice getting around you easily a few times. After you feel they are controlling their speed and changing directions easily, apply a little more pressure.

1.7 All of the people with a ball, stand still. Those without a ball, find a new partner close by you. [Repeat tasks 1.4 through 1.6 as needed.]

2.0 Let's practice kicking for a goal with the inside of the foot. Get a partner and two cones. Set the cones up in between the two of you, six to eight steps apart, and practice kicking goals standing about 15 steps away from the goal.

2.1 As you prepare to kick the ball, be sure to plant your nonkicking foot next to the ball and keep your eyes on the ball as you kick it. Don't look at the target!

2.2 As you contact the ball with the inside of your foot, remember to keep your ankle very firm and keep your kicking knee over the ball as you kick. Don't let your foot turn or your kick will be off target.

2.3 Make your kicking foot and leg follow through to the space between the cones.

2.4 Work hard to make contact with the ball at or above the midline or center of the ball. This will keep the ball on the ground and make it hard for a goalie to defend because it won't be up in the air, easy to catch.

2.5 See how many times you and your partner can kick the ball through the goals before one of you misses your target.

2.6 Keep working with your partner and, instead of standing still to practice kicking goals, both of you move back and dribble 5 to 10 yards and kick for a goal without stopping.

2.7 Now, as one player practices being the attacker kicking for a goal, the other person practices being the goalie and tries to keep the ball from passing between the cones. Remember, soccer goalies are allowed to use their hands to block or catch the shot at the goal.

2.8 When you are protecting the goalie position, move quickly to get in front of the ball, catch it in your arms so it doesn't get away from you, and then throw or roll the ball back to the kicker. Make the kicker reposition to receive the ball by sending accurate lead passes. After six or eight turns, trade places.

2.9 When the goalie rolls or throws the ball back in play, see how quickly you can settle the ball and start dribbling to prepare immediately to take another shot on goal.

3.0 Let's see how two of you can pass the ball with the inside and the outside of your foot so the ball goes right in front of the feet of your receiver as you both are running down the field. Don't make the receiver have to speed up or slow down to receive your pass.

3.1 As you both are running down the field side by side, work extra hard to make your passes accurate by anticipating where the receiver and the ball will meet and extending your kicking leg toward that spot as you pass the ball.

3.2 This is very important! You must watch your spacing and keep an open space between you. Remember, if two players on the same team are too close, one person can guard both of them; if they are too far apart, an opponent can easily intercept the ball. [Unskilled players need lots of continued help to not converge on the ball.]

3.3 Dribblers, keep that open space between you and your receiver and this time see if you can accelerate and decelerate before you pass the ball—just as you often do playing soccer. Receivers, don't crowd your dribbler. Match the dribbler's changes in speed by staying opposite each other as you travel down the field.

3.4 When you pass the ball, try to plant your nonpassing foot next to the ball just as you did when you practiced kicking for a goal. Remember, contacting the ball with your foot in the center of the ball keeps it on the ground.

3.5 When receiving a pass, don't stop the ball. Return it immediately while it is still rolling. You may have to reposition your whole body to place your nonkicking foot next to the ball to redirect it back to your partner.

3.6 One of you dribble the ball fast as you and your partner run side by side down the field. The dribbler suddenly steps over the ball and stops it quickly with his or her heel. [Demonstrate stop.] Your partner [or later a defender] will not be expecting you to stop so quickly and probably will run two or three steps past you, giving you a moment to change directions or to pass to a teammate. Dribble and stop suddenly about five times and then switch places.

3.7 As you dribble, focus ahead of you in front of the ball. This helps you see the ball and anyone in front of you. Better dribblers can control the ball without looking at it.

3.8 [Group students to play a game of "Keep-Away" with two versus three players. Each group decides how many passes the offensive team must complete to score a point.] Play a game of 'Keep-Away' by having the team with the extra player be the offensive team. Decide how many passes in a row the offensive team must make to earn a point and how many points you will play before one of the guards rotates in to play offense. Set your boundaries for your game and begin. [As they play, focus their attention on content in 3.0 through 3.7, reinforcing acceleration, deceleration, passing so the receiver does not have to stop to get the ball, and maintaining open spaces between teammates.]

3.9 As you play 'Keep-Away,' be sure everyone on the offensive team is feeling a part of the game by having frequent opportunities to pass and receive the ball.

4.0 Let's play a game called 'Three-Against-Three Soccer.' Each team will consist of six players: one goalie, three attackers [offensive players], and two defenders. The object of the game is for the three offensive players to score a goal while two defenders and a goalie from the other team try to intercept the ball and pass it back to their attacking players. Everyone must stay on their own half of

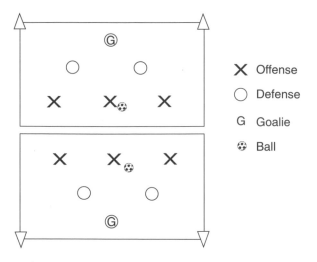

X   Offense

◯   Defense

G   Goalie

⚽   Ball

Three-Against-Three Soccer

the field. If the ball goes out of bounds or is touched by the hands of any player except the goalie, give a free kick to the opposing team at the spot where the mistake occurred. Get in groups of six and find a playing area. Decide who will be the three attackers, two defenders, and the goalie. Get a ball for each group and begin your games with a kick-in by one of the defensive players standing on the center line. [Rotate attacking and defending positions every two or three minutes, giving everyone a chance to play both positions and goalie.]

4.1 Keep your passes on the ground by contacting the ball in the middle with the inside or outside of your foot.

4.2 Make it easy for the receivers to handle your pass by passing the ball slightly ahead of them so they don't have to slow down.

4.3 Watch your spacing. Staying too close makes it easy for one person to guard two people. Staying too far away makes it easier to intercept the pass.

4.4 See how you can maneuver around the defenders by accelerating and decelerating as you dribble—instead of trying to dribble right through them.

4.5 Pass often to keep the defenders on their toes and to make every person on your team feel that they are an important part of the game. [Continue to observe for skill development. Stop play and focus the attention of the players on relevant tasks that you have previously covered.]

4.6 Offense, remember how we learned to make a triangle with clear passing lanes so the person with the ball always had two options for passing?

4.7 Defenders, quickly block those passing lanes the offense has made. Take the clear pass and shot on goal away from the offense.

ASSESSING SOCCER STRATEGY

List three or more important strategies for your soccer play. Which is easiest for most of you? Which is hardest? What can you improve the quickest in your strategy?

Offensive and Defensive Strategies in Softball

5 or 6 lessons

FOCUS Developing offensive and defensive strategies in softball

MOTOR CONTENT

Selected from Theme 7—Introduction to Complex Relationships

Relationships

Player placement—positioning to cover the area about the base rather than standing on the base

Ball placement—throwing the ball ahead of the base runners to cut off the lead run, throwing to get the easy out

OBJECTIVES

In this unit, students will (or should be willing to try to) meet these objectives:

- Field and throw the ball quickly to get the lead runner out or to go for the sure out.
- Position to cover space to the inside of first and third base and to the left of second base rather than standing too near or on top of the base.
- Understand the rules and strategies of the game.
- Accept teammates with varying skill levels and adjust the speed and placement of their throws to accommodate different catching abilities.

EQUIPMENT AND MATERIALS

For every 5 to 10 students: One 5-inch ball (Whiffle, foam, or "mushball"); four bases; ond bat; one batting tee. *Optional:* Baseball mitts. (You may want to ask students to bring their mitts from home.)

LEARNING EXPERIENCES

1.0 [Organize class in groups of five and have each group decide who is to play catcher, shortstop, and first, second, and third bases. Each group will need a playing area with four bases.] Begin throwing the ball around the infield, trying to get the ball to go as straight as you can from one base to the next.

1.1 If you feel the bases are too close or too far apart, move them so each of you can throw an aerial ball in a straight line to another base. Work hard to get the arches out of your throws.

1.2 Try hard to throw the ball straight to your receiver by releasing the ball as your hand points directly at your receiver. [Monitor closely and, if necessary, remind them to step forward on the opposite foot as they throw.]

1.3 If the ball does not come right to you, reach or run to make sure you catch the ball. Tag the edge of your base with your foot when you have the ball in your hand. Then throw the ball quickly to the next base.

1.4 Catchers, throw the ball into the infield and, as you throw, name the base where the receiver should throw the ball. No matter which fielder receives the throw, continue to throw the ball to every player, then back to the catcher.

1.5 Infielders, stay awake! Cover your own space and stay ready to charge the ball. The minute you see where the ball is thrown and hear the call from the catcher, run to cover your base and be ready to catch the ball by having your hands up in a catching position to give the thrower a target.

1.6 Make your catches and throws as smooth as you can by having the give in the catch blend right into the preparation for your throw.

1.7 Catchers, throw the ball toward third base. Third basemen, charge the ball and throw all the way to first. First, throw to second; second, to shortstop; shortstop, to third; and third, to catcher.

1.8 This time, catchers, throw the ball to your shortstop. Shortstops, throw the ball to the first basemen; first, to second; second, to third; and third throw back to the catcher.

1.9 Catchers, throw to the shortstop again and see how quickly you can get the ball back to the catcher. Remember, if you can get the arch out of your throw, the ball will get to your receiver faster.

1.10 Try making your throws go in a straight line so you get the ball around the bases faster. Ready? Throw!

1.11 Catchers, throw the ball so the ball lands in the infield. Then, as soon as you throw, run quickly to beat the throw to first base. When you get to first base, stop. Then everyone rotate counterclockwise [point] so everyone can take turns being the catcher.

2.0 [Reorganize to have no more than 10 in a group: two teams of five throwers and five infielders to maximize practice chances.] In your groups at your own diamond, let's play a game of softball where the ball is thrown instead of batted. Throwing helps put the ball in play faster so you will get more practice in fielding the ball and throwing to get the runner out. Batters must throw the ball overhand so it lands in the infield. The minute you throw the ball, run to first base. The game is played just like softball so the team out in the field needs to hustle to try to field the ball and get the runner out.

2.1 Fielders, cover as much of the area next to your base as you can by taking a couple of big steps away from your base toward another baseman. Get into a ready position with your weight forward on the balls of your feet in a slightly crouched position. Be ready to get back to cover your base quickly if the batter doesn't throw the ball into your area.

2.2 Throwers, don't wait to see if someone catches the ball. Keep your eyes focused on first base and run as fast as you can.

2.3 When you throw the ball out to the field, be prepared to run past first base. Don't slow down before you get there. You can turn toward the sideline and come back safely to first base or you can round the base and turn toward second base if you think there is a chance you can make it to second.

2.4 Remember, your most important task is to catch the ball. If you are playing a base, stretch your hands and arms way out toward the ball as it is being thrown to you by taking a big step and bending your front knee toward the ball. If you can, keep the back edge of your foot touching the base as you reach.

2.5 When playing a base, know if a force-out is possible and try to put the lead runner out by catching the ball and stepping on the base. [Be sure the students understand they need not tag a runner who is running to first base or to any other base when the base behind them is occupied.] Basemen, when you have the ball, you can make a force-out if the base behind the runner has someone on it. You only need to touch the bag the runner is trying to reach. You only have to tag the runners when the base behind them is empty.

2.6 Runners, know if there is someone on the base behind you before you run. If there is, you must run to the next base before the baseman steps on that base while holding the ball and puts you out. If there is no one on the base behind you, you can choose to run back to the base you left and the baseman with the ball has to tag you to put you out. Run your fastest and try to touch the inside of the base if you are rounding the base and going on to the next base to help you turn the corners fast. If you are not forced to go to the next base, be prepared to go back to your base if you think the throw is going to reach the next base before you do.

2.7 Fielders, position for a throw so the throw will not hit the runner.

3.0 [Divide the class into groups of 12 or fewer to play a modified game of softball. Have each group number off 1 through 12: 1 through 4 are up to bat, 5 through 8 are the catcher and the three basemen, 9 through 12 are the shortstop and three fielders. [Eliminate the catcher and some fielders in groups having fewer than 12. One of the players at bat can play catcher.] Have the batters hit the ball from a tee to speed up play to give students maximum practice in fielding and running the bases. Each member of the batting team gets one turn at bat before the groups rotate. The four batters rotate to the three outfield positions plus shortstop, the outfielders and shortstop move to the infield positions, and the infielders come in to bat. The figure below shows the setup of two teams on Field 1 and diagrams the organization of four playing fields.]

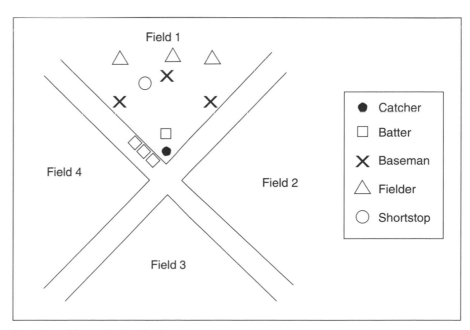

A setup of four playing fields.

3.1 Fielders, charge the ball and see how fast you can get the ball to the baseman.

3.2 Outfielders, plant your rear foot firmly on the ground, lean back on the planted foot, and step toward your receiver. Planting your back foot, leaning back before you throw, and stepping toward the target with the opposite foot all help you throw the ball farther. [If some students are still having trouble getting complete weight transference, break this task into three separate parts with one directed toward the action of the rear foot, another focused on the body leaning back, and the third toward the stepping foot.]

3.3 As soon as the four batters have had a turn to bat, rotate. The batters will go to the outfield and shortstop positions, the outfield and shortstop will move to the infield, and the infield will become the batters. [You may need to walk them through this.]

3.4 [Watch the basemen and fielders to see if they are playing their own area and not that of another fielder or baseman.] Fielders and basemen, be sure you are covering your own area and not creeping into an area covered by another person. Call for the ball if you think someone else is trying for it, too.

3.5 [Question groups where they would throw the ball and whether the runner needs to be tagged.] If runners are on first base [throw to second base]; first and second base [throw to third base]; second base [throw to third base and tag the runner]; second and third base [throw to home and tag the runner]; first and third base [throw to home and tag the runner]. Many times when playing softball or baseball, where you throw the ball depends on the number of outs, where the ball is hit, and on who the runners are. When playing softball, work hard to stop the lead runner from going to the next base.

3.6 [Group students who can hit a pitched ball and those who can get the ball over the plate fairly consistently together. Give them a choice of hitting a pitched ball or using the batting tee to practice place hitting. Review some of the earlier tasks as warranted by the skill levels of the individuals in the group.]

3.7 Basemen, as the batter steps up to bat, be in your ready position on the balls of your feet with your hands ready to catch. Cover the space about your base to catch any ball that comes near you and then quickly cover your base to receive a throw from a teammate.

3.8 This is the strategy if you are not forced to run: Runner, lead off part of the way when the ball is hit and decide whether to go to the next base or stay on the base where you are; fielders, decide which out [force or tag if these are options] is the more sure out and quickly play to that base.

ASSESSING SOFTBALL SKILLS AND STRATEGIES

On a card, write three ideas to help others play better. We will post these on the wall so do *not* write your name on the card.

Unit 8 — Throwing, Catching, and Dodging

5 or 6 lessons

FOCUS
Throwing, catching, and dodging, emphasizing passing ahead of the runner, backing up the throw, and repositioning away from the ball

MOTOR CONTENT

Selected from Theme 7—Introduction to Complex Relationships

Relationships

Player placement—Offense: repositioning away from the ball. Defense: backing up the throw to a teammate, and backing up the throw when thrown at the runner
Ball placement—Defense: throwing to base or teammate ahead of the runner.

OBJECTIVES

In this unit, students will (or should be willing to try to) meet these objectives:

- Reposition quickly to receive or to back up a ball thrown at or ahead of a runner or to another player.
- Change speeds and pathways quickly while running away from the ball to avoid being tagged.
- Understand that (a) good defensive play requires quick, accurate passes ahead of a runner and constant repositioning of teammates who do not have the ball in order to back up a throw or to be in a more advantageous position for getting the runner out; and that (b) good offensive play requires the runners and teammates waiting to run to be aware of where the ball is at all times and to run in the opposite direction.
- Work together as a team, passing the ball quickly to those who are closer to the runner and have a better chance of putting the runner out.
- Remember to throw the ball below the waist of the runner and to be sensitive to the force of the throw.

EQUIPMENT AND MATERIALS

One 8- to 10-inch vinyl ball for each group of four to six students; tape to mark bases and restraining lines for each game played. (Place the balls about the room by the wall so they are easily picked up by the students. Divide the gym into two or three sections, depending on the size of the class. You can have two or three games being played at once, giving every student maximum opportunity for participation. See diagram on page 34. This game may be played outside as well.)

LEARNING EXPERIENCES

1.0 Today we are going to practice two skills needed in our game. The first will be throwing the ball ahead of a runner to get the ball to a teammate as close to the runner as possible before trying to tag the runner. Second, we'll practice backing up each throw at the runner. Fielding team will do this by repositioning a receiver behind the runner in line with the thrower so someone is always in a position to catch the ball if the player with the ball does not tag the runner. In groups of five, six, or seven, you will have one runner and four to six fielders. Each runner will throw the ball into the playing field and try to get to the base without being tagged. The player fielding with the ball is going to try to tag the runner below the waist before the runner crosses the safety line. Each person in your group will have a number from one to seven, so they know when it is their turn to become the runner. Number one goes first and so on. Fielders, pass the ball quickly, always keeping it ahead of the runner. Try to tag the runner below the waist. Get in groups of five, six, or seven with boys and girls in all groups. You will need one ball per group. Begin.

1.1 Runners, watch where the ball is being passed and run in the opposite direction away from the ball. Try not to be tagged by the person with the ball.

1.2 Fielders, make your pass go as straight as possible to your intended receiver and at a catchable speed by taking a step in the direction of the pass and following through with your hands and arms. Remember, you are working together as a team to put the runner out. You want your passes to be caught easily.

1.3 Throwers, be sure you are throwing the ball into an open space and then running in the opposite direction of your throw to make the fielders pass the ball to the other side of the playing area.

1.4 Everyone in the group be on the move except the person with the ball. Once you have the ball in your hands, you cannot take more then one step. Try to pass the ball straight ahead of the runner to keep the runner from reaching the safety line easily. This pass is the same lead pass you worked on in basketball, soccer, and 'End Ball'.

1.5 Runners, as you are running to the base, try to change your speed and pathway to confuse the throwers. Make them guess where you might run next.

1.6 Fielders, check your playing area to see that you have all the space covered with players as evenly as you can. Stay on the move and be sure there is always someone ahead of the runner to receive the pass. [Stop the class and have the students hold their places to see if they are covering all the space evenly or if some are too close together. If they are too close together, have them reposition and start again.]

2.0 As you were working on repositioning to have fielders ahead of the runner, how many times did you have to chase the ball after it was thrown to another fielder? Why? Right. No one was behind the runner and in line with the thrower to catch the ball if the thrower missed the runner. Let's see if we can think how to include repositioning to get behind the runner and in line with the thrower so we have no loose balls. [You may have to demonstrate this concept

Working together as a team.

for the students. Have three students get in a line each about eight feet from each other. One student has the ball, the middle student is the runner, and the third student is backing up the throw. Have the student in the middle move and see if the one backing up the throw stays in line with the moving player and the thrower. Again, stop the play and check to see if the students are moving to get in line with the throw by having them stop and check to see if anyone is in line with the runner and the student with the ball.]

2.1 See how many times you can catch the thrown ball and prevent it from going out of your playing area by being in back of the runner and in line with the thrower.

2.2 Runners, be on your toes and watch where the fielders are positioning themselves. If they all tend to go to one side after the ball, run to the empty side. If they have stayed well-spaced, you will have to do some fancy running by starting and stopping quickly to confuse them or throw off the timing of their throw.

2.3 Fielders, you also need to think about backing up your receivers in case they drop the ball. Let's see how many fielders can be quick thinkers and movers and back up the person closest to them when they are receiving a throw.

2.4 Keep thinking and be alert at all times to know where the ball is in relation to the runner and try to anticipate where the runner may be headed so you can throw the ball ahead of that spot.

2.5 Let's be sensitive to the runner when you throw the ball. Try to hit the runner below the waist and consider the force of your throw.

2.6 Let's see which groups can really keep the ball moving in their playing area by backing up every throw made at the runner. If everyone is really being alert and repositioning, no one should have to run after a loose ball.

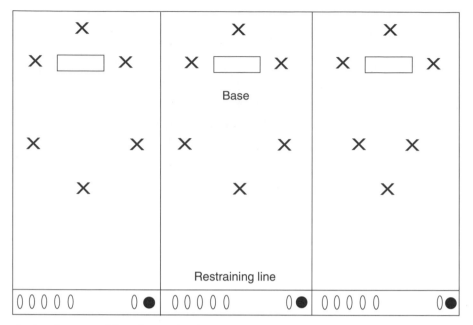

A plan for organizing three simultaneous games.

3.0 We have been working hard on repositioning to back up a throw and on directing lead passes ahead of a runner. Instead of having one team in an area, we are going to try putting two teams in one playing area to play a game called 'Field Dodge.' In the game of 'Field Dodge,' you have a fielding team and a running team. The running team stands behind the safety line while the fielding team positions out in the field as we have been doing. The first runner will throw the ball out into the field away from the fielder, run to the base, and back to the safety line, trying not to get touched with the ball. If the runner is touched with the ball, the next runner runs immediately, and the tagged runner goes to the end of the running line. When a runner gets back to the safety line without being touched by the ball, the next runner immediately starts to run to the base and back. Play continues without stopping until everyone on the running team has had a turn to run. All players then exchange places; the fielders become runners, and the runners become fielders. Fielders must hustle to get the ball and try very hard to tag the runner below the waist before the safety line is crossed. One point is scored for each runner who returns to the safety line without being tagged by the ball. Remember, the base is not safe. There is one ball on each playing field where the running team will begin. Quickly get into groups of five, six, or seven. You may start as soon as you are ready.

3.1 As you are playing the game, work to improve your ability to throw the ball ahead of the runner to another person on your team. Straight passes are more effective than arching ones because they get to the receiver or tag the runner faster.

3.2 Runners, keep your eye on the ball and try very hard to reposition away from the thrower. Dodge in and out as you run.

3.3 Fielders, keep the ball moving. Don't hold the ball because that gives the runner time to reposition.

3.4 Runners, remember to run in a zigzag pattern. Why do you think this is best? [To elude the thrower.]

3.5 Fielders, try your very best to not let the ball go out of the playing area by repositioning to back up every throw made to another person or at the runner.

Fifth Grade Gymnastics

Unit 1 — Creating Shapes in Flight

5 or 6 lessons

FOCUS Creating shapes in flight when vaulting or dismounting

MOTOR CONTENT

Review of content from Theme 1—Introduction to the Body; Theme 2—Introduction to Space; Theme 4—Introduction to Relationships of Body Parts; and Theme 5—Introduction to Weight

Body

Activities of the body—flight, vaulting, takeoffs, and landings
Shapes of the body—body shapes in the air

Effort

Speed—accelerating
Force—firm takeoffs, soft landings, and appropriate muscle tension during flight to create body shapes

Space

Directions—changing directions

Relationships

Of body parts—legs and feet to hands or to each other and to the apparatus

OBJECTIVES

In this unit, students will (or should be willing to try to) meet these objectives:

- Accelerate during the approach to the apparatus by gradually increasing speed and the length of the stride as appropriate in vaulting.
- Perform different vaults by changing the relationship of the feet or hands and both hands and feet to the apparatus.
- Vary their direction and landing (fixed or resilient) when vaulting to achieve greater versatility during and after flight.
- Understand that to perform different vaults selecting and producing appropriate muscle tension in flight helps to achieve control essential to changing the shape of the body and the relationships of the feet and hands to the apparatus.
- Sustain a working atmosphere in class by quietly observing the work of others when they are resting or waiting their turn.

EQUIPMENT AND MATERIALS

For every four to six students a selection of vaulting boxes; stools; benches; bars; planks; tumbling and landing mats. (With careful planning, you may be able to use the stage or platforms located in the instructional area safely.)

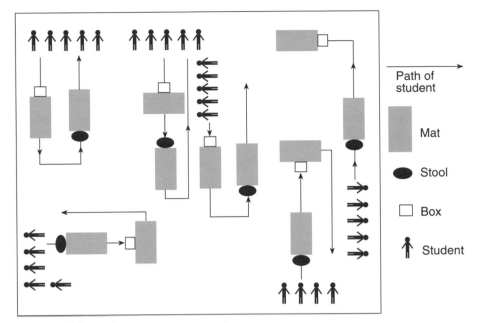

One possible equipment arrangement.

LEARNING EXPERIENCES

1.0 Take care to first walk out a working pathway just for you, making sure your path does not cross the paths of others. In your own pathway, start with a nicely lifted upper body and take four or five light, running steps and finish with a jump, landing very softly on both feet.

1.1 We call this a vertical jump when we are trying to get height with our jumps. Practice doing a vertical jump, landing in the same spot as your takeoff. Try not to travel forward as you jump.

1.2 Concentrate on making your landing very soft by landing on the balls of your feet, giving with your ankles, and bending your knees so your heels touch the floor very lightly.

1.3 Keep running short, new pathways and end each short run with a vertical jump and a nice springy pop-up.

1.4 Make your landing from your high pop-up right on the same spot as your takeoff.

2.0 Get in groups of four to six and stand away from a piece of apparatus about six steps to give the performer working space. The first person in each group, stand facing the box [apparatus] with your feet close to the box. Place both palms firmly on top of the box, fingers pointed forward. Keep your hands pushing against the top of the box with strong hands and arms, make a springy, two-footed takeoff, and land with your feet close to the box. Practice this springy takeoff four or five times each turn you take.

2.1 Some of you may want to run one or two steps to get more height in your springy takeoff. Landing close to the box will help send your hips straight up above your hands.

2.2 The takeoff spot for many of you is still too far from the box. Some of you may need to put a chalk mark on the floor [a piece of masking tape] rolled

FLEXIBILITY, STRENGTH, AND ENDURANCE

Stand on a stair step on the balls of both feet, holding on to the stair rail, or lean one hand against the wall for support. Rise up on the balls of your feet and hold this position for 10 seconds. Then lower your heels slowly until they are below the level of the step, holding this flexed position for 10 seconds. Repeat extension and flexion of the ankles 10 times.

about 12 inches away from your box to remind you to take off close to the box in front of your mark.

2.3 Push hard with your feet against the floor and press with your hands on the box to keep your elbows straight and make your arms very strong. Pushing with your feet and pressing with your arms should help you shoot your hips up high. [Encourage students to create a pike position while in the air by flexing sharply at the waist, forming a "V" with their hips and legs. This "V" relationship helps the feet land on the takeoff spot and fosters the feeling of hips over hands needed in performing a variety of vaults.]

2.4 Push with strong shoulder muscles as you practice four or five bouncy springs up into the air, seeing if you can send your hips higher each time.

3.0 Begin to make your takeoff send you up on top of the box. Then hold a balance for a moment and, exaggerating stretching, twisting, or curling, make a clear body shape in the air as you dismount.

3.1 Now begin to land in a fixed [glued] landing with your feet shoulder-width apart, back straight as a wall and your shoulders over your feet. Control your landing by flexing your hips, knees, and ankles.

3.2 Watch the person in front of you and try to make your shape in the air really different than the one you see them doing. [If this fails to achieve greater variety in body shapes in the air by each student, begin to ask the class to show specific kinds of shapes, such as wide, twisted, round, and long.]

3.3 Add three or four running steps to your approach to the box, remembering to take off close to the box. Still work on making clear shapes in the air as you dismount, keeping your shoulders straight above your feet as you land.

3.4 Limit the length of your approach and make the size of your steps grow as you run. Start with a small step and increase the size of each step as you approach the box, making the last step very long.

3.5 As the size of your steps increases, increase your speed also so you are running very fast when you take off. Most of you are slowing down just as you take off. Slowing down reduces your power and momentum. Then you don't get the height and the strength in your takeoff.

4.0 Combine your best accelerated run and takeoff close to the box, and see how you can take your legs and whole body over the apparatus and land on your feet on the other side. Remember to push on the box using your hands, arms, and shoulders.

4.1 Each time as you perform, really think about muscle tension in your arms and throughout your legs to the tip of your toes as you go over the apparatus. Practice your fixed [glued] landing, making an effort to keep your upper body vertical [lined up] over your feet with your hands out to the side of your body for balance.

4.2 Watch the relationship of the legs of the person in front of you as they vault over the box. See if you can describe the relationship their legs have to each other. Then, as you do your vault, plan carefully the relationship you want to show with your legs. Some of you might like to make both legs go to the same side as one of your hands. Plan what body shape you will make.

4.3 When we can change the relationship of our feet and legs as they pass over the box, we create new shapes with our bodies, and we also create new

STRENGTH AND ENDURANCE

Arm and shoulder strength is important to push forcefully for vaulting. Bench pushing can help here. Sit on a step or bench. Support your weight only by your arms and heels as you walk your legs away from your arm support. Bend and then straighten your arms, keeping your body as straight as possible. Try to increase your number of bench push-ups during the next two weeks.

vaults. Keep thinking about and changing the relationship of your legs and feet as they go over the box—but don't forget to create good speed in your approach and a nice two-footed takeoff. Your vaults will be only as good as your approach and your takeoff.

4.4 Now select one of your favorite vaults and try to perfect your muscle tension and exaggerate the shape of your vault. If your legs are supposed to be straight, stretch them way out, making one straight line from your hips to the tip of your toes. If your vault calls for you to be tucked up in a ball, draw those knees up tightly to your chest.

4.5 After you land, see if you can add one of your best rolls, then finish by traveling, transferring weight from your feet to your hands.

5.0 [Arrange apparatus to encourage continuous mounting and dismounting. Place several pieces of apparatus for each group of four to six students with landing mats appropriately placed to elicit changes in pathways.] Take care to do this next activity safely, watching out for others in your group. See how you can mount or vault different pieces of equipment in your working space, intentionally changing the shape of your body or the kind of vault you make. Also change the way you land and travel to each piece of apparatus.

5.1 As you vault on and off various pieces of apparatus and travel to new pieces, smooth out your traveling. Look and feel like a gymnast all of the time by thinking of muscle tension and by tightening your muscles to make clear, tight lines with your body throughout your entire performance.

5.2 [Two or more people may be able to work simultaneously, depending on the skill of the students and the amount of apparatus and working space. They can match the performance of one another or they may perform at the same time, each making their own sequence. Continue to monitor the size of the steps, the speed of the approach, and the relationship of the feet to the box in the takeoff and the placement of the hands in the vault.]

ASSESSING TAKEOFFS AND LANDINGS IN VAULTING

Accelerates to increase stride length and speed at takeoff.	Varies relationships of feet, and feet and hands to apparatus to perform different vaults.	Performs both fixed and resilient landings when dismounting.	Changes direction in vaults to create more versatility.	Uses moments of inactivity to quietly observe and analyze others' work.
T. Rand	A. Raymond	J. Barr	K. Liber	L. Holloway
C. Mink	K. Philipio	D. Jantis		M. Day
J. Lietto	G. Garcia			
	T. Liu			

List the names of those who need special instruction or needs additional help to perform consistently.

Unit 2
Traveling On and Off Apparatus

4 to 6 lessons

FOCUS — Traveling on and off apparatus while contrasting ongoing and stoppable movement qualities

MOTOR CONTENT

Selected from Theme 1—Introduction to the Body; Theme 4—Introduction to Relationships of Body Parts; and Theme 6—Flow and Continuity in Movement

Body

Locomotor activities—traveling on and off apparatus

Effort

Flow—free and ongoing or stopped and controlled qualities; continuity in combining gymnastic movements

Relationships

Of body parts—base of support to the apparatus and placement of body parts to form their base

OBJECTIVES

In this unit, students will (or should be willing to try to) meet these objectives:

- Work to show a clear contrast between ongoing and stoppable movements.
- Understand that ongoing movement in gymnastics produces the feeling and appearance of continuous motion while bound or stoppable movement may be stopped at any time.
- Understand that contrasting ongoing and stoppable movement requires hard work and, when attained, adds variety and skillfulness to a gymnastic routine.
- Consciously select and place body parts in relation to the present base of support or to the apparatus so they can plan and refine the flow and continuity of their movement.
- Help the class establish a positive attitude by working quietly, sharing space with others, and making a serious effort to improve their own performance.

EQUIPMENT AND MATERIALS

A selection of gymnastic equipment, such as benches; vaulting boxes; stools; tumbling and landing mats. (Arrange apparatus with or without student help to encourage safe, ongoing gymnastic movement punctuated by moments of planned stillness. See diagram on page 42 for some ideas for apparatus placement.

LEARNING EXPERIENCES

1.0 To get started, arrange two mats in relation to each other so that you can travel, balance, then travel down or across both of the mats, trying to look your best as a gymnast. Get into groups of four, place your mats thoughtfully, and begin. [Group size can vary from two to six, according to the number of mats available, or students can pair up to help each other arrange the mats and then work alone. Observe the placement of the mats to ensure the working path of one group does not cross the path of another group.]

1.1 As you take your turn, don't be satisfied with only one form of locomotion. Work to include several different kinds of rolls, moments of flight, and going from your feet to your hands to your feet all in one turn.

1.2 Break up your moments of traveling by planning a balance. Travel into a stationary balance, then carefully travel out of the balance and continue traveling.

1.3 Constantly think of your entire trip down and across the mats as a performance. Make each phase of your movement and each part of your body feel special by tightening your muscles and caring about how the movement feels to you and looks to an observer. Show us your best work!

1.4 Each time you balance, see if you can come out of the balance by going immediately into some form of locomotion. To be successful at combining the balance with locomotion, you really have to think ahead and know which body part is going to take your weight and become your new base and what form of locomotion is going to follow the balance.

1.5 Some of you are ready to make your sequence more interesting. Those of you who can, intentionally change your direction so observers will be constantly surprised. Too often performers tend to move in the same direction over and over. As you come out of your balance, surprise us with a change in direction.

1.6 See if you can make your performance longer by adding several more planned balances and several changes in direction. But don't sacrifice quality for quantity. As you make your performance last longer, be sure to keep that lifted and tight feeling in all parts of your body so the lines and angles you create with your body are always clear and sharp.

2.0 Sit and think for a moment of the arrangement of your mats and where you could place a piece of apparatus. Can you use the apparatus to help you add the unexpected move or balance, adding more excitement to your work? Consider where you will want to land and where you can mount the apparatus. Try to place the apparatus to give you several options for mounting and dismounting in different directions. Take care to have enough people carry it safely. Remember to bend your knees to grasp it and straighten your knees to lift it. Keeping your elbows straight to make the big muscles in your back and legs do the work is the safe and smart way to lift heavy apparatus. [The diagram on page 42 shows several different arrangements you might suggest if you feel uncomfortable having students determine the placement of the apparatus.]

2.1 Before you approach the apparatus to take your balance, plan what body part or parts will be your base of support on the apparatus and what body part or parts you will place on the mat or floor to begin traveling again after coming out of your balance.

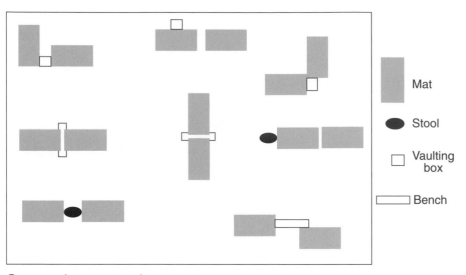

Suggested apparatus placement.

2.2 Coaches always say that basketball and football are games of inches. Skilled performances in gymnastics are determined by inches, too. Plan ahead so you don't make even tiny unnecessary movements. Avoid having to make little adjustments. Start your mount from the exact spot you need in order to place your new base of support on the apparatus for your balance or on the mat or floor for your dismount.

2.3 As you mount and dismount, notice how far away your base of support is from the apparatus. Some of your bases of support are so far away from the apparatus it is almost impossible to transfer your weight to and from the apparatus without falling. Work on ending your traveling movement very near the apparatus and starting very near the apparatus as you come out of your balance.

2.4 [Some classes may find rotating groups during a lesson stimulating because it allows them opportunities to experiment with a variety of apparatus arranged in different ways. Other groups work best when permitted to work at their individually arranged apparatus for the entire lesson.]

3.0 Let's intentionally try to keep our traveling looking and feeling free and ongoing by working to eliminate any moments of hesitation. Make sure the pauses in your gymnastic work come only as you perform a balance. Remember, the balances may be on the mats or on the apparatus.

3.1 Planning ahead and knowing the order of each form of locomotion will help to improve the free flow of your gymnastic sequence. Try to repeat each movement of your sequence in its exact order while keeping your weight moving smoothly from one base to the next.

3.2 To help you develop a free and ongoing feeling, make your gymnastic traveling last longer. You may need to add more rolls, roundoffs, cartwheels, or your own special ways of traveling between your balances. Some of you may need to travel on the floor as well as on the mats to give you more traveling space. Remember safety at all times.

3.3 Imagine this feeling of ongoing movement first before starting your turn. You may need to think, 'Keep moving; don't stop' before you will be able to make one action flow right into the next without stopping. Talk to yourself.

Keep saying, 'Keep moving; don't stop!' See if that helps to get you to make your movement more continuous, more ongoing.

4.0 As you come out of each balance, see how smoothly you can place your new body part down to be part of your base. Act like a slow-motion TV camera has caught you in your performance and every little action of every joint in your body is being shown on TV.

4.1 See how many different places in your movement you can pause as you come out of your balance. Think of the photographer taking several pictures of you as you come out of your balance. Pose for each picture.

4.2 As you come out of every balance, work to feel very much in control of every part of your body. Be in such perfect control of your body that you can stop each body part and hold the new shape just like somebody had zapped you with a ray gun and frozen you in that position.

4.3 You are working on what we call *bound* or *stoppable* movement. To be able to control and stop each part of your movement takes a lot of muscle tightness, but it adds interesting contrasts to your gymnastic sequence. Start your free and ongoing locomotor [traveling] part of your sequence and go into your balance. Then see if you can show a terrific contrast by making each shift in body position very controlled as you come out of your balance.

4.4 Take care in forming your new base of support. Place the body part near the old base of support so you can restart your traveling very quickly.

4.5 When you are working on a contrast, always exaggerate the differences between the two things you are contrasting. Say, 'Keep going; don't stop!' during the ongoing moments and, 'Stop—let the photographer take several pictures!' during the bound, stoppable moments.

4.6 [Use this task more than once in teaching the unit. Repetition gives children continuing motivation.] Take time to enjoy the work of other people around you. Take turns showing each other a sharp contrast between your ongoing, gymnastic work and your very stoppable moments as you come out of your balances. All of you appreciate how hard it is to select and control the flow of your movement in gymnastics. As observers, see if you can notice how sharply contrasting flow makes each person's gymnastic sequence much more exciting to watch.

ASSESSING UNDERSTANDING OF FLOW CONCEPT

Estimate the percentage of each class that consistently performs each criterion. Use these estimates to plan subsequent instruction.

Criterion	Class 1	Class 2	Class 3
Shows clear contrast between free and bound flow.	75%	75%	75%
Positions body parts to support and aid flow qualities.	75%	50%	30%
Transitions smoothly between flow aspects.	50%	40%	30%

Unit 3

Developing Sequences With a Partner

4 to 6 lessons

FOCUS Developing short, matching sequences with a partner

MOTOR CONTENT

Selected from Theme 7—Relationship to Others

Relationships

Of individuals and groups—matching, copying

OBJECTIVES

In this unit, students will (or should be willing to try to) meet these objectives:

- Develop skill in rhythm, timing, and covering space, enabling them to move at the same pace and distance as another.
- Observe actions, time (speed), space, flow, and weight of the movement carefully to copy or match the actions of another.
- Take responsibility for adapting their own actions when working with others to accommodate each other's skill levels and to achieve mutual satisfaction.
- Be aware of the variety of relationships that are possible when they are matching actions with a partner, selecting the one which is most appropriate for their sequence.
- Understand that they must duplicate all aspects of a movement exactly to copy or match another's movement.
- Value accuracy in duplicating their own performances so they help their partners repeat the actions exactly.

EQUIPMENT AND MATERIALS

Landing and tumbling mats; benches; bars; boxes (all to increase the challenge and elicit interest in demonstrating greater variety of movements).

LEARNING EXPERIENCES

1.0 With your partner, work out a short sequence of movement that both of you can do very easily in which you are moving at the same time and performing

FLEXIBILITY

Before rolling, always stretch your back, shoulders, and neck. Use steady, slow movements—no bouncing. Stretch your neck up and away from your shoulders, then hide your neck inside your shoulders. Then do steady, easy stretching to the side—no neck circles.

the same actions. [Select from the list of sequences, develop another, or allow students to create one on their own. Sample sequences include the following:

- Back roll into an asymmetrical shoulder balance that leads into a back shoulder roll, with weight being taken on knee, shin, and top of foot, followed by a forward roll.
- Roll sideways into a balance on two hands and one foot and resolve the balance into a forward roll.
- Forward roll into a balance facing a new direction, with a balance on two shins or one shin and one foot (leg extended to the side), followed by lowering hips and rolling backward over one shoulder.

You may wish to select different sequences for various lessons or to use more than one in the first lesson.]

1.1 As you practice, pay very close attention to each body part that takes your weight. Both of you try very hard to place that part on the mat exactly at the same time.

1.2 Think about your starting positions and try several of these before you make your final decision: standing side by side, facing the same direction; standing side by side, facing different directions; standing back to back; standing one behind the other, facing the same direction; facing each other in a mirror-like relationship; facing each other in a nonmirror-like relationship, for example, both of you move to your own right.

1.3 Once you have selected your beginning position, stick with it and practice going through your sequence. Then add an ending. Work to improve your matching relationship.

1.4 Check to see if you are doing each movement in exactly the same way, at the same time, at the same speed, with both of you trying to make your movement cover the same amount of space.

1.5 [Separate the movement characteristics mentioned in 1.4 as needed into an isolated task.]

2.0 Now that you have a feel for matching your partner's actions, you may choose to continue to add to your sequence or to develop another matching sequence. Be sure you include movements and balances you both can do.

2.1 Select and work on actions that both you and your partner feel comfortable doing and make you both look good.

2.2 It is important to remember what you do, how you do it, and where you do it. You decide what needs improvement. Is it the speed, the flow, the relationship of body parts or your relationship with your partner, or the space aspect of your sequence that needs polishing? Work to polish whatever needs improving. I am going to come around and ask what you are working on to improve.

2.3 Count how long it takes to do an action so that both of you can feel the same rhythm and work more closely together. It is okay to watch your partner, but watching may make you be a little behind. You might prefer to develop some spoken signals or gestures to help you time your movements better so you can move exactly at the same time.

3.0 Great! Everyone has been matching each other and moving at the same time. Some of you might want to try to hold a position very still while your partner performs a part of the sequence, then holds a position while you copy your partner.

3.1 If you hold a balance together, you might want to switch who travels out of the balance first.

3.2 See if you can make your matching and copying parts blend right into each other so they really make up one smooth flowing sequence. Don't stop in between the two sections unless it is a planned balance.

3.3 If you are having trouble copying or matching, make your sequence shorter. If your sequence is showing great matching and copying, you might want to make it a little longer by adding another short phrase of matching or copying to your sequence.

3.4 Let's take time to share what you and your partner have accomplished. [Show in sets of three or four pairs.]

ASSESSING GYMNASTICS PHRASES DURING PARTNER MATCHING

[As students near finalizing a sequence, have them design a "script" of the sequence on paper, preferably on a computer.] Your sequence script must show your pathways, the positions of both partners, and any equipment you use. You must include a graphic way to show strength and speed of movement. If possible, show the difference between moving and still parts in your sequence, especially when one partner moves while the other stays still. Use your script as you improve your sequence. [Use the script to help you assess understanding of continuity, contrasts, and performance quality.]

Unit 4

Balances, Traveling, and Changing Body Part Relationships to Apparatus

4 to 6 lessons

FOCUS Linking balances and traveling at different speeds while changing relationships of supporting body parts to apparatus

MOTOR CONTENT

Selected from Theme 1—Introduction to the Body; Theme 3—Introduction to Time; and Theme 4—Relationship of Body Parts to Each Other

Body

Nonlocomotor activities—balances
Locomotor activities—rolling and stepping actions

Effort

Time—moving into and out of balances at different speeds

Relationships

Of the body to apparatus—changing the relationship of the base of support to the apparatus

OBJECTIVES

In this unit, students will (or should be willing to try to) meet these objectives:

- Develop a sequence of balances and traveling actions that show different relationships of the supporting body parts to the apparatus and a contrast in speed.
- Work to eliminate extraneous movements when traveling in and out of balances; show a lifted, buoyant posture to improve the quality of their performances.
- Select changes in speed to create variety in gymnastic performances and to help them combine certain movements.

EQUIPMENT AND MATERIALS

Available gymnastic equipment, such as boxes, benches, ropes, stools, trestles, climbing apparatus, adjustable bars or planks, tumbling and landing mats.

LEARNING EXPERIENCES

1.0 [Arrange or allow students to arrange the mats. Reduce the number of students working at one mat by using all available mats.] Each of you take a balance that is easy for you to hold. Now take one free body part and slowly lower it so that free body part becomes part of your base. Hold this new balance position, then roll to your feet. Keep practicing until you feel in perfect control of the balance, the placement of the new body part, and your roll into a standing position.

1.1 Begin to focus on showing a contrast in speed when moving out of your balance without losing control. Find places where you show sudden changes in speed.

1.2 [Select and describe a specific balance or have a student demonstrate a balance all students can do, such as a scale. In the scale, the body is supported on one foot with the knee straight. The free leg and torso are held in one straight line, parallel to the floor, with both arms stretched out away from the sides of the body. You could ask the students to lower the free knee to the mat, roll, and stand up. After talking the students through or demonstrating this short sequence, ask them to repeat it several times.]

1.3 Sometimes come out of your balance very slowly and then safely repeat the scale and roll out of it very quickly.

1.4 Take turns being the leader and make a balance, hold it, lower a body part to the mat, and see how carefully you can roll out of it and stand up. Watch your leaders and notice their base and what new body part they lower to the

Notice the extension of fingers and toes in this scale balance.

mat. Try to make a photocopy of the short sequence. Leaders, watch your group members as they try to copy your sequence. Repeat your sequence exactly. Copiers, work to improve your photocopy.

1.5 Each new leader take a different balance to give your group good practice in coming out of a variety of balances. Show definite speed changes, too.

2.0 On your own, take a balance you can hold. Then, after you lower a body part to the mat, see if you can make three or four stepping actions to take you into a second balance that is very different from your first. Roll out of your second balance and stand up.

2.1 Remember your sequence. Balance, lower a body part, step, step, step, step, and hold a new balance, lower a body part, roll, and stand up. Those of you who are waiting, see if you can observe this sequence in the performance of the person ahead of you, including changes in speed.

2.2 As you make stepping actions, see if you can get several different body parts to do the stepping. I've seen some people step with their knees, hips, shoulders, shins, forearms—lots of different body parts. Everyone, get more body parts involved in your stepping actions.

2.3 As you step, feel each new body part support part of your weight. Be able to stop your action on each new stepping body part.

3.0 Try combining rolling and stepping to come out of a balance. Balance, place a free body part down on the mat, and roll into a new balance. Then lower a free body part, take three or four stepping actions, and hold a second balance.

3.1 Some of you have the order of your sequence learned. Perform it several times without stopping except in your planned balances.

3.2 Get rid of all unplanned movements—even little ones.

4.0 [Allow students to select and arrange their own apparatus or draw floor plans showing the placement of the apparatus. In either situation, ensure that mats are located where they will protect the students as they mount and dismount the apparatus in different ways from different places.] Find a way to balance by forming a base of support on two different levels with part of your base on the floor or mat and part of your base on the apparatus. Hold your balance, then travel out of it onto the mat or onto the apparatus. [Observe carefully to see if the students create their base at two different levels.]

4.1 As you come out of your two-level balance, see if you can go immediately into a balance on the apparatus. Take care in practicing this. If the relationship of the part of your base on the floor is too far from the apparatus, it will be difficult for you to hold a balance immediately on a new base on the apparatus.

4.2 Each time you take a balance on the apparatus from your two-level base, remember to place the base on the floor close enough to the apparatus so you can create your new balance without any extra wiggles to get balanced over your new base of support.

4.3 When you feel comfortable going from a two-level balance into a balance on top of the apparatus, see if you can go directly into another balance with rolling or stepping actions.

4.4 Keep adding other balances. Include new two-level balances as well as balances performed entirely on the floor, along with balances on top of the apparatus. Remember your previous balances as you add new balances.

Form a base of support on two different levels.

5.0 Select five to eight balances that show great variety in your bases of support as well as variety in the way you come out of some of them with stepping actions and rolling. See how smoothly you can put them all together in a planned sequence. Change your speed when you can control the sequence and its flow.

5.1 Rather than stop and start your sequence all over when you make a mistake, try to finish it so you begin to know the exact order of the sequence through making yourself practice your whole sequence. This is also fairer to those who are waiting for a turn. It will give each of you about the same amount of practice time. [Observe the relationships of the bases of support to the apparatus. Some students will need help in recognizing that they are attempting things that are almost impossible because one base is too far from the place where they expect to form the new base.]

5.2 Keep in mind as you develop your sequence that you need to have some two-level balances where part of your base is on the floor and part of it is on the apparatus.

5.3 If you can repeat the order of your sequence, intentionally show a change in speed. Make one phase in your sequence very slow and deliberate and one phase very fast, but safe and controlled, to add variety and interest to your sequence.

5.4 Make your stepping actions and rolls take you away from or toward the apparatus. Some of you may be able to perform some of your rolls and stepping actions on top of your apparatus.

5.5 Rid your sequence of all extra movements that you didn't plan. Plan ahead and control your movements and speed. Plan your speed and the relationship of each base carefully so you have sufficient space to place each new base correctly.

5.6 All of you have been working hard and have come up with some interesting balances and ways to travel into and out of them to sharpen your performances. Begin your sequence by concentrating on that beautiful, proud posture that gymnasts have throughout their whole performance. Keep a feeling of buoyancy and lift throughout your whole body.

ASSESSING BALANCES AND SMOOTHNESS

[Have one pair of partners perform while a second pair observes.] Make two accurate and positive comments to the performing pair and one suggestion for improving balancing or linking movements in the sequence. [Change roles. After subsequent practice, each pair writes how the feedback was used to improve their sequence.]

5.7 [Have each group perform for the class. Each time a new group performs, ask the observers to watch for a different part of the content, such as observing for changes in speed, seeing if the performers have rid their sequences of unplanned movements, or watching for the lifted, buoyant posture throughout the sequences.]

Introducing Counterbalance and Countertension

3 to 5 lessons

MOTOR CONTENT

Selected from Theme 1—Introduction to the Body; Theme 6—Flow and Continuity in Movement; and Theme 7—Relationship to Others

Body

Locomotor activities—traveling into and out of countertension and counterbalance

Effort

Flow—developing smooth transitions between partner work and individual work

Relationships

Of individuals or small groups supporting and being supported

OBJECTIVES

In this unit, students will (or should be willing to try to) meet these objectives:

- Create and refine a gymnastic sequence with a partner traveling in a variety of ways into and out of balances showing counterbalance and countertension.
- Understand that to develop countertension with a partner, both place their bases of support close together and pull or lean away, holding on to each other until they are mutually supported. To develop counterbalance, both position their bases of support far enough apart so each partner leans against the other for balance or support.
- Recognize that in countertension and in counterbalance both partners are dependent upon each other for support, making it unsafe for one to attempt to come out of the partner balance until both are prepared to regain their own balance.
- Respect the confidence their partner has in them when performing countertension and counterbalance, communicating clearly with each other before coming out of balances so both have a safe, satisfying experience.

EQUIPMENT AND MATERIALS

For the last task: Large tumbling and landing mats, benches, boxes. *Optional:* A large chart showing counterbalance and countertension.

LEARNING EXPERIENCES

1.0 [Demonstrate countertension by talking two students through an example.] You will be experimenting with some different kinds of balances. This first kind is called *countertension*. To start, both [Robert and Deborah] clasp each other's hands and place their toes very close to form one narrow base of support. Both carefully lean away from their narrow base, making their arms straight until they feel responsible for each other's balance. When you make this kind of balance with someone, you have to be serious and trust each other because the balance of each one depends upon the other. To regain their own balance, they just strengthen their pull, gently bending or flexing their elbows. This pulls them back to a standing position in full charge of their own balance. Get a partner and slowly try making a partner balance showing countertension. [Partners of approximately the same height and weight support one another more easily than those whose body builds vary greatly.]

1.1 Try this same countertension balance, being sure you place your toes close to your partner's, hold on tight, and carefully lean away. Once you feel the two of you responsible for each other's balance, pull back up to a standing

In countertension, you and your partner share a small base of support.

position by bending your elbows. Do this several times. To trust each other, you have to be very serious because you are responsible for each other's safety.

1.2 The two of you are working together to create countertension. Both of you must time your effort closely with your partner. Lean slowly away at the same time with the same amount of tension to carefully become balanced over the same narrow base. If you are losing your balance, it probably is because you haven't matched [synchronized] the speed and tension of your leaning away. When only one of you moves, neither of you can balance.

1.3 As you lean away, do not let your hips sag. Make your shoulders, hips, and feet like one block of wood. The straight line of your body helps to control the leaning away and makes this partner balance easier to achieve.

1.4 Remember this firm feeling in countertension and make your base of support very narrow. Hold on to each other in another way or start in a different position instead of standing to create a new balance forming countertension. Remember to be serious about each other's safety.

1.5 Great! I saw people hooking elbows—some standing with the sides of their feet close together and next to their partner's and leaning away sideways. Keep trying different positions and joining different body parts. Each time you will develop a new balance showing countertension. Remember to come back to get your own balance before either of you let go.

1.6 Most of you have been forming balances starting and staying at a rather high level. Try starting at a lower level and create new balances showing countertension.

1.7 Change partners. Be patient when working with the new person until you can again feel the pull come just at the same time and with just the same amount of force. [Change partners two or three times and perform the same balances. Each time they change, consider repeating some of 1.1 through 1.6 to help them adjust to new partners.]

1.8 [You may wish to repeat all or some of the tasks from 1.0 through 1.7 with the class working to make balances in small groups of two to five on apparatus. In groups of three or more, work on apparatus with countertension only after the students have demonstrated seriousness in their work by maintaining contact until all regain their own balance.]

2.0 In *counterbalance*, your base of support is away from your partner and you lean against each other. You must remember you are responsible for your partner's balance and safety. Everybody walk through this as I say it: Stand back to back with your shoulders and your heels touching your partner's. Pressing your shoulders against your partner's, both of you step straight away from your partner. Feel yourself leaning away from your own base. To regain your own balance, walk your feet back toward your partner. Repeat this balance and come out of it several times until you trust each other and feel dependent on each other for balance. [Some may want to hook elbows as they do this.]

2.1 It helps if both of you press up with your shoulders and head, keeping your back straight with the wall as you move your feet away from your partner's. Do not lean backward or forward at your waist because you will likely overpower the other person or be overpowered.

2.2 Begin to experiment doing other counterbalances, making different body parts be the contact point with your partner. Try your palms, the side of one shoulder, or another body part.

2.3 Some of you try sitting facing each other. Place your palms flat on the floor, just to the side of your hips. Lift your feet and put the soles of your feet flat against your partner's. Now with slow, steady, even pressure from both of you, begin to push your hands strong against the floor, press your feet against your partner's feet, and push them toward the ceiling. See, some of you have lifted your seat off the floor, and you and your partner have formed a counterbalance with just your hands as your base of support. Come out of your balance soon by lowering your seat and easing off with the pushing by your feet.

2.4 Can you see that if you don't work precisely together at the same time with the same pressure pushing in the same direction, neither of you can maintain your balance? Continue to develop this teamwork and mutual respect while starting in different positions with different bases of support.

2.5 [Change partners and revisit any of the tasks 2.0 through 2.4. You may wish to give these same tasks to students working on apparatus.]

3.0 Develop a sequence including countertension or counterbalance and traveling out of your balance in a planned way. [For example, by rolling, cartwheeling, spinning, turning, and the like.]

3.1 Watch your muscle tension as you travel out of your partner balance onto your own new base. Don't collapse. Think about your performance posture constantly.

3.2 This time, do your same partner balance and your same traveling gymnastic movement but add a balance you can hold on your own without your partner.

3.3 Be sure you practice both counterbalance and countertension. Some of you are showing a strong preference for one and not practicing the other.

3.4 Plan how you come out of your individual balances. Place your body parts on the mat or floor carefully and stand tall by making the space between your belt and your chest as long as you can.

3.5 This half of the class, sit down and look for variety in the balances and for lift in the performance posture. This half, working two at a time on the mat, show your best performances. [Change roles.]

4.0 Start with countertension or counterbalance, then travel away from your partner and go into individual balances. Plan a way to travel back to each other and go right into either countertension or counterbalance.

4.1 Show variety in the way you travel to and from your partner. Include not only rolling but also step-like actions and maybe even moments of flight.

4.2 Don't make unplanned stops or movements that distract from your planned sequence. As you come out of your partner balances, signal to each other without talking to make your departure very smooth, blending your own base and your own way of traveling with your partner balance.

4.3 You are really working to refine your sequence. Now watch the space you use as you travel back to your partner from your individual balances. Sometimes you misjudge and end up having to make extra, unplanned movements to return to your partner.

4.4 Those of you who would like to share, raise a hand. While we watch, let's enjoy the tremendous effort each of the pairs [groups] have given to developing and refining their sequence. This is one time where hard work really has paid off. [You may have more than one group share at a time to save time.]

4.5 [You may wish to allow students to incorporate apparatus into their sequences. The interdependent partner balances or their individual work may be made on top of the apparatus. In either case, urge the students to work to get their mounts blending right into their balances and their dismounts blending right into their traveling.]

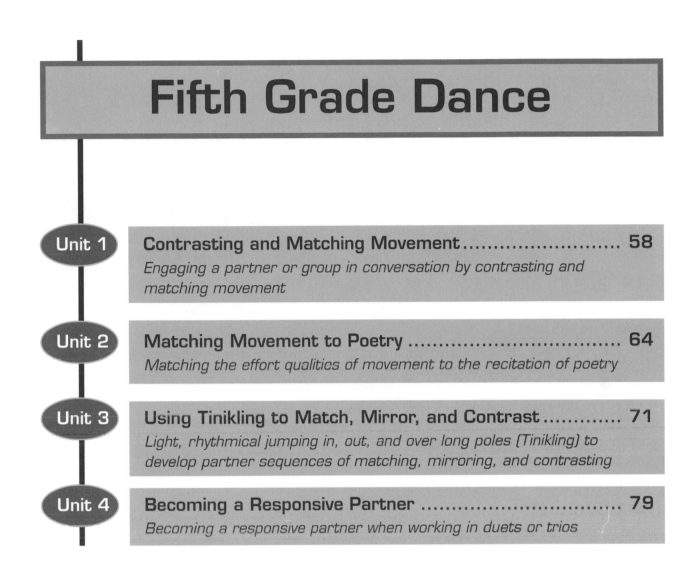

Fifth Grade Dance

Unit 1

Contrasting and Matching Movement

3 or 4 lessons

FOCUS Engaging a partner or group in conversation by contrasting and matching movement

MOTOR CONTENT

Selected from Theme 5—Introduction to Relationships; and Theme 8—Occupational and Everyday Rhythms

Relationships

Interpersonal—following, leading; meeting, parting; matching, copying; contrasting, opposing a partner and group

Special relationships—moods and rhythm of actions, gestures, and conversations

OBJECTIVES

In this unit, students will (or should be willing to try to) meet these objectives:

- Improvise, create, and perform "question-answer" movement conversations with a partner or small group.
- Understand and demonstrate that one's movement may be totally different from a partner or group (contrasting and opposing movement); exactly the same as others with no variation or differences (matching and copying movement); or a combination of these. Show clear transitions between these movements (reflects National Standard in Dance 2a).
- Work cooperatively with a partner or small group and share movement ideas using "statement" and "question-answer" formats; understand that in dance an interpersonal relationship occurs between two or more people during a movement conversation because they are actively exchanging ideas (reflects National Standard in Dance 2d).
- Observe and demonstrate how dance differs from everyday gestures or actions (reflects National Standard in Dance 3a).
- Create and perform their own movement conversation dance based on an emotion or motion of personal significance (reflects National Standard in Dance 3d).
- Demonstrate appropriate audience behavior and discuss their opinions of peers' dances in a supportive and constructive way (reflects National Standard in Dance 4b).
- Create dance sequences that reveal understanding of English language sentence structure and form (reflects National Standard in Dance 7b).

EQUIPMENT AND MATERIALS

Music: Selection A—"The Prologue" from *West Side Story*; Selection B—"Stars and Stripes Forever" or "Washington Post" by Sousa; Selection C—"Shepherds' Dance" by Menotti from *Amahl and the Night Visitors*.

LEARNING EXPERIENCES

1.0 Who can explain what happens when you have a conversation with someone? Right! One person talks, one listens, and then the listener often replies. Sometimes one person asks a question and the other person answers. Let's try these ideas using movement instead of words. [Mary] will 'make a statement' or 'ask a question' in movement and we will 'answer' her with our very own movement. [For example:

(Mary): "Run, run, run, run, *explode!*"

Class: "Run, run, run, run, fizzle."

Let's try again and remember to watch what (Mary's) movement is "saying" or "asking":

(Mary): "Sink, crawl, crawl, crawl, roll, freeze?"

Class: "Sink, roll, roll, roll, freeze."]

Let's continue having a movement conversation. [Explore a variety of movement statements and questions with the entire group, then divide into pairs or small groups and let one student in each group "make a statement" or "ask a question." Change leaders often.]

1.1 As we have our movement conversations, look for the most important part of what is being 'said' by your leader, then respond. For example, what do you remember most about [Mary's] first statement? Yes, '*Explode!*' And you responded to that strong action with an opposite action, 'Fizzle.' Listen to and watch what is being said in movement, then give a clear response.

1.2 Not all conversations are happy. Some are sad, angry, pouting, or defiant. Watch as I express a mood or action, and then you answer in movement:

[Teacher: "Leap! Running steps and kick. Punch the air!"] Now it's your turn to move [students respond].

[Teacher: "Walk slowly . . . turn around and sit down, cupping chin in hands."]

Your turn to move [students respond]. Let's work in groups of three to five. Leaders, try to clearly express a mood or feeling in your movement so the followers can easily answer or reply. Find your group, decide who will be the first leader of your conversation, and start.

1.3 Leaders, try to show a variety of different feelings such as sad, angry, surprised [elicit student responses]. [Rotate leaders so everyone has a chance to make an initial statement or pose a question.]

1.4 One possible reply or answer to a movement statement is 'Yes! I absolutely agree with you!' When your movement agrees completely with the original movement, it's called matching or copying. Let's try it together. [Select one leader to demonstrate a short movement phrase.]

Student leader: 'Stamp, stamp, stamp, clap, clap, *jump!*'

Class: 'Stamp, stamp, stamp, clap, clap, *jump!*'

Try this idea in your groups. Show you agree with everything the leader says. [Keep changing leaders.]

1.5 Another type of movement response is to disagree completely so your movement contrasts with the leader's movement. As your leader moves, your group will do the opposite in some way. [Groups demonstrate.] If leader number one shows big movements, spreading arms wide, the group could move in small ways with arms in close. If leader number two steps cautiously toward the group, they might spring backward, up or away, in surprise. Practice contrasting your movement with what your leader 'says' or 'asks.'

1.6 Watch your leader's movement carefully. Answer the question or make a statement that clearly shows you either agree or disagree with your leader.

1.7 Agree with some statements or questions and disagree with others. Show both matching and contrasting movement during your conversation.

2.0 See if you can carry on a longer movement conversation as a duo [with a partner]. Each person will reply to a statement or question made by the other. Keep your movement conversation going with no long pauses or hesitations. Find a partner and begin.

2.1 Watch your partner's movement closely to get an idea of how to respond. Be sure you actually reply to the statement or question.

2.2 Make your movement answer very clear. Show you agree totally by copying your partner's movement exactly or that you disagree completely by moving in contrasting ways.

2.3 After you answer your partner's question, ask one of your own. So we have

First person: [Performs a "question."]

Second person: [Immediately "answers" and without stopping asks a new "question."]

Each of you provides and answers and poses new questions. Your conversation is ongoing. [Provide adequate time for exploration.]

2.4 Sometimes we 'talk' quickly on the run. Partner number two, lead this energetic conversation with fast traveling [steps, turns, jumps, and so on], scrambling to get somewhere. Partner number one, follow in a merry chase, then take over the lead! [Divide class in half to provide additional performing space. Play music B or other lively piece.] Be very careful of others.

2.5 Pause from time to time . . . then show sharp, excited gestures. Have an animated, amusing conversation. Include lots of questions and statements. No voices—let your body do the talking.

2.6 Sometimes there are moments when we are together, but no one 'talks.' Let's share those quiet moments by traveling with your partner side by side. [Play music C as students travel.] Partner number one stop where you are, ask a question with movement, and the two of you, without voices, have a movement conversation on the spot. Here we go: 'Travel . . . travel . . . travel . . . pause. Right where you are ask a question and answer on the spot.' Again, 'Travel . . . .'

2.7 Show in your movement you are having a calm, caring, supportive conversation. Find different ways to demonstrate slow, steady movement with sustained pauses.

2.8 As you travel, meet up with another couple and have a four-way movement conversation. Each person take turns to question or answer each of the other three dancers. Respond. Say 'good-bye' with your movement and travel on to meet another set of partners. [Repeat.]

AEROBIC
ACTIVITY

At home after a lot of activity, take an exercise heart rate (take a pulse for 15 seconds and multiply by 4). Wait one minute and take this again. Repeat once or twice more. Record the scores. How many minutes did it take for your heart rate to return to within 20 beats of your resting heart rate?

2.9 Let's end class today with a 'farewell' gesture. As you line up or get your belongings, say to your partner or group, 'Good-bye! You did a great job!' No voices, only body language.

3.0 Let's design a small group dance in which the movement conversation passes rapidly from person to person, with some of you agreeing, some interrupting, and sometimes all of you 'talking' at once! Form groups of three to five, select the order of your 'answering' and begin.

3.1 Include in your dance both traveling activities and gestures or body actions performed on the spot. Your movement conversation should be filled with unexpected moments. [Revisit Fourth Grade Dance Unit 4, if you wish.]

3.2 Practice and refine [perfect] your movements so the audience can clearly tell whether you agree or disagree. Perhaps you have a different, but complementary idea? Make your agreeing movements match exactly. To disagree, perform sharply contrasting movements! To complement, show variations on a movement idea.

3.3 I will play two or three musical selections. Listen and decide which selection best matches the mood of your conversation. Try out your group dance with the music. [Play selected parts of music A or B.]

3.4 Some of you may decide to contrast moments of traveling together with moments of breaking away, and having a short movement conversation with one or two others in your group, then rejoining as a traveling group. For an

In visual arts class, students make imaginative drawings or paintings based upon their personal experiences. Artwork, like dance, invites us to identify the artist's point of view and to participate in a conversation.
Brush painting with chalk by Peymei, age 10.

instant, the conversation spotlight would focus on the solo person, couple or trio, then return to the group. Take a few more minutes to practice and refine your sequences.

3.5 [Play slower tempo music C and revisit 3.0 through 3.4, enlarging traveling activities and actions and gestures.] Notice how changes in movement quality affect the mood or feeling of your conversation. What do slow, strong movements say? How much space is used?

3.6 [Another day.] Select an emotion for your group to 'discuss' in movement. Perhaps one person is sad and the others offer comfort and sympathy. Perhaps you are all angry with each other about something. Design a dance that expresses how you feel. Include both matching and contrasting movements. ["The Prologue" and "The Rumble" from *West Side Story* are excellent for accompanying dramatic movement conversations.]

3.7 Set the order of your movement conversation. How will you begin? What happens next [middle of sequence]? When should your conversation end? [Practice and refine sequence.]

3.8 As we rehearse our conversations, think about how important your whole body shape is to the expression of your movement. How do your face, torso, hands, and other body parts contribute to the overall effect? Don't distract us with unplanned movements or a lack of commitment. Even eyes wandering detract from your conversation if they are not a planned part of your dance. Focus is important! Think about what you are expressing in movement and say it with every body part.

3.9 Let's watch our dances. Audience, look for matching and contrasting movement ideas. How do the performers use their bodies to express certain thoughts or feelings? [If two or three groups have a similar "theme," group them for performing and play the same musical selection. After initial performance, discuss observations and questions. Explain scoring rubric below for final student performance. Hold an additional rehearsal to refine dances.]

ASSESSMENT: GROUP PROJECT

Each group will design, refine, and perform a movement conversation dance for peers. Teacher scores

- 4 points if students clearly demonstrate matching and contrasting movement, transition without distracting actions, and a topic (emotion or motion of personal significance).
- 3 points for clear demonstration and presentation with few omissions.
- 2 points for clear demonstration, but incomplete presentation.
- 1 point for partial demonstration of movement skills and concepts.
- 0 points for unclear demonstration and presentation.

4.0 [Collaborate with classroom teachers by having students write sentences featuring "action words," then bring sentences to movement class (see examples on page 63).] We can create a movement conversation with a partner or small group based on your own writings. Choose two or three sentences and perform the main actions. Repeat your actions, making each movement as *large* as

Declarative (statement):
> The deer leaped out of the forest and through the fields.
> The car followed the curving road through the mountains at high speed.
> The top spun itself off the table.
> The well-dressed couple danced every polka at the wedding.
> When I'm older I would like to travel around the world.

Interrogative (question):
> Did you tell them the news yet?
> Did the storm wake you last night?
> Does it take that high-speed train a long distance to stop?
> Can you freeze as if you were a statue?
> Are those kids throwing stones or are they skipping stones in the water?

Exclamatory (exclamation):
> The firecrackers exploded in the sky!
> He slid into home plate for a home run!
> I can't stop laughing at your jokes!
> This sidewalk is too hot for my bare feet!
> How cold the water is!

Imperative (command):
> Walk, don't run with scissors in your hands!
> Wiggle out of that inner tube and toss it to me!
> Skip over all the cracks in the sidewalk.
> Jump over the puddles to keep your shoes dry.
> Never go swimming during a lightening storm.

Examples of sentences.

possible—stretch out, exaggerate each and every movement! [Revisit Fourth Grade Dance Units in the third book of this teaching series to help students effectively demonstrate differences between miming and abstracting gestures.]

4.1 What is the mood, feeling, or attitude of each sentence? Fast, slow; strong, light; direct, indirect; cautious, flowing? Show these moods in your movement. [Rotate among students, offering suggestions and giving feedback.]

4.2 Does each sentence have a clear beginning? Try out various movement ideas with your partner or group. Make the first action of each sentence stand out like a capital letter.

4.3 How can you show a comma, period, question or exclamation mark? Exactly, pauses or rests in movement are like commas. A clear, held position [body shape] might be a period. An uncertain ending with indirect movement asks a question, while an abrupt ending using direct movement requires an exclamation mark!

4.4 Endings are important. Explore different ways to end your movement statements or questions. Which way do you like best?

4.5 Consider your use of floor or air patterns. Does the size and design of your movement in space [curved, straight, zigzag] fit the mood of your statements or questions? Do you need to cover more or less space? Remember how direct movements draw straight lines on the floor [or in the air] and abruptly stop! Indirect movements create wavy, curvy lines that flow.

4.6 We'll take turns demonstrating our movement sequences. Audience, watch closely. Can you identify the mood, feeling, or attitude of the movement? Be ready to point out how dance is different from everyday gestures and actions.

Unit 2

Matching Movement to Poetry

4 to 6 lessons

FOCUS Matching the effort qualities of movement to the recitation of poetry

MOTOR CONTENT

Selected from Theme 5—Introduction to Relationships; Theme 6—Instrumental Use of the Body; Theme 7—Awareness of Effort Actions; Theme 9—The Awareness of Shape in Movement

Body

Shapes of the body—round, straight, wide (spread), angular, twisted; shapes in movement and patterns
Activities of the body—jumping, stepping, sliding, balance, off-balance, turning, stretching, extending, curling, bending, twisting, rising, sinking, opening, closing

Effort

Contrasting strong and light (weight), sudden and sustained (time), direct and flexible (space) actions

Relationships

Interpersonal—individual to group, leading, following; matching sudden and sustained actions with verbal recitations having the same effort qualities

OBJECTIVES

In this unit, students will (or should be willing to try to) meet these objectives:

- Demonstrate the principles of balance, applying force, and alignment by maintaining low, rounded shapes near the floor and sequentially straightening the spine to achieve tall, reaching shapes with alert, aligned postures (reflects National Standard in Dance 1a).
- Explore the principles of instability and fall and recovery by leaning to shift the center of gravity, achieving off-balance positions and controlling falling and turning (reflects National Standard in Dance 1a).
- Maintain a focal point at some distance when jumping, turning, or pausing and focus on a spot nearby when rising, sinking, or gesturing.
- Match the effort quality of their movement with the words of a poem "Leaves" and observe and explain how accompaniment (spoken text) affects the meaning of a dance (reflects National Standard in Dance 3b).
- Explore how lighting and costuming contribute to the overall effect of a dance (reflects National Standard in Dance 3c).

EQUIPMENT AND MATERIALS

Drum; students' voices; a large printed copy of the poem "Leaves."

Leaves

Growing
Settling
Growing
Settling
Growing
Crinkled, crunchy, down
Leaves, turn, brown
Hesitating
Swirling
Whirling, whirling, round
Settling
Leaves, turn, brown
Leap, bounce, skid, and scuddle
Across the woodland floor

From Barry McBride, Nonington College, England.

LEARNING EXPERIENCES

1.0 [Exaggerate your enunciation of all italicized words in this unit.] Crouch down near the floor with your head lowered. When you hear the drum, begin to rise and unfold the body slowly as if growing in slow motion. [Tap slow, even drumbeats and say the word "*Growing.*"] Use every beat to grow as tall as you can . . . feel your body opening, lengthening, reaching, extending upward.

1.1 Crouch down again with a very curved back. Starting at the base of your spine, slowly uncurl the upper torso [body], building each part of your back onto the next until you stand straight and tall. Your spine supports your upper body like a strong column supports a tall building. [Repeat.]

1.2 Feel your back slowly roll up and straighten. Your neck and head will be the last parts to arrive in a straight line. Keep lifting through the top of your head. You now have fabulous alignment!

1.3 Curve your arms gently as your movement grows, lifting and spreading the arms wide. Keep muscle tension in the arms so your arms don't look droopy.

1.4 Everyone, say the word, 'Growing' with me. See if you can really draw the word out so it sounds like it is growing. Ready, '*Grrroooooooooooowing.*' Great! Let's say it again. [Repeat several times, tapping the drum or saying the word along with students.]

1.5 See if you can 'grow' slowly in different ways each time you repeat the word 'growing.' Stretch, extend, lengthen your whole body. Reach upward, outward—arching, spreading, shooting out body parts into angular shapes on "ing."

1.6 Our next action is 'Settling' back to the ground. Let's break this word into three syllables, 'Set-tl-ing,' so we have three, distinct sudden collapsing actions at three different levels. Twist your body and fall a little, twist again and drop, twist once more, collapse. [Practice several times.] Feel all your body parts falling together or giving way with each collapsing action.

1.7 Let's combine the first three words of our dance poem: 'Growing,' 'set-tl-ing,' and 'growing.' Remember to draw out the word 'Growing' and to break the word 'set-tl-ing' into three parts. First, we'll say the words together and then put our actions with the words. [Repeat this sequence several times. Have one student start by saying and leading the action "growing"; the others quickly follow. Next, do the same on "settling" and "growing" with different students leading.]

1.8 Show a contrast between your rounded shapes that slowly grow upward, lifting and spreading into tall reaching shapes, and your angular twisted shapes that suddenly collapse, lose air, taking you back to the floor.

1.9 Let each twist, or change in body shape 'set-tl-ing,' take you to different sides, in front, behind. See the photo on page 69.

2.0 The next action words are, 'Crinkled, crunchy, down.' Say each word so you hear every letter sound and make these words crinkle and crunch as you say them. Let your voice trail off and become fainter on the word 'down.' [Review phrase many times, helping students say these words with expression.]

2.1 What kind of actions do the words 'Crinkled, crunchy, down' suggest? Yes, quick, sharp, short, actions; contracting, shrinking, shriveling, sinking. Show three, quick sharp actions with a pause between each word. [If you wish, allow students to demonstrate their ways.] Now we can put the whole first part of the dance together! [Rehearse 1.0 through 2.1.]

2.2 On the next line of the poem, 'Leaves, turn, brown,' we will repeat familiar actions but show variations on the movement. Take a low curved shape on the floor; crouch down or curl up in your own rounded shape. As you begin to rise up, take a few running steps into a tall, reaching shape. Keep your head tucked until your shoulders begin to straighten to help you maintain a nice, curved, rounded back as you travel, rise, and roll up smoothly. [Practice until students are able to rise easily with a few running steps and hold a tall, reaching shape.]

2.3 When you arrive in your tall, stretched shape, pause a moment, then lean or fall into an off-balance position that takes you circling back into a curled, rounded shape.

2.4 Let your hands and arms lead your body off-balance and into a turning action. See how free and easy your hands and arms can be as they help you turn and go back to a curved, rounded shape.

2.5 Let's say, 'Leaves, turn, brown,' and draw the words out, letting our voices get louder as we say, 'Leaves, turn,' and trail off in volume on 'brown.' [Repeat several times.]

2.6 Let your running steps take you into a high reaching shape that grows and spreads. Say 'Lllleeeeavvvessss' in a loud, rich resonant voice as you travel and move into your high reaching shape. Everyone does not have to do this at precisely the same time. Let's have one person start, then everyone else follow, a few at a time. Leaders who start first [name volunteers], hold your shape until the last people move into their tall, reaching shapes. [Repeat several times, changing leaders if others would like to go first.]

2.7 Now we'll add the turn. Who would like to be the leader to say, 'Turn'? [Emily], when you are ready, say, 'Turn' and begin to lean [fall] off-balance into a turn. Everyone else, follow [Emily], a few at a time. [Practice turning, then combine actions in 2.6 and 2.7. Cue students, saying, "Travel [run], rise, pause, fall, and turn."]

2.8 Make your traveling from a low position gradually rise upward to form a tall, reaching shape [pause]. Being in a long stretched-out position will help you fall off-balance and move right into the turn, then circle around easily and end in a low, curled shape. In dance, one movement flows into the next and the next.

2.9 [Choose three different students to recite the three words "leaves, turn, brown" and to lead this movement. Initially, call (cue) the leader's name to start.] We have three new leaders. When [Andrew] says, 'Leaves,' everyone will travel, rise, and pause in a tall, reaching shape. [Juan] will sense that moment of stillness [when everyone stops] and say, 'Turn.' As soon as everyone falls into a turn, [Jessica] will say, 'Brown,' and you end in a low, curled up shape.

3.0 Look at the poem [large printout] and whisper the next word, 'Hesitating.' What does it mean? Yes, 'To hold back, to pause, to avoid something.' Take a few steps and demonstrate the meaning of 'hesitating.' Walk, step, or gesture in careful, cautious, uncertain ways; wavering, faltering, pausing. [Give students time to explore and develop hesitating steps, then develop a group rhythm.] [Thomas], show your hesitating steps. Notice how he pauses a moment after each step, 'Step, pause, step, pause, step, pause, step, pause.' Let's all try this together. With each step you take, say one syllable of the word, 'Hes-i-tat-ing.' Say each syllable distinctly [clearly] and be ready to stop at any moment!

3.1 In dance, the word 'swirling' is just the opposite of 'hesitating.' It has a smooth, soft, gentleness to its sound. Imagine leaves blowing around in little circles in the wind. Pick a spot on the wall at about eye level to focus on. As you turn around in place and your eyes are pulled away from the spot, quickly turn your head to refocus your eyes on the same spot and finish the turn.

3.2 Let your arms and upper body wave or swerve gently to help make your turns look soft and gentle. Swirl around, drawing two or three small circles with your arms.

3.3 As you turn on the spot, say in a light, whispery voice, '*Swirling.*'

3.4 Say the next three action words of the poem. How do these words sound different than swirling? 'Whirling, whirling, round' does sound faster and stronger! There is a lot of energy used when something is whirling in space. How do the words make you feel as you say them and move at the same time?

3.5 Contrast your turn on the spot with two traveling turns that build energy and speed, making you feel like you are whirling round and round. Look for a big, open space and travel, 'Whirling, whirling, round.' Can you jump and turn in the air on the word 'round'? [Repeat sequence, checking for safe spacing.]

3.6 Let your arms help drive these powerful turns by swinging them out away from your body and in the direction you are going. Feel your whole body 'Whirling, whirling, round [turning jump]'!

3.7 Now the poem repeats two lines, 'Settling' and 'Leaves, turn, brown.' We'll review these actions, then put our dance poem together so far. Remember, each movement should flow or pour into the next. Transitions are important to skillful performance in dance. [Rehearse the first 12 lines of the poem.]

4.0 'Leap, bounce, skid and scuddle' are the next action words. Practice a leap from one foot to the other in your own space. Push off hard from the ball of your foot to generate power to get up into the air.

4.1 To get a forceful leap, bend in the ankles, knees, and hips, then extend these parts strongly. Drive your arms upward in opposition as you extend your

AEROBIC ACTIVITY

People who exercise at least every other day for 20 minutes or more at their target heart rates should recover very quickly after vigorous [hard] exercise. Often, their heart rates drop to near resting in several minutes after stopping exercise. This quick recovery means they need only a little rest before exercising again. Professional dancers work several hours a day performing exercises and routines and interpreting movement. This builds up their aerobic endurance, allowing them to recover rapidly after vigorous jumps and turns.

legs to get more height in your leap. Check for adequate open space ahead of you before each leap.

4.2 A bounce is a very small jump off both feet. Bend your ankles, knees, and hips as you jump lightly. Bounce a few times and then put your leap and bouncy jump together. [After exploration:] Watch [Lee], 'Leap, bounce.' Try it! There is no extra step to get ready into the leap or bounce. One action leads right into the next.

4.3 All together, let's try this combination with the words, 'Leap, bounce.' A leap is strong and powerful and should be said that way while a bounce is smaller and spoken quietly. [Say words several times with students to refine the verbal accompaniment, then practice with actions.]

4.4 Next is a 'skidding' step. Take a big step sideways with one foot and drag the other foot along the floor up to it. Hold both arms out to the same side. Use enough muscle tension to look as if you are sliding your arms and hands along a smooth surface.

4.5 As you practice your skidding [sliding], say the word '*skid*' out loud in a long drawn out way, accenting the 'id.' [Have students play with this movement idea, then put "Leap, bounce, *skid*" together.]

4.6 There is one more word in this phrase: 'scuddle.' As you say this word, do your feet want to take large or small steps? Small, little steps. Try some short, choppy, shaky, scuddling steps like a tottery old man shuffling down the street.

4.7 I'll cue you the first few times we put 'leap, bounce, skid, and scuddle' together, then you can take it on your own. *Ready*, '*Leap*, bounce, skid, [*ssskkkiiiiiiiddd*], and scuddle [*sssccccuuuuuuuuudddllle*].' [After practicing this phrase, assign the words to a student who will say and start the group's actions.]

4.8 Our poem ends with the phrase, 'Across the woodland floor.' How could we move to this phrase? Practice your favorite ways. [For example, traveling freely, lifting arms and legs; rolling or tumbling over until momentum ends; skipping and turning or jumping lightly.]

4.9 Draw your movement pattern on the floor with your finger. Travel and follow the pathway. Say the phrase as you go, letting your voice and movement fade at the end, 'Across the woodland *floor*.' [Pause.]

4.10 [If students need help choreographing their ending, you might suggest the following:] Can you sink slowly to the floor and roll until your words die out? Think of a lonely leaf floating down to the ground, tumbling over and over in the wind as it blows across the ground, and finally coming to rest against a rock.

ASSESSMENT: DOCUMENTATION

Videotape short segments (30 to 120 seconds) toward the end of various units throughout the year for individual classes or selected sample classes to provide a permanent record; to assess group progress; and for comparison with subsequent performance. Pictures can also be taken for the same purposes and to provide a showcase or bulletin board.

5.0 Let's review our poem from the very beginning. Who remembers the first action? 'Growing.' Everyone, take your low, rounded shape, ready to grow. [Have the same students say the words or ask for new volunteers. Alternatively, half the class could recite the spoken text while the other half performs; change roles. Or small groups could accompany each other.]

5.1 [Students may need more practice enunciating words or saying the words with expression. Consult the music teacher in your school who may be willing to assist; consider recording a sound score of the students' voices on audio tape.] Now that we have rehearsed the spoken text and the actions, it is time to plan for our final production. Some of you have made detailed drawings of leaves that can be used in lighting the dance [use an overhead projector on wall or scrim] or to design costumes. Others have taken slide photographs of 'leaves' and the environment [during art class], which we can project onto the wall [scrim]. Others will explore combining poetry with movement images created on the computer [in the classroom].

Show a contrast between your rounded shapes that slowly grow upward, lifting and spreading into tall reaching shapes, and your angular twisted shapes that suddenly collapse, lose air, and take you back to the floor. Let each twist, or change in body shape, take you to different sides, in front, or behind.

5.2 [Revisit this unit during fifth and sixth grades as students read various plays and poetry and write their own Haiku. Focus on effort qualities and shape in movement.]

Haiku

From thin, silken threads

the spider hangs free-floating

then falls and lands firm.

—*Yolanda Danyi Szuch*

Movement Interpretation

[straight, narrow body shapes or pathways in air]

[suspended, buoyant, floating actions]

[off-balance into a firm, angular shape].

Using Tinikling to Match, Mirror, and Contrast

4 or 5 lessons

FOCUS Light, rhythmical jumping in, out, and over long poles (Tinikling) to develop partner sequences of matching, mirroring, and contrasting

MOTOR CONTENT

Selected from Theme 5—Introduction to Relationships and Theme 6—Instrumental Use of the Body

Body

Activities of the body—combining the five basic jumps (two feet to two feet, two feet to one foot, one foot to two feet, one foot to same foot, one foot to other foot); sequences of activities

Relationships

Interpersonal—matching, mirroring, contrasting partner's movement

OBJECTIVES

In this unit, students will (or should be willing to try to) meet these objectives:

- Skillfully demonstrate basic steps, positions, and patterns of "Tinikling" and their own step-jump combinations by jumping lightly and quickly on the balls of their feet in, out, and over stationary and moving poles (reflects National Standard in Dance 1b).
- Keep a steady beat by tapping long poles in 3/4 time (or 4/4 time) with the music.
- Create a partner sequence showing three of the five basic jumps, clear transitions, and relationships of matching, mirroring, and contrasting movement (reflects National Standards in Dance 2a and 5a).
- Understand the definitions of "matching movement," "mirroring movement," and "contrasting movement."
- Show concern for others' safety by keeping poles low to the floor while tapping a rhythm and quickly releasing the poles if a dancer's feet accidentally touch the pole.
- Demonstrate appropriate audience behavior and discuss their observations and opinions in supportive, constructive ways (reflects National Standard in Dance 4b).

EQUIPMENT AND MATERIALS

For every two to four students: Two 8- to 10-foot poles (bamboo or plastic tubing); two 2-foot boards (two-by-fours or unit blocks) to place under each set of poles (mark lines on each board 18 inches apart and centered); two 8- to 10-foot lengths of rope (floor tape, chalk lines) laid on the floor in parallel lines 18 inches apart; recording of "Tinikling" by Kazan, "Tinikling" from *Young People's Folk Dance Library,* or "Tinikling—Philippine Stick Dance." (You may substitute music with a moderate to quick 3/4 rhythm. If students need one extra beat for smooth transitions between steps, select music [folk or contemporary] with a moderate 4/4 rhythm.)

LEARNING EXPERIENCES

1.0 [Tinikling is a Philippine Island folk dance performed by dancers who step, hop, or jump in and out of two, long bamboo poles rhythmically beaten together in a 3/4 rhythm. Steps and gestures of the dance suggest movements of the Tikling bird, an olive green rail, or wading bird, found in marshes and grain fields in the Philippines. Tiklings have long legs and very long toes, allowing them to run silently on soft mud and hop among tall grasses, reeds, and branches.] Listen to 'Tinikling' music and lightly clap the rhythm; there are three beats to a measure. [Play music.] Ready to go, 'Clap, clap, clap.' The authentic Tinikling rhythm is beaten lightly with long bamboo poles, 'Open, open, close.'

Try this hand rhythm right where you are. You may kneel or sit with legs folded in front or to one side. Slap your thighs twice, then clap your hands once. Ready to go? 'Slap, slap, clap.' [Repeat several times.] Let's do the same rhythm, facing a partner nearby, but this time lightly pat or tap the floor in front of you, 'Tap, tap, clap.' [Repeat several times until students feel the 3/4 rhythm and hand action, "Open, open, close."]

1.1 Tinikling challenges you to jump in and out of the moving poles without stopping or breaking the rhythm pattern! This takes some practice. First we'll practice without poles to explore light ways of jumping, then with parallel floor lines [simulating poles] to practice various step-jump combinations. Finally, we'll jump in and out of the moving poles.

1.2 [Play music softly.] Find your own space and practice stepping lightly to the beat of the music, 'Step, step, step.' Lift the knee high—keep your footwork going.

1.3 Think of other ways to step, hop, or jump lightly to the rhythm. On the spot, 'Step, step, jump; step, hop, hop; hop, hop, jump; jump, jump, jump; [and so on].' [Have students show their ways.]

1.4 Let's all try 'jump, jump, jump,' trying hard to stay with the beat. Keep your jumping light and springy by landing on the balls of your feet and letting your ankles bend.

1.5 Can you change the relationship of your feet so they are together for two jumps and apart on the third jump? Say to yourself, 'Together, together, apart.' [Repeat many times in place.]

1.6 Try adding a half-turn on count three when your feet are apart. 'Together, together, turn [apart].' Each time you turn, try to land with your feet apart. [Repeat many times.] What are some variations of this jumping pattern? Right, you could turn on count two, 'Together, turn [together], apart.' Or, turn on count one, 'Turn [together], together, apart.' Practice turning to your right and left sides, always landing on the spot.

2.0 How many of the five basic jumps do you remember from last year? [One foot to the same foot; one foot to the other; two feet to two; one foot to two; and two feet to one.] Practice these jumps with a partner as you move in and out of parallel lines on the floor. [Have students lay ropes or tape on the floor in parallel lines, approximately 18 inches apart, simulating poles.]

2.1 Can you copy or match your partner's movement by facing the same direction and jumping the same way? Who is the leader? Yes, the jumper in front.

2.2 As you jump in different ways, begin to repeat a favorite matching pattern, 'In, in, out [of the lines].' Repeat one way for eight measures; then change—try a new way. [Play music. Encourage light, quick jumps in time with the music; matching movements; and changes every eight measures, or 24 counts or jumps.]

2.3 Choose three of your favorite jumping patterns and combine them into a longer 24-measure [72-count (72-jump)] sequence. Practice until you can go from one jumping pattern to the next jumping pattern smoothly, without stopping, in time with the music. [Play music.]

2.4 Can you add a half-turn to make the sequence more interesting? Or cross one foot in front of the other to land inside or outside the parallel lines? Who becomes the leader when you turn?

2.5 Partner behind, try to copy or match the leader's movement. Jump exactly the same way at exactly the same time.

2.6 If we add a final 8 measures to our sequence, we'll have a 32-measure [96-count (96-jump)] matching dance! Think of a way you and your partner would like to end your sequence—the last 8 measures. On the final count [96], hop or jump outside the parallel lines to let us know your dance is finished.

3.0 In traditional Tinikling dances, there are two important skills. First, jumping in, out, and over the poles with a partner. Second, tapping the bamboo poles together in time to the music. To carry and set up the poles, you must be very careful of others. When I say, 'Begin,' get into groups of four and set up. Two people will get the poles and two get the blocks. The safest way to carry the poles is to pick up two poles, place the poles together, cover the pole ends with your hands, and carry the poles to your space. Put two blocks under the poles, one at each end.

3.1 People who carried the blocks will beat the rhythm first. Hold the pole ends lightly, as if shaking hands. Keep your thumbs on top for safety. Lightly tap the poles twice on the blocks [lines marked 18 inches apart], then slide the poles together to hit once. Keep the 3/4 rhythm going, 'Open, open, close [hit].' Be sure to keep the poles low by sliding them along the board when opening and closing. [Repeat several times, then exchange places so both sets of partners have a turn tapping the rhythm. Encourage students to repeat cues to themselves until the rhythm is up to tempo.]

3.2 Quickly decide which set of partners will jump first. Jumpers, stand with feet together inside the two poles, facing each other, one arm's-length apart. Jump twice in place, then jump with your feet landing apart outside [straddling] the poles. [See diagram on page 74.] Say to yourself, 'In, in, out; in, in, out.' Rhythm players, remember your cue is, 'Open, open, close; open, open, close.' Try not to catch anyone's feet between the poles. If you see the jumper is going to miss, quickly drop the poles. Three counts to go. Ready to go? 'Jump, jump, jump; in, in, out; in, in, out.' [Repeat jumping phrase "in, in, out" 16 times,

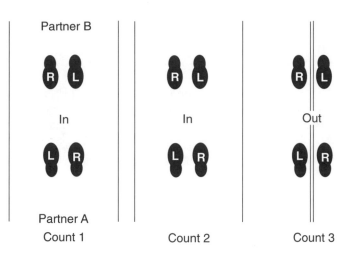

Partner B

In   In   Out

Partner A
Count 1   Count 2   Count 3

Straddle jump: jumping two feet to two feet [Kazan 1972].

then jumpers and rhythm players change roles. Play music as students show readiness.]

3.3 Count measures as you jump saying, 'One, two, three; two, two, three; . . . [up to] eight, two, three.' Quickly add a half-turn [you now have your back to your partner] and repeat your eight measures of jumping. Finish by hopping outside the poles to face your partner on the last count, 'Eight, two, three, [hop]!' You know the whole straddle pattern! [Jumpers exchange roles with rhythm players; repeat.]

3.4 As you practice your straddle pattern, focus your eyes on your partner [front-to-front position] or the rhythm player [back-to-back position]. Don't look at your feet.

3.5 You have just learned how to mirror your partners movement. *Mirroring* means to face your partner[s] and reproduce their movement as if you were a reflection. Let's try another jumping pattern. Face your partner standing on *the same side of one pole*. [Check positioning.] If you jump onto your right foot, what foot would your partner jump onto? Yes, their left foot! Let's see if you can jump in and out of the poles using a 'one-to-the-same-foot' pattern. [See diagram at the top of page 75.] You will jump-hop onto your right foot in the center of the poles [counts one and two] and jump back to the same side onto your left foot [count three], 'In, in, out; right, right, left.' [Partner mirrors, "Left, left, right."] You will always come out of the poles on the same side. [Practice with poles held still to prevent rolling or slipping on pole, then try with partners rhythmically tapping poles. Accompany with music as students show readiness.]

3.6 Stay on the balls of your feet with easy ankles and knees as you jump. This will help keep your movement light and springy.]

3.7 Say to yourself, 'In, hop, out; in, hop, out.' Keep the rhythm going. Don't stop after you step out. On the very next beat, you must have one foot back in the center of the poles. [Practice diagram at the top of page 75 from other side of pole. Change roles with rhythm players.]

3.8 Create your own jumping patterns, mirroring your partner's movement. Decide who will be the mirror and the reflection. Practice your mirroring without the poles until you know the jumping patterns well, then try mirroring with the poles. [Music.]

3.9 Mostly, your hands have been hanging down at your sides as you jump. Make your hands a planned part of the dance, seeing if you can mirror where

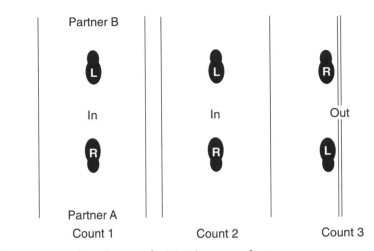

Jump-hop pattern: jumping one foot to the same foot.

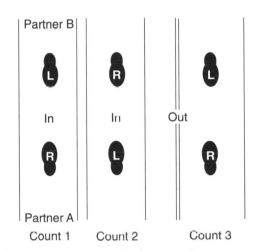

Step sideways to the right starting with the right foot.

you place them. You could join hands, place hands on hips, put hands behind your backs, or swing them up and out to your sides. Try different arm actions as you mirror your partner.

4.0 We have been working on the relationships of matching and mirroring. Let's try a third relationship called *contrasting* movement. What does the word *contrasting* mean? Yes, to make something look different or the opposite. Many of the traditional Tinikling dance steps [jumps] use the idea of contrasting. For example, 'Side step right (3 counts), now side step left (3 counts).' [See second diagram above.] Start by standing, facing your partner, on opposite sides of the two poles. One pole is near your starting position and one is farther away. As the poles are tapped apart on count one, you both jump in with the foot closest to the *near* pole. On count two, jump onto the other foot inside the poles [to same spot as foot one]. On count three, jump onto the first foot outside the *far* pole. You have just gone from one side of both poles to the other side. Now to return to your starting position, do the opposite. Begin with the foot close to the pole nearest you. *Ready?* Three counts to go. [No music.]

4.1 The whole pattern from the beginning is, 'Jump right [in], left [in], right [out]; jump left [in], right [in], left [out].' [Practice the sequence until smooth, then try it with the music.]

4.2 Say to yourself, 'In, in, out.' Keep the rhythm going. Don't stop after you jump out. On the very next beat, you must jump back inside the poles.

4.3 Jumping inside the poles to start your sequence is a challenge! From your starting position [outside the poles], tap your toe to the floor twice inside the open poles [counts one and two], and lift the knee [count three], ready to jump in. To help you feel the rhythm, repeat this once or twice *before* you actually jump in.

4.4 Make up your own contrasting sequence. Think of different ways to start your jumping. [One person could begin inside the poles, the other person outside. Or, both people could begin in the middle, facing different directions; one could jump out to the right, one to the left. Or, you might face each other but use contrasting arm actions.] Let's have one person start a jumping pattern on the floor without poles. Your partner will observe the pattern and do the opposite in some way.

4.5 Remember to keep your jumps light, bouncy, and continuous. Keep going from one jumping pattern to the next to make smooth transitions.

4.6 *Find new ways* to contrast your partner's movement. Change your direction, level, jumping actions, and hand and arm gestures. [Have students decide when they are ready to try their new sequence with poles and up to tempo with music.]

5.0 Let's try putting three sequences together to demonstrate the relationships of matching, mirroring, and contrasting. Each sequence will be 16 measures [48 counts (jumps)]. With your partner, practice three of your favorite jumping patterns to show a variety of relationships. Include some turns to make your dance challenging and exciting to watch!

Keep your jumping light and springy. Can you add a hand, arm, or leg gesture that clearly shows your partner relationship?

5.1 Remember all the different starting positions you have worked on? Back to back; face to face; inside or outside the poles; on the same side of the poles or opposite sides; one partner inside poles, the other outside. Explore the possibilities and decide what you like best.

5.2 Begin to make some definite decisions about the order of your sequence. Will you perform matching, mirroring, or contrasting movement first? What kind of relationship will be next? Practice repeating the order in the same way. [Accompany with poles.]

5.3 Make the relationships you have chosen clear. Would an audience be able to identify each part of your dance as either matching, mirroring, or contrasting? Make your hand and foot positions clear and crisp. [Play music and strike poles.]

5.4 Let's watch our Tinikling dances. [Half of the class performs.] Be sure to show us clear starting positions, light jumping, a variety of relationships, and deliberate hand gestures. Audience, select a group to watch and try to guess the order of the dancers' matching, mirroring, and contrasting movement. [Following the performance, audience meets with dancers in small groups to share their observations and opinions; change roles. Partners jot notes on their records and write a brief summary statement.]

ASSESSMENT: PEER AND SELF-ASSESSMENT

Your dance sequence should have a specific order of jumping patterns and partner relationships. Record this information so we can compare your plan with your performance. End your dance with a spontaneous, unplanned jumping pattern, created on the spot.

Sample

Names: _____

Measures: 1-4
Jumping: Two feet together inside poles and two feet apart outside poles.
Relationship: Matching—starting on the same side, both facing the same direction, with hands on hips.

Measures: 5-8
Jumping: Right foot in, left foot in, left foot out.
Relationship: Mirroring—starting on outside of poles with hands on partner's shoulders.

Measures: 9-12
Jumping: Right foot in, left foot in, right foot out.
Relationship: Contrasting—one person starts on the right side of the poles, and the other on the left.

Measures: 13-16 "The End"
Jumping: Freestyle
Relationship: Free (spontaneous)
Summary statement: _____

_____

_____

6.0 [Revisit this unit later in the school year or in sixth grade. Challenge students to learn more difficult, traditional Tinikling steps—the crossover, crossover and turn, "the chase of the Tikling birds" (see instructions accompanying recordings listed in equipment list). In addition, students could develop and practice increasingly more difficult variations of the five basic jumps.]

7.0 [Invite a community member to give a presentation on traditional Filipino costumes, customs, dances, foods, and celebrations. Compare traditional and contemporary dance in the Philippines today. Modern dances often include movement qualities or step-jump combinations that originate in traditional dances.]

Unit 4 — Becoming a Responsive Partner

3 or 4 lessons

FOCUS Becoming a responsive partner when working in duets or trios

MOTOR CONTENT

Selected from Theme 5—Introduction to Relationships

Relationships

Interpersonal—leading and following; mirroring, copying, matching; moving simultaneously in duos and trios

OBJECTIVES

In this unit, students will (or should be willing to try to) meet these objectives:

- Participate capably in both leading and following roles to become a more versatile mover and to broaden and clarify their own movement ideas.
- Watch their leader at all times while mirroring or copying and matching movement and, with practice, transfer visual cues into a kinesthetic awareness of moving together in unison (reflects National Standards in Dance 1c and 1f).
- Identify aesthetic criteria for evaluating dance, such as ability of performers to move in unison, originality of movements, and variety in levels and directions (reflects National Standard in Dance 4d).
- Work cooperatively in duos and trios as a leader by selecting and demonstrating movement ideas that are challenging, but attainable, and as a follower by accepting the leader's movement ideas and working hard to perform in unison (reflects National Standard in Dance 1d).

EQUIPMENT AND MATERIALS

Musical selections featuring a variety of moods: quiet and slow paced, faster and up-tempo, classical and currently popular. (See Chappell, Nakai, Kitaro, Windham Hill, Winston, and Winter in Resources.)

LEARNING EXPERIENCES

1.0 In your own personal space, face me and move the same way I move. [Slowly move arms, legs, torso very simply without traveling:] 'Stretching, curling, lifting, lowering, rising, reaching, sinking, kneeling, leaning, closing, opening the body.' As I turn around, continue moving and copy or match my

FLEXIBILITY

Pause and hold a stretched position. Holding a stretch for 10 or more seconds can help your muscles improve their ability to stretch and be flexible. This is a very slow process, taking weeks and months of stretching at least every other day. Without frequent use and stretching, muscles lose some of their ability to stretch. 'Follow my movement *slowly*, reaching high and hold; leaning to one side [hold 10 seconds] . . . the other side [hold]. Now continuous movement, lowering, kneeling, curling, rising, lifting, stretching on the spot.'

movement. [Briefly turn your back to the class and move slowly without making sudden or abrupt actions, keeping movement large and visible to students.]

1.1 We are moving in unison—exactly the same way at the same time. All together now, let's turn around to face [Marty]. [Select a student in the back to demonstrate as leader.] When [Marty] moves, we should all move the same way, face-to-face, mirroring [Marty's] movement. Now as [Marty] turns [his or her] back to us, continue to watch closely and copy or match each movement.

1.2 Try very hard to watch your leader and perform every movement the same way at the same time. The audience should not be able to clearly tell who is leading. Find a partner and begin.

1.3 Practice moving in unison [together] by mirroring, then try the very same actions by matching your leader's movement. Which way is more difficult?

1.4 [Divide class into four or five groups. Accompany work with soft, slow, unobtrusive music.] Name an individual in your group to be leader number one. Leaders, turn around and *slowly* move in such a way that your group can match exactly what you do. Keep your movement *large* and easy to see. Followers, copy the movement of your new leader, then after one or two minutes, another person should take over the lead. [Allow sufficient time for all students to lead. Expect breaks in the flow of movement when changing leaders.]

1.5 Leaders, stay in front of your group with your back to others. Remember to keep your arm and leg movements *big* and out to the side. Your followers cannot see movements you make in front of your body.

1.6 [Play moderately slow music (walking tempo).] Leaders, this time move your followers off their spot by traveling a short distance. Keep it simple without complicated steps. Try repeating the same movement idea over and over to give your partners a chance to pick it up before changing your way of traveling. [Change leaders at regular intervals so all students may experience leading and following.]

1.7 When you become the leader next, lead your group to a different level or in a new direction. Remember to keep your movement simple and moderately slow at first, especially when traveling.

1.8 Pause from time to time and hold a position of stillness. Be sure your followers are with you. Look to the sides without turning your head [use your peripheral vision] and demonstrate *large*, clear movement. Work toward feeling the whole group moving together.

1.9 [Play moderate or moderately fast tempo music.] Leaders, challenge your group by varying the way you travel and the speed of your movement. Do something new with those feet!

1.10 Leaders, avoid turning to face your group because then your followers must also turn away from you! Find ways to change directions and levels so your followers can watch you all the time.

2.0 [Accompany tasks with selections of moderately slow music.] In pairs, the leader will move so a partner can easily follow. Make up simple actions with your arms, feet, whole body—movements you can remember and repeat several times. Find a partner, quickly decide who will be the leader, and begin.

2.1 Leaders, make your partner really travel through space. Move in ways your partner can follow. Let them clearly see your every movement.

2.2 Followers, face the same direction as your leader. Your leader must always be in front of you as you move.

2.3 Leaders, make your partner change levels and directions often. Remember to make changes slowly. Slow, simple movements are easier to follow.

2.4 Partners, try to anticipate what movements will come next as you follow your leader. Feel yourselves moving in unison. [Change leaders, repeating 2.0 through 2.4.]

2.5 As you lead and follow, convey the feeling to the audience that no one else exists but your partner. Stay focused and attentive.

2.6 Design a leading and following dance. Make it up as you go. Determine in advance who leads first and for how long, then try to make the transition to the next leader a secret. The audience should hardly notice when you change leaders because the two of you are working as one. [Practice and refine dance studies, 1 to 2 minutes in length.]

2.7 I will play two selections of music quite different in feeling. After moving awhile to each selection, decide with your partner, 'Which selection suits the mood of your dance study?' All of you who want selection one, take a quick seat while we watch partners who have chosen selection two. Then, you will have a turn to perform. [Accompany dances with music one or two.]

2.8 Audience, remember we are looking for smooth transitions between the leader and follower. Are partners working hard to move the same way at the same time? Do they make a good duo? [After the initial performance, have students list other criteria for judging their dances (see assessment below). Provide additional rehearsal time to refine movement studies and hold a final performance. If using self-assessment, videotape partner dances.]

ASSESSMENT: PEER- OR SELF-ASSESSMENT

Your dance sequence should demonstrate:

1 point = Traveling to cover a lot of space
1 point = Frequent changes in levels and directions
1 point = Slow, large movements that are challenging but easy to follow
1 point = Sharing of leading and following roles
1 point = Focus, concentration

Name _____

_____ Total   Peer _____

3.0 [Demonstrate leading and following in groups of three by selecting two reliable students to accompany you.] In our triangular formation, I will begin moving while the other two follow me. Now watch what happens when the leader changes direction to face a different place. We have a new person in front. This person is now the new leader. Every time the leader turns to face a different direction, a new person is in front and becomes the new leader. This works best if the group stays in a triangular formation and if you stay spread an equal distance apart from one another. Quickly join two others to make a trio. Start in a triangular formation, the middle-height person [for example] be the first leader.

3.1 Followers need to be alert and ready to assume leadership instantly when the leader turns to face a new direction. New leaders, be ready to keep your trio moving by making the transitions smooth. Don't turn and pause. Keep your motion going. [If this task is too challenging, allow breaks in the flow of movement and revisit 3.0 through 3.8 in sixth grade. Alternatively, explore relationships between dance and drama through learning activities such as "Mirrors, Shadows, and Diamonds," "Slow Motion," and "Tableau/Still Image." See Flynn, 1994. These activities are a progression toward developing an "Awareness of Shape in Movement" (Theme 9) and require increasing cooperation with others (Theme 5).]

3.2 Leaders, share the leadership role equally among you. If you find yourself passing the leadership role on too quickly, keep it awhile longer next time. Remember that your partners can benefit from following your unique movements. Leaders, if you just love to lead, pass it on sooner so all of you become better dancers.

3.3 When you are leading, try to cover a lot of floor space as you move your trio to open spaces. If you move your group *through* another group, move cautiously, trying not to disrupt the work of the other group.

3.4 Show us different speeds: light, quick jumps; small runs across the floor; a leap that surprises [fast]; large, slow gestures of the arms, shoulders, head, hips, or knees [slow]; an unexpected kick or jolt, or a scramble to get somewhere fast! Move only as fast as your partners can follow.

3.5 Before passing on the leadership role, work hard to explore a variety of changes in levels, directions, speeds, and body actions. Followers, watch your leader's movement at all times. Be ready for these changes.

3.6 Design a short dance [1 to 2 minutes in length] in which all three of you have the opportunity to lead and follow. After each of you have taken the leadership role, complete your dance with a sinking action [controlled falling] to the floor. Hold a still position to end your dance.

3.7 Let's spend some time choreographing [planning] a leading and following trio dance to music. Remember to work hard to make the transitions between leaders smooth and unnoticed. [As in 2.7, you may want to allow students to listen to two or three musical selections while working so they can decide which selection suits the mood of their study.]

3.8 For performing, let's have all the trios using music number one perform in one group. Then we will watch the number two music group and the number three group. Audience, we are watching for concentration and smooth transitions. Performers, focus on your leader at all times and try not to distract the audience by letting your eyes wander. This element of concentration makes you a better follower and gives your dance work authority and magnetism. Capture the attention of your audience and hold it!

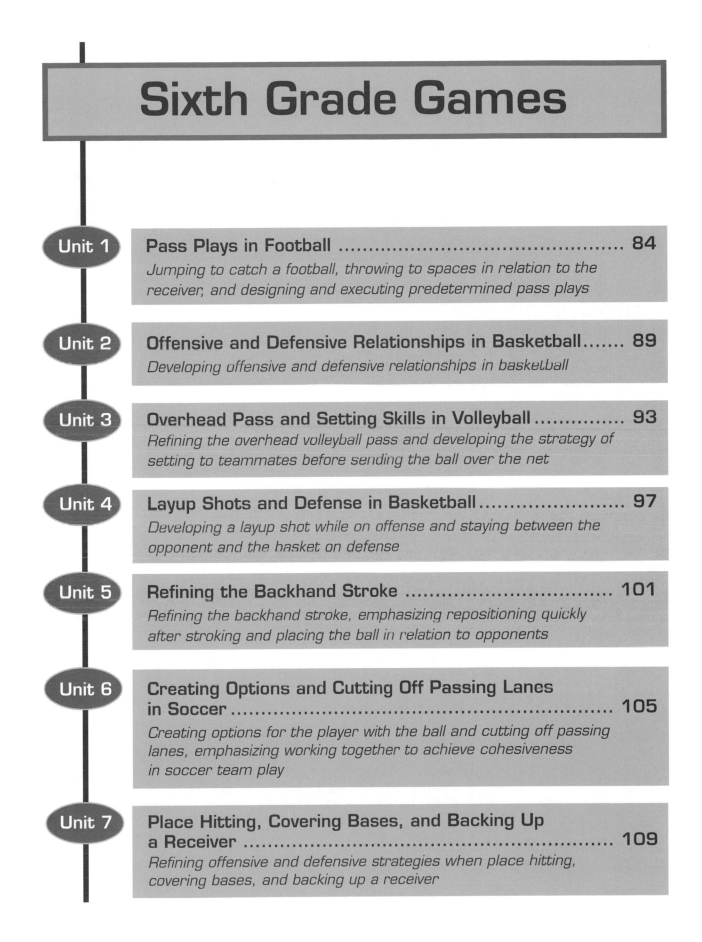

Sixth Grade Games

Unit 1 — Pass Plays in Football

5 or 6 lessons

FOCUS Jumping to catch a football, throwing to spaces in relation to the receiver, and designing and executing predetermined pass plays

MOTOR CONTENT

Selected from Theme 6—Advanced Body and Manipulative Control and Theme 7—Introduction to Complex Relationships

Body

Locomotor activities—jumping to catch a football

Relationships

Passing the ball over the shoulder of a receiver running away from the passer; passing to predetermined places; running different offensive plays in relation to sidelines, opponents, and teammates

OBJECTIVES

In this unit, students will (or should be willing to try to) meet these objectives:

- Jump and catch the ball while in the air, catching a ball arriving to them from over the shoulder as they advance down the field (reflects National Standard in Physical Education 1).
- Loft the pass over the shoulder of a receiver who is running away from the ball so the receiver can continue running toward the goal and passing the ball to a space above the head and in reach of the receiver to give the receiver opportunity to practice jumping to catch (reflects National Standard in Physical Education 1).
- Remember the ball must be thrown at a spot in relation to the path and speed of the running receiver, not at the receiver (reflects National Standards in Physical Education 1 and 2).
- Respect the feelings and needs of others by accepting any classmate as a teammate, by sharing the desirable roles of passer and receiver with all who play on the team, by working to their individual potential, and by abiding by the rules selected by the teams to increase the enjoyment for everyone (reflects National Standards in Physical Education 1, 5, 6, and 7).
- Recognize that enjoyment in acquiring football skills is more likely to be achieved in team games if all players learn to work together, subordinating their own wishes to the needs of the group, and when they equalize the skill ability on opposing teams (reflects National Standards in Physical Education 2, 5, 6, and 7).

EQUIPMENT AND MATERIALS

One junior-size football for every two students; one "flag" and belt or 20-inch strip of cloth about 2 inches wide for each person; four traffic cones for every 10 to 14 students. Some students who are still not comfortable in catching the harder ball may prefer soft, sponge footballs. Also, some students may be more mature and skilled enough in passing and catching a football to grip the regular-size football. You may want to permit them to bring theirs from home. Those using the regular-size, if it is made of harder material, such as leather or plastic, should be spaced so the larger, heavier ball does not endanger or intimidate those whose skills are less developed.

LEARNING EXPERIENCES

1.0 Pair up with someone who has about the same passing ability as you have, mutually decide on what kind and size football you prefer to throw and catch, find a space away from others, and begin to practice throwing and catching your very best spiral passes.

1.1 [By the sixth grade there is likely to be a wide range in commitment to football as a personally satisfying experience; several of the students could be far more experienced than others. You must, as always, be alert to the range of motor development and social maturity of your students and try to personalize instruction by selecting each task to accommodate individual needs. Those who are skilled in passing and catching a football still delight in being given the opportunity to do so in a physical education class and will not mind the attention you give to others to help them achieve greater skill. You need to closely observe each student in the act of throwing, focusing attention on the special aspect needing attention. The tasks listed here under 1.1 are representative of the kinds of tasks that are likely to be needed by less-advanced students to help further develop their skills in passing the football.]

- Make sure your little finger side of your throwing hand is pointing toward your receiver as you throw the ball. Don't let the front of your hand face the receiver. Create a feeling of chopping or slicing the air with the side of your hand like you see when someone does a karate chop.
- Lean back when you prepare to throw and take a step with the foot on the side opposite your throwing arm. Leaning to prepare to throw and the step with the opposite foot will help you get more power into your throw. Really go for power and distance.
- Make your throwing arm travel fast. Hold the ball nearer one end and grip the ball with your fingers spread wide so you can get the ball to spin off your fingers into a spiral.
- Plant the foot on the throwing side firmly on the ground behind you and then push with it and step with the opposite foot as you throw the ball. This will help to get those big leg and back muscles working as you throw to give your throw greater distance.
- Point the front tip of the football up high to help you get more distance, but don't forget to lean back on the rear foot as you prepare to throw. [Some students will need to stay with tasks like these in 1.1 longer than others; however, a brief period of practice in improving the pattern of the throw is helpful for the entire class and you could use several of these as a daily warm-up or introductory task.]

FLEXIBILITY

To help you become a more skillful receiver and catch passes thrown high, low, and in front and in back of you, practice twisting at your waist with your arms extended to the sides each morning when you get up. Do this slowly so you feel a stretch in your side muscles.

1.2 When you and your partner are able to get the ball spiraling through the air, begin to work on throwing it farther—but don't lose the importance of completing each pass. Keep taking a step or two away from each other each time you are both able to get the ball to your partner.

1.3 See how far apart you can be and still complete your spiral passes.

1.4 Catchers, make a big basket or bowl for the ball to land in by spreading your fingers apart and cupping them. Be prepared and give in the direction of the force of the ball at the moment the ball contacts your hands.

1.5 See if you can get your throws so accurate that your receiver doesn't have to move their feet to catch your pass.

1.6 Move up to a point where you and your partner can pass and catch five passes without making the receiver move more than one of their feet to catch the ball.

2.0 Often in football, you need to be able to jump high into the air to catch the ball because the passer misjudges your speed or because the ball has to be thrown over the opponents to keep the pass from being intercepted. Still standing close enough so both of you can make pretty accurate throws nearly every time, some of you may like to see if you can aim your pass a little high so your receiver has to jump and catch the ball when the ball is high. [The roles of the passer and receiver alternate, since the students are in partners for this task and all other tasks in this grouping unless noted differently. Some students may still need work selected from 1.1 to develop the throwing pattern of the pass. Do not push the entire class into this more advanced placement of the ball. Encourage those who need further refinement of the throwing pattern to work on passing and catching with partners standing opposite each other.]

2.1 Receivers, don't jump to catch the ball unless the ball is so high you can't reach it standing on the ground.

2.2 Receivers, spread those fingers and keep your two thumbs close together when you make that catch. Be sure to 'give' with the catch and bring the ball into your body.

2.3 Passers, watch the speed. Don't throw too hard. Remember your receiver and you will be on the same team and you want each pass to be completed.

2.4 Receivers, try to jump high enough so you can catch the ball and bring it in up under your arm as you give with the catch. Try not to let the ball bounce off of your hands or body.

2.5 Passers, get the front tip of the football pointed higher so you can release the ball at about a 45-degree angle [demonstrate] to send the ball higher.

2.6 If you are able to jump and catch the ball high in the air staying in your own space, some of you may like to travel and see if you can run and jump and catch the ball high in the air. Passers, remember you are going to have to throw lead passes so aim that ball out in front of your receiver and send the ball high.

3.0 This is really going to be a test of accuracy for the passers. The receivers will stand near their passer and face in the same direction as the passer. The receivers will jog out in front and away from the passer, trying hard to glance over their shoulder to keep the ball in view as they run. Passers, loft a pass over the head of the receivers so the ball drops in front of the receivers into their hands while they are still running forward.

3.1 Can someone tell me why lofting a catchable pass over the head of the receiver is important in any kind of a football game? That's right. The receiver can continue to run at full speed, probably making more yardage, and can even score a touchdown because they don't have to change their pathway or slow down to catch the ball. It is a very difficult pass to defend because the defender is likely to be in back of the runner and the runner's body blocks the ball from the defender.

3.2 As your passer gets better at judging your speed and the distance you are traveling, speed up your run. This will make it harder on the passer to judge the distance they need to throw. When you are the passer, remember you are throwing to a spot out in front of your receiver.

4.0 [Observe the students as they work on passing. Group those who are ready for a game situation and discuss the game with them. Getting two teams into the game more quickly than others gives them needed practice for demonstrating to the rest of the class. Often, however, some students prefer and will benefit from continuing to work in partners on jumping to catch or on making the loft pass over the head of the receiver. Do not rush to get all students into a game situation. Be sure to keep the teams small with several different games being played at the same time, affording maximum learning time in the game situation. In addition, if you encourage the students to develop rules compatible with their skills, it becomes easier to accommodate individual differences in the game situation.]

Does anyone remember the game of 'Flag Football' and how it differs from regular football? Right, each player tucks a flag—a piece of cloth in the belt in the middle of the back—and, instead of tackling the player with the ball, you pull their flag out. The other difference is the blockers must stay on their feet to block the opponent. Both of these rules help to eliminate falling to the ground and pushing, making the game safer when you play football like we must do in class without the protective equipment football players usually wear.

FLAG FOOTBALL (SIMPLIFIED)

The game is played by two teams of no more than seven players each with rules similar to regular football. Each player tucks a strip of cloth in the middle of their back waistband or belt with about 15 inches of the strip hanging on the outside. Two important exceptions to the regular football rules are: (1) There is no tackling and (2) you must block while standing. A person with the ball is downed when the flag is pulled from their belt. The next play begins at a line where the flag was removed. When a team does not advance 10 yards in four downs, the other team gets the ball. All players on the offensive team may receive a pass. Either team may pick up a fumble and advance the ball. Students and the teacher agree which fouls are major rule-breakers and award 15-yard penalties for these. For less important rule-breakers, award 5-yard penalties. Each touchdown scores six points. After a touchdown is scored, the ball is placed about 10 steps from the end line and a try for an extra point can be made by the scoring team. They have one play to run or pass to the goal to earn one extra point.

4.1 Wait until all the directions are given before you get up. You will need to have four traffic cones for each two teams for marking the end lines and sidelines of your field. Each of you will need a flag tucked in the middle of the back of your belt or waistband with about 15 inches hanging out. Then get with a person who has football skills that nearly match yours. Get into even (if possible) groups of 10, 12, or 14 and divide into two matched teams. For better competition, the person who has skill which matches yours should be on the other team opposing you to make equal teams. Sit in the middle of your field facing your opponents and decide on the rules of your game. [Ensure that everyone has chosen adequate rules, inserting the no tackling and no blocking with the feet off the ground rules to eliminate dangerous play. It also may be advisable to penalize straight arming. If the students demonstrate an inability to equalize teams, you may have to prearrange the teams before class. You will also need to be alert to the need for changing roles within a team so all students get a chance to play quarterback and receiver. Distribute a football to each group when they have their rules and teams clearly defined.]

4.2 Let's take time out from our game to have all teams work out some pass plays. What are some pass plays you have used on the playground or in your backyards? Yes, down and out, down and in, hook, Z out, curl in, hook and go. All of these are good plays. Decide as a team which ones you would like to practice. Then either get up and practice the play as a team or break up into smaller groups and practice several plays at once. Each team practice your plays on your own side of the field. If you need more balls for practicing, get them. [Post a chart of pass patterns. Intersperse this task and those which follow with periods of game play. In addition, give these tasks at the beginning of some of the later lessons or at different times during a lesson when you see that the students need greater variety in the plays they are using.]

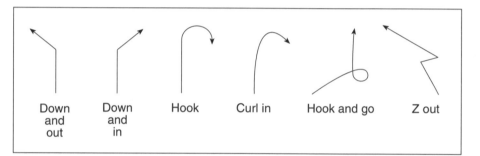

| Down and out | Down and in | Hook | Curl in | Hook and go | Z out |

Six pass plays.

ASSESSING FOOTBALL PLAYS AND STRATEGIES

Draw at least three different pass plays. Explain with the drawing and words exactly what the players on offense need to do. In another color pencil, draw where the defenders may position best at the beginning of the play and where they need to go when the play starts. Be very clear about where to make cuts and how much distance defenders need to give receivers until the pass is thrown.

4.3 As you develop and practice these plays, have at least one play include that lofting pass to a receiver who is running full speed down the field. It is the kind of pass the football announcers call the *bomb*.

4.4 Sit down a moment and think about your team's defensive play. Make sure each of you knows your responsibility. Discuss who is going to rush the quarterback and who is going to try to intercept the passes.

4.5 Take some time for your team to practice one or two plays that involve running with the ball instead of passing the ball. Your team will do better when it can keep the other team guessing whether you are going to have a running play or a passing play. Each team will need at least one ball for this practice.

4.6 Have the receiver and the passer decide on the spot where a cut is to be made so the passer knows exactly where they are to throw the ball. Remember a 'cut' is made by the receiver running in one direction, then making a sharp change in their pathway and running into a new direction to lose their guard.

Offensive and Defensive Relationships in Basketball

5 or 6 lessons

FOCUS Developing offensive and defensive relationships in basketball

MOTOR CONTENT

Selected from Theme 4—Movement Flow and Theme 7—Introduction to Complex Relationships

Effort

Flow—keeping the ball moving; receiving and passing the ball quickly; hustling to reposition

Relationships

Game strategies: Offense—throwing into spaces to make the receiver cover space; repositioning away from teammates to spread defense. Defense—repositioning to stay near the opponent, between the basket and the opponent, keeping the opponent and the ball in view.

OBJECTIVES

In this unit, students will (or should be willing to try to) meet these objectives:

- Pass the ball quickly and reposition away from other teammates and the guard to receive another pass (reflects National Standards in Physical Education 1, 2, and 4).
- Make high, quick passes as soon as they receive the ball to make it more difficult for the defense to set up and to allow a teammate to break open for a pass or a shot (reflects National Standards in Physical Education 1 and 2).
- Guard by repositioning themselves between their opponent and the basket, keeping the opponent and the ball in view when guarding (reflects National Standards in Physical Education 1 and 2).
- Understand basketball-type games require constant physical and mental alertness by everyone to keep the mind and body poised to react to the ever-changing game situations (reflects National Standard in Physical Education 2).
- Understand and show that passes about chest high are easier to catch and pass off more quickly than low passes because the eyes of the receivers do not have to focus downward to catch the ball, allowing them to stay focused on the changing positions of their teammates and their opponents (reflects National Standard in Physical Education 2).
- Share the ball and game responsibilities willingly with any classmate and alter the speed of their passes and aggressiveness with the capabilities of

their opponents and teammates (reflects National Standards in Physical Education 5 and 6).

EQUIPMENT AND MATERIALS

One 8-inch playground ball or junior-size basketball for every four students in class.

LEARNING EXPERIENCES

1.0 I am sure most of you have seen some basketball played recently at a game or on television. I hope you have noticed how important completed passes are to the winning team. Let's concentrate on making our passes go to the receiver right about chest high to make it possible for the receiver to keep their eyes looking straight ahead when catching. You will need some working space, four people to a group, and one ball per group. [It is a good idea to change grouping often, taking time to comment on the importance of working with anyone and being able to adjust the speed of their passes to accommodate different receivers.]

1.1 Make every pass catchable. Don't throw harder as you try to get rid of the ball quickly.

1.2 Watch the path your ball makes in the air! Make the ball go in a straighter line. Looping passes are slow, giving the opponent more time to intercept your pass. [Later you may need to add that looping passes sometimes can help when a guard is between the receiver and the passer.]

2.0 Just as you release the ball, look for an empty space away from the ball and your teammates and dash for it to be ready to receive another pass.

2.1 Speed is important. As you go to that empty space, really hustle—*but* keep your eyes in the game. Don't turn your back on the ball.

2.2 As you break to the empty space, staying in your group's working space, look for every person in your group and position yourself away from the others. Positioning away from other teammates will help to spread the guards that we will be adding soon.

2.3 Now as you break quickly for those empty spaces, let's see how many catchable, quick passes your group can make in 30 seconds. Remember, throw lead passes ahead of your receiver.

2.4 In your group, the four of you line up shoulder to shoulder and number off one, two, three, four. Now quietly walk over and face another line of four. The ones and the threes switch groups so each group now has two new members. Let's see if your new group can beat the number of passes you just made in 30 seconds.

3.0 Get with a person who has just about the same skill you have in these kinds of games. Now go with your partner and get into groups of 8 [or 10] and sit down with your partner facing you. Partners, please play on opposite teams and guard each other to give you more competition by making your teams evenly skilled. Let's concentrate on guarding. Guards have to learn to hustle, too. When guarding, you need to stick to the person you are guarding like glue. When the team with the ball completes four passes, they can shoot for a basket. We will play half-court. The groups in the middle will shoot for the wall targets. The groups at the end will shoot for the regular baskets. Get one ball, decide who will take the ball out of bounds, and begin to practice repositioning to

ENDURANCE

To be a good basketball player, you must have endurance to run up and down the court. Practice jogging each night after school for 10 to 20 minutes or longer to increase your endurance. The longer you can jog (without discomfort), the more energy and endurance you will develop.

Stick to the person you are guarding like glue. Stay between the forward and the ball, trying to intercept.

receive chest-high passes with the guards repositioning to stay between their forward and the ball trying to intercept the ball. [Change groups shooting at targets and baskets often.]

3.1 Think about the relationship you are trying to maintain as a guard! You want to keep repositioning so you can stay near the person you are guarding and between them and the basket. If you let the player you're guarding get behind you, it is very easy for them to get a pass and take a shot.

3.2 Guards, keep your weight forward on the balls of your feet and move immediately right along with the person you are guarding.

3.3 When the ball is caught by the person you are guarding, move in close, extend your arms, and keep moving them about and above the ball to make it difficult for your opponent to pass the ball.

3.4 Now as you are guarding, try to split your attention between the ball and the person you are guarding. If you can watch both the ball and your opponent, you can see when the ball is coming, and you will have a better chance of intercepting the ball. [Reorganize groups often, commenting on their ability to work with many different classmates—both boys and girls.]

4.0 The team with the ball, begin to watch the space between you and your teammates. There should be a clear path between you and the receiver. Don't pass the ball to a teammate unless they have traveled fast to a big empty space. Receivers, hustle—really go! You are working for your opponents when you lope along, not really running, because you are easy to guard.

4.1 Passers, make every pass catchable for your receiver. Remember when your receiver is on the run, that ball must be thrown in front of them.

4.2 Making your steps a little smaller as you start your run will help you accelerate faster. See how fast you can start when you break to that open area and, remember, don't turn your back on the ball. If you are on offense, your eyes should be checking to see where each person on your team is all of the time. If you are a guard, your eyes should be keeping track of the ball and the person you are guarding.

4.3 Don't forget, throwing passes to the chest of the receivers will help them to be able to watch the ball and their teammates.

4.4 Hold the ball only long enough to see an open teammate and pass to that person. If the ball is moving constantly, the defense has difficulty repositioning and cannot set up well to guard.

4.5 Offense, as you reposition, you need to think about breaking for the basket. Shoot when you are close to the basket.

4.6 Watch the person with the ball. Sometimes you might have to break back to the ball when you or the passer is being guarded closely.

SELF-ASSESSMENT: BASKETBALL GAME PLAY

Write the date and a percentage describing how successful and consistent you are for each of the following behaviors:

	Date/%	Date/%	Date/%
I hold the ball only long enough to decide to pass or shoot.			
I pass crisp, catchable passes, aimed at shoulder height.			
I reposition away from teammates to create offensive space.			
I guard staying between my opponent and the basket.			
I watch my opponent but know where other players are.			
I use faking and arm movements to distract passers and offense.			
I share the ball and duties with teammates.			

Overhead Pass and Setting Skills in Volleyball

5 or 6 lessons

FOCUS Refining the overhead volleyball pass and developing the strategy of setting to teammates before sending the ball over the net

MOTOR CONTENT

Selected from Theme 5—Introduction to Basic Relationships

Relationships

Squaring the body to the intended direction of the hit; reestablishing court position to cover court space; offensively setting the ball to teammates to intentionally distract defense

OBJECTIVES

In this unit, students will (or should be willing to try to) meet these objectives:

- Run quickly to get in line with an oncoming ball, reassuming a ready position with knees bent, feet in a forward stride position, hands above forehead with fingers relaxed and spread, and elbows bent (reflects National Standard in Physical Education 1).
- Contact the ball with the finger pads of both hands in front and above the forehead, simultaneously extending the knees and arms to set the ball high in the air to a partner or teammate who will either set for another person or send the ball over the net (reflects National Standard in Physical Education 1).
- Continue to work with all class members to help them improve their skills, show "with-it-ness" by maintaining an alert, ready-to-travel position to receive a ball, and quickly reestablish court position after each hit (reflects National Standards in Physical Education 1, 5, and 6).
- Understand that a ball set in a high arc gives a teammate more time to reposition than a ball set in a lower arc (reflects National Standard in Physical Education 2).
- Recognize the skill of others on the team and give them opportunities to play the ball (reflects National Standard in Physical Education 7).

EQUIPMENT AND MATERIALS

One vinyl ball for every one or two students; nets and standards for every six to eight students.

LEARNING EXPERIENCES

1.0 See how gently you can toss a ball straight up in front of you above your head. Reach up and push it back up with the finger pads and second joints of both hands, trying to contact the ball when it is still higher than your head. [Demonstrate.] Work alone in your own space. Get a ball and begin.

1.1 Contact the ball when it is high so your fingers are pointed up. Try not to let the ball drop down so you are tapping with your palms.

1.2 While the ball is in the air, try to look through the space formed by your fingers and thumbs and watch the ball as it comes down. Make your finger pads contact the ball softly.

1.3 Bend your ankles, knees, and elbows, then extend them quickly as your hands contact the ball to give you more force to send the ball higher.

1.4 As you develop skill in sending the ball high, see if you can make your hands and arms follow the ball to a high spot in the air where you want the ball to go. Keep your hands pointing where you thought your ball would go. Try to make your hands and arms point to this spot every time you send the ball high in the air.

2.0 One of you will toss the ball softly up in a high arc so it comes down above the head of the setter. The setter then tries to set it in a high arc back to the tosser. Take about 10 turns and trade roles. Tossers, make sure you are giving the setters the best toss you possibly can so they get many good sets back to you.

2.1 Setters, you will be more able to send the ball high back to the tosser if you reposition your body each time the ball is tossed. Be waiting for the ball to drop down in front of you with your hands up in front of and above your forehead, your feet in a forward stride position with one foot in front of the other, and your knees and elbows bent. [Demonstrate as you give this information.]

2.2 Listen to your hands touch the ball. Make your touches as soft as you can by spreading your fingers and contacting the ball with all of your finger pads.

2.3 If the setter taps the ball high back to you, some of you may want to see if you can keep the ball going by setting it back and forth to each other. Really try to set the ball so it drops on your partner's forehead.

2.4 Work hard to send the ball high and make your feet take you under the ball. Set it back to each other when the ball is high in the air. Take pride in counting how many times you can set the ball back and forth with your partner.

2.5 Change partners and see how many times you and your new partner can set the ball back and forth.

3.0 This time, let's see if we can purposefully make our receivers reposition to return the ball. Set [or toss] the ball to the spaces out about the setters so the setters must take one or two steps to reposition their whole bodies to get their feet and shoulders under the ball. [Increase number of steps for those pairs ready for a greater challenge.]

3.1 Receivers, keep your eyes on the ball and reposition quickly to get directly in front of and under the ball. Always try to contact the ball high with the finger pads on both hands.

3.2 Watch and make your elbows bend just before you tap the ball. As you contact the ball, extend your elbows and knees quickly to give you the power to send the ball back in a high arc.

Setting the ball high in the air.

3.3 Setters [or tossers], the minute you send the ball back to your partner, move to the right or the left so your partners have to square their shoulders to where you repositioned.

3.4 If you have been tossing the ball to your partners, you may now want to challenge yourselves so both become setters. See how many times you can set the ball to each other, making the other person reposition two to four steps to send the ball back. Count the successful sets you make when you have to reposition.

4.0 [Set up six-foot high nets for the students to use. Have them work in groups of two or four, depending on the space you have.] See how many times you can set the ball over the net working with one or two on each side of the net.

4.1 Try to send the ball about four to five feet over the net so your partners have time to get under the ball to send it back to you. Keep the ball going so you get as much practice in setting as you can. Try not to be ball chasers.

4.2 Keep your head, eyes, and body in the game. You will need to keep your weight on the balls of your feet, waiting to run for the ball. Don't ever take your eyes or mind off the ball. [Getting the students to remain focused and concentrating on what they are doing is a very important skill. Emphasize this point many times.]

4.3 Begin to make it a little harder for the receivers across from you by setting the ball deeper, to the sides, or in front of them. Receivers take pride in not letting the senders outwit you. Keep your eyes and head in the game. Travel quickly to send the ball back. You do not want your ball to hit the floor or the net.

4.4 Each time you play the ball, show you have your head in the game by traveling immediately to reestablish your position to cover your part of the court.

[Discuss with the students how they know which is their part of the court to cover. They need to think in terms of covering a large circle of space around them.] Any time the ball comes into your area, it is your responsibility to get it. There are some areas that will overlap with another person. In this case, the nearest person to the ball must call for the ball, and the other person steps out of the way to support or back up the receiver if there is enough time.

4.5 As you set the ball, get your hips and shoulders facing the precise spot where you want to send the ball.

5.0 [You want to increase the size of the groups to three on a side. If you do, and you designate front and back line players, the following task may be helpful.] Front line players, think about the space near the net. That space is your responsibility. Back line players, why should you not stand near the back line? [In setting the ball, you want to play the ball when it is high, and any ball coming high will go out of bounds if you are standing too near the baseline.] Back line players, try to take two or three big steps from the baseline. Remember to keep the space covered. Return the ball with either the overhead set or the forearm pass and see how many times you can keep the ball going. [If students are not bending their knees and getting one foot forward, or if they need to practice extending their knees to lift their arms to contact the ball, refer to Third Grade Games Unit 4 (the third book in this series).]

5.1 Begin to have two or three players play the ball on each side before sending it over the net. Each time the ball is touched, everyone on both sides of the net should show 'with-it-ness' by adjusting their feet to square their hips, feet, and shoulders to the ball.

5.2 [You or the students can develop a method of scoring and play a competitive game, or any group or class can work cooperatively to see how many times they can set the ball, reestablishing their position in relation to their territory and practicing "with-it-ness."] In your game, the server can start the ball by tossing the ball over the net or serving the ball by striking it with one hand underhand [or overhand] over the net.

5.3 Try to make your game a team game by completing at least one or two passes with teammates before sending the ball across the net. This makes the defense stay alert because they don't know when the ball is coming over.

ASSESSING STATISTICS IN VOLLEYBALL PLAY

During game play with three or four on a side, several other students record the number of passes on one side before the ball is sent across the net. Tally the number of one, two, and three passes for the entire game. In subsequent game play, use these data to set a goal for increasing the number of two and three passes and for reducing the number of single hits.

SELF-ASSESSMENT: VOLLEYBALL PLAY

Write three or more sentences to describe how well you align your body to the ball, pass, reposition, and cooperate with teammates. Then share the ones you need to practice most.

Unit 4 — Layup Shots and Defense in Basketball

5 or 6 lessons

FOCUS Developing a layup shot while on offense and staying between the opponent and the basket on defense

MOTOR CONTENT

Selected from Theme 4—Movement Flow; Theme 6—Advanced Body and Manipulative Control; and Theme 7—Introduction to Complex Relationships

Body

Manipulative activities—developing the layup shot

Effort

Flow—combining the dribble and the layup shot into one continuous action

Relationships

Offense—passing the ball in front of the receiver so the ball and the receiver reach the same spot at the same time; receivers timing their speed and arriving at a certain spot the same time as the ball. Defense—positioning to stay close to the opponent and between the opponent and the basket.

OBJECTIVES

In this unit, students will (or should be willing to try to) meet these objectives:

- Watch for a player breaking for the basket and throw a lead pass that enables the player to shoot a layup without breaking stride (reflects National Standards in Physical Education 1 and 3).
- Play defense effectively (reflects National Standard in Physical Education 1).
- Help the passer complete the pass by adjusting running speed to meet an early or late thrown pass and by faking one way and breaking another when tightly guarded (reflects National Standards in Physical Education 1 and 5).
- Understand that the momentum from the run helps put height into the layup as well as aids in covering space quickly to shake the defense (reflects National Standard in Physical Education 2).
- Willfully accept anyone in the class as a teammate and appreciate close competition as being a good learning experience (reflects National Standards in Physical Education 6 and 7).

EQUIPMENT AND MATERIALS

One playground ball or junior-size basketball for every two to four students; two to six baskets (lower the baskets to six to eight feet high if adjustable). (If baskets are insufficient for every group to have their own, outline 16-inch baskets on the wall for some to use. Rotate groups so all get to work at the baskets each period.)

LEARNING EXPERIENCES

1.0 Try your best to be off the ground as you shoot a layup shot. See if you can lay the ball gently on the backboard about 10 inches above the basket or in the square above the basket. Get in groups of four with one ball, go to a target or basket, and begin.

1.1 As you approach the basket or target, try to come toward it from an angle. You may come in from either side but shoot with your strong shooting hand.

1.2 Really try to make your bent knee pull you high in the air. Swing that right knee up [if they are shooting right-handed; left knee if shooting left-handed] strong and fast to help you get height in your jump. This is just like the hurdle step you used in gymnastics to get height in your spring.

Lift your bent knee forcefully to pull you high into the air during a layup.

STRENGTH

When shooting a layup shot you must be able to run and jump off one foot to get as close to the basket as possible. Practice running and jumping off one foot, seeing how high you can get. Running up and down the stairs will also help build strong leg muscles.

1.3 Add a run to the beginning of your shot. Let the momentum from the run help you get height in your hurdle jump.

1.4 Jump for height. See how close to the backboard you can get your shooting hand as you lay the ball softly against the backboard into the basket.

1.5 Stretch your body as far as you can as you release the ball—toes, ankles, knees, hips, arm—your total body should be fully stretched.

1.6 Make your shot very soft by pretending the ball is an egg as you lay it gently on the backboard.

1.7 After you have made several layup shots from one side, you may want to try shooting from the other side or the front of the basket. Those approaching the real hoop from the front shouldn't let the ball touch the backboard. Lay the ball over the rim.

1.8 As you take turns shooting, see how many shots out of five you can make from the right, left, and front of the basket. Try to break your own record.

2.0 One line will be the passing line, and the other line, the shooting line. Passers will pass the ball at chest level so the shooter can go immediately into the layup shot. The shooter goes to the end of the passing line. The passer gets the rebound, passes the ball to the next shooter, and goes to the end of the shooting line. Make two lines of four players at every basket or target and begin.

2.1 Passers, be sure you pass the ball crisply ahead of the shooter at chest height so the shooter doesn't break stride receiving the pass. Remember, you are passing to a space, not a person.

2.2 Shooters, run fast and make a high hurdle jump, laying the ball gently on the backboard with one hand.

2.3 Give the passers a target with your hands. Passers, remember they are showing you exactly where they want the ball.

2.4 Shooters, really try to lift your body high and completely stretch to get as far off the floor as you can.

2.5 As you pass the ball to the shooter, run in quickly and time your jump to get the rebound as high in the air as you can.

2.6 Both the shooter and the passer really work to see who can get the rebound. Watch the ball carefully, trying to judge where it may rebound off the backboard. Get to that spot as quickly as you can.

2.7 With your partners, keep track of how many baskets you each scored because of an accurate pass. Assists are just as important as the basket.

3.0 When you have the ball, everyone in your group should be traveling to new spaces. Look for the player who is breaking toward the basket for a layup. Pass the ball quickly ahead of the breaking person. Get in groups of four and begin.

3.1 Break to the basket every chance you get. When you see a teammate break, cut in the opposite direction and give the passer more than one option.

3.2 Passers, share the ball with all teammates. Keep your eyes open for the cutting person.

3.3 Starting from midcourt, work the ball toward your basket or wall target. Complete at least three passes before going for the layup. [Rotate groups to give everyone practice shooting at a basket.]

3.4 Receivers, keep repositioning quickly. Cut to the basket from an angle, always focusing on the ball.

SPEED

To change directions quickly and cut sharply requires a lot of practice of controlled and fast cutting. If you want this skill, you will need to practice this at home often and hard by running to a spot and quickly changing direction.

3.5 Let's see how long it takes your group to score 10 points. Catchable passes thrown ahead of the shooter will be the key to success.

3.6 In groups of three or four, one person plays defense and tries to intercept the ball. When the ball is intercepted, the passer becomes the defender and the offense starts play again away from the basket. If the offense makes two baskets before being intercepted, the player making the second basket and the defensive player change places.

4.0 Get in groups of five. Two of you play defense [guards] and practice repositioning to stay between the basket and the three forwards. Forwards, practice short, quick, lead passes toward the basket. For awhile, guards, try not to be too aggressive to give the offense a chance to practice layups without much pressure.

4.1 Forwards, pass the minute the player breaks for the basket, remembering not to travel with the ball.

4.2 Reposition quickly to an open spot after you pass. Pass the ball several times before breaking toward the basket to catch the defense off guard. Remember, chest high passes are easier to catch on the run.

4.3 Forwards without the ball, run a far enough distance to lose your guard. Then make a sharp, sudden change in pathway, breaking toward the basket to receive the pass. Forward with the ball, stay alert and pass the ball ahead of the receiver the moment another forward breaks for the basket.

4.4 Now guards, begin to tighten your defense. Stick with the person you are guarding, keeping your arms high to block the shot.

4.5 Let's play a 10-point game. We have been working on not traveling with the ball and not making personal contact. In this game we will add three new rules: no dribbling, all shots must be taken from inside the free throw line, and layups count for three points.

5.0 Let's play three against three at your basket or wall target. You will have to work harder to complete your passes. Break after you pass to get free for a layup. When the defense intercepts the ball, they are to work the ball back to the top of the court, then reverse roles immediately and go for the layup.

5.1 Make short, quick passes. They must be hard enough to keep the defense from intercepting them but still accurate so your receiver can catch them.

5.2 Offensive players without the ball, don't forget to change your pathway sharply cutting toward the basket. Passers, pass the ball in front of your receiver the moment your receiver breaks for the basket.

5.3 If you want to be the one that shoots the layup, you must break while moving close to the basket to score. [Keep reminding teammates to stay away from each other so they have room to run and pass the ball. They will tend to cluster around the ball or stand still.]

5.4 As you reposition quickly, look for an open spot nearer the goal and make your break suddenly. If your open spot plugs up, move back quickly toward the foul line and break again.

5.5 Receivers, you must be ready to do something with the ball the minute you receive a pass. Assess your situation quickly and pass to someone who is positioned for a layup or shoot if you have a sure two points.

5.6 Take a shot if you are free and within six feet of the basket. Remember, layups will count three points and all other short shots score one point. Any shot from the free throw line or farther away will lose two points.

FOCUS — Refining the backhand stroke, emphasizing repositioning quickly after stroking and placing the ball in relation to opponents

MOTOR CONTENT

Selected from Theme 1—Introduction to Basic Body and Manipulative Control and Theme 7—Introduction to Complex Relationships

Body

Manipulative activities—refining the backhand
Locomotor activities—footwork

Relationships

Placing the ball away from the opponent; positioning to return a shot; and repositioning to cover space

OBJECTIVES

In this unit, students will (or should be willing to try to) meet these objectives:

- Refine the backhand by positioning the back of the racquet shoulder toward the net or target (reflects National Standard in Physical Education 1).
- Keep the feet in motion, returning to the ready position after each stroke to enable quick repositioning to return the ball (reflects National Standard in Physical Education 1).
- Recognize that footwork is critical to the game of tennis because players must constantly adjust their positions to return the ball (reflects National Standard in Physical Education 2).
- Understand scoring of a game in tennis (reflects National Standard in Physical Education 2).
- Accept responsibility for the enjoyment and skill development of others by remaining serious and by trying to keep the ball playable (reflects National Standards in Physical Education 5 and 7).

EQUIPMENT AND MATERIALS

One racquet and ball for each student; standards and ropes or nets. (The black plastic racquets and high-bounce foam balls, which are available commercially, have proven to be extremely satisfactory, especially for indoor instruction, as have the short-handled racquets with strings.)

LEARNING EXPERIENCES

[You may choose to teach all these experiences with the students stroking the ball over a net in a more game-like situation.]

1.0 Today, see if you can start out by seriously trying to produce your best tennis strokes to help your partner return the ball. You will need a racquet, a partner, and one ball for the two of you. You may begin.

1.1 Everyone stand and show me your position for a backhand. Good, you have all remembered to point the racquet side of your body toward the net and use your nonracquet hand to steady the throat of the racquet. As you rally back and forth over the net, try to reposition so you practice only backhands. Your backhand should feel like you are throwing a deck tennis ring over the net. Get the hitting side of your body pointing toward the net before you stroke the ball. Try to direct the ball to the backhand side of your receiver.

1.2 Discipline yourself to let the ball bounce out in front of you before you try to return it. Remember how you turned your body to throw the deck tennis ring? Be sure to have the whole racquet side of your body to the net and your feet set to stroke the ball backhand.

1.3 Remember, you need to control where the ball lands when you're returning it. Direct [swing] the racquet face toward the spot just out in front of the nonracquet side of the receiver to help your receiver return the ball with a backhand stroke.

1.4 Receivers, anticipate where the ball is going to land. Adjust your feet and body position so you can contact the ball out in front of you as you wait for the ball to bounce. Hit the ball softly back to your partner.

1.5 Remember to step toward the net, shifting your weight from your back foot to your front foot, as you stroke the ball.

1.6 When you contact the ball, your arm should be relatively straight. Work on extending your arm as you contact the ball. Reposition your feet a little farther from where the ball bounces so you are reaching for the ball.

1.7 Count and see how many backhands you and your partner can make in a row. You must stop and restart your counting if you stroke the ball before it lands on the floor [court], if you miss, or if you stroke the ball with a forehand. [Challenge students to beat their previous records.]

1.8 Sometimes our record is higher with different partners. Let's see if we can maintain our best record with a different partner. [Have students change partners frequently. Notice which pairings produce the best work.]

2.0 You need to focus on your feet. When performing in games, sports, or dance, your performance is only going to be as good as your footwork. To improve your footwork in any activity and especially for tennis, you must make each step light and springy. Concentrate on making your feet light and springy as you reposition to play the ball.

2.1 To start, get your weight on the balls of your feet with your knees in a slightly relaxed position with your body facing the wall. Grip the racquet with your stroking hand, letting it rest lightly in your other hand. Hold the racquet out in front of your body with the head of the racquet pointing to the wall. After

AEROBIC ACTIVITY

You were quite active today throughout the lesson, which helps build your aerobic capacity. How fit you are aerobically will determine how tired you get or don't get during physical activity. If you exercise regularly, your aerobic condition improves. If you are not active for several weeks or months, your aerobic condition decreases. To keep improving your aerobic fitness, do activities like jumping rope or playing games and sports that require a lot of continuous movement.

each stroke, quickly go back to this ready position while you're waiting to return the next ball.

2.2 You really need to hustle and get squared to the wall. Return to the balls of your feet after each stroke. Be ready to travel in any direction. You don't jog in tennis. You must think and run quickly!

2.3 Don't lock your knees when you are in your ready position. Did you ever see any animal jumping or ready to pounce? Their leg joints are crouched, ready to spring into action. Keeping your knees bent a little, weight forward on the balls of your feet, and your feet spread a little makes it easier to get started quickly and move fast in any direction. Bent knees spring into action faster than locked knees.

2.4 Intentionally try to alternate sending the ball first to your partner's forehand and then to your partner's backhand. This will make them adjust their position and move their feet on each stroke.

2.5 Have a seat and let's watch the footwork of [Terry and Patti]. Notice their feet are alive and springy. They move quickly and get in their ready position after each stroke. Go back and see if you can get more bounce and spring in your knees and ankles.

2.6 Challenge the person closest to you and see who can send the ball back against the wall the most times. Concentrate on your footwork.

3.0 [Go over scoring in advance of giving them a choice of competitive or cooperative game play. A poster showing the scoring method for tennis (see below) helps to clarify scoring discussion. Students can refer to it during their game.] To start each point you can either let the ball bounce and then send it over the net with a forehand or some of you may want to toss the ball in the air and use the regular overhead serve. You can play singles or doubles. If you prefer, you can play a cooperative game and see how long you can rally the ball back and forth without missing. Before you begin, decide on your boundaries and whether you prefer to play a competitive tennis game or a cooperative rallying game. [Games will need to be played on courts greatly reduced in size unless unusual facilities are available.]

3.1 Many of you will be playing on public or private courts this summer. Let's work on court etiquette. Does anyone know what you should do when your ball goes into another court? Right, wait until the other players' point is finished and then ask them for your ball. See if you can practice this in your game.

3.2 Some of your games are beginning to show good forehands and backhands. Let's not forget to keep our footwork light and springy. Really try to get set before you stroke each ball.

SCORING
LOVE, 15, 30, 40 GAME

If the score is tied at 30 or 40 all, it is called 30 or 40 deuce and *two more points* must be played and *won* to win the game. The first point won is "add in" if won by the serving team or "add out" if won by the receiving team. If the next point is won by the opposite team, the score goes back to deuce. *You must win two points in a row to win the game after it has gone to deuce.*

3.3 Don't be satisfied just returning the ball. Try to place your shots when you have plenty of time to set up, getting ready before you stroke the ball. Concentrate on the face of your racquet and your follow-through. Guide the ball to an empty spot on your receiver's court by making the face of the racquet point right to your target.

3.4 If you have always played a cooperative game, play a competitive game now so you are familiar with the tennis scoring method.

ASSESSING THE BACKHAND STROKE			
Class list	Positions back of racquet shoulder toward net or target.	Contacts ball out in front of forward foot.	Returns to ready position in center of their space after returning ball.
Sandy	4	4	3
Tosha	5	4	3

Scale: 5 = Almost always   4 = Consistent at least half the time   3 = Has to be reminded or must really attend to in order to achieve   2 = Seldom   1 = Very rarely or never

Creating Options and Cutting Off Passing Lanes in Soccer

5 or 6 lessons

FOCUS Creating options for the player with the ball and cutting off passing lanes, emphasizing working together to achieve cohesiveness in soccer team play

MOTOR CONTENT

Selected from Theme 7—Introduction to Complex Relationships

Relationships

Offense—creating a clear pathway between the player with the ball and the receivers by always forming a triangle with the ball and another teammate. Defense—repositioning to block the pathway between the person with the ball and the receiver.

OBJECTIVES

In this unit, students will (or should be willing to try to) meet these objectives:

- Pass the ball to a teammate after three or fewer touches (dribbles) (reflects National Standard in Physical Education 1).
- Work as an offensive unit to create options for the passer by moving to an open space away from another teammate to form a triangle with him and the passer (reflects National Standard in Physical Education 1).
- Work as a defensive unit by having one person challenge the player with the ball while other teammates cut toward the open passing lanes to intercept a pass (reflects National Standards in Physical Education 1, 5, and 7).
- Understand and show that the ball needs room to move and should be kicked or passed to spaces—not people (reflects National Standard in Physical Education 2).
- Pass the ball to others on the team, accommodating the skill level of the receivers by passing the ball to their feet at a speed that receivers can easily handle (reflects National Standards in Physical Education 5 and 6).

EQUIPMENT AND MATERIALS

One soccer or utility ball for every three or four players; cones or goalposts for each playing area.

LEARNING EXPERIENCES

1.0 [You need a space at least 20 by 40 feet for every 6 to 12 students. Accurate passing is the key to success in soccer. Continually stress the importance of passing quickly and accurately, passing to the feet of the receiver, timing the pass to arrive at the feet of the running receiver, adjusting the speed of the pass to accommodate the skill of the receiver, and supporting players showing themselves to the ball by repositioning away from other teammates to an empty space, and form a triangle to receive the pass.] Today, let's concentrate on creating better options for the passer by repositioning to show yourself to the ball while forming a triangle with the passer and another teammate. Get in groups of six with four playing offense [attackers] and two playing defense. [These numbers may vary between five and seven but always try to have two more playing offense than defense.] The offense scores a point each time they complete seven passes in a row. The defense scores one point each time they intercept the ball. The person who intercepts the pass trades places with the one who passed the ball. Get in groups of six, divide your group into four offensive and two defensive players, pick up a ball, and begin.

1.1 Offense [attackers], keep repositioning to maintain spaces between each other and clear passing lanes between you and the passer. Always be ready for a quick pass. [Watch carefully to make sure the students are not hovering over the ball. The habit of creating open spaces instead of clustering around the ball takes time to learn. Remind students everyone has a job on the team and a position to play.]

1.2 Passers, pass the ball before you dribble [touch] the ball four times. Be alert! Look for the open receiver and pass immediately. Don't keep possession of the ball. Get rid of it quickly.

1.3 Receivers, reposition continually away from your defenders and other teammates to stay open for a pass. Passers, pass the ball quickly to the open receivers or those breaking open for a pass. Make sure your receiver is on the move.

1.4 Defenders, reposition to cut off the shortest two passing lanes. Make the passer kick a long pass that is easier to intercept.

1.5 Passers, pass the ball quickly, then run past the person marking [guarding] you to prepare to receive a pass. Always keep an open pathway between you and the ball. Move—no one should ever be in that path.

1.6 Defenders, work together. The one nearest the ball, stay close to the ball to put pressure on the person with the ball. Others cut off a passing lane by repositioning to stay between the passer and the receiver you are marking. Don't let the person you are marking get between you and the person with the ball.

1.7 Try to make every pass quick and accurate at a speed your receiver can handle. Remember, a missed pass usually ends up in the possession of the defender.

1.8 Receivers, don't wait for the ball to come to you. Run toward the pass to get to the ball as quickly as you can. A defender is going to be racing to beat you to the ball.

2.0 [Accommodate varying skill levels by grouping the more skilled together to play three versus three and the less skilled to play four versus two.] Continue to work on sharpening your passing and repositioning skills by sharing the ball and passing after two or three touches. The offense [attackers] gets one point every time they complete five consecutive passes. The defense gets one point for intercepting the ball. Always look for the open receiver. [Change the number of touches needed to score a point to accommodate the skill level of the students or allow each group to determine the number of touches needed.]

2.1 When you are marking [guarding] the attacker [offense] with the ball, put pressure on the ball by staying close to the person with the ball. Work to make your opponent give up the ball. [Watch to see they are not marking too closely, allowing the attacker to cut easily around the defender.]

2.2 As pressure is put on the ball by one defender, the other two defenders should try to block the open passing lanes. Don't follow the person putting pressure on the ball. [Students will tend to converge on the ball. Stop them; show how bunched up they are. Keep stopping to urge them to maintain open spaces. If they continue to converge on the ball, you may need to revert to three versus one for awhile.]

2.3 Passers, don't give the defense time to put pressure on the ball. Look for an open teammate and pass quickly. Receivers, spread out to give the ball handler options when passing.

2.4 Supporting players [those not immediately handling the ball], spread out far enough to form a triangle with the ball, giving the passer clear passing lanes. Be sure you are giving yourself room to run and space to receive a pass.

2.5 Attackers, keep the ball moving quickly from one person to the other so the defense can't get set up to block a passing lane. Try to use no more than three touches so you can pass the ball before the defense takes it away from you.

3.0 [Keep the teams small to give each student greater opportunity to develop skills highlighted in this unit. Arrange the students in groups of four versus two, three versus three, or four versus four, depending on their skill level, or let

Stay close to the dribbler—but not too close.

them choose their teams. Later, give the students opportunity to regroup.] If you want to kick for a goal, make goals by setting two cones at each end about six feet apart. Continue to work on keeping a free path between yourself and the ball, passing the ball after two or three touches. One rule: Three passes must be made before you take a shot for the goal. [The higher their skills, the fewer the touches allowed. Let the students decide how to put the ball in play following a goal.]

3.1 Pick out an open receiver before you pass the ball. Reposition quickly after you pass to create an open lane for your receiver to return a pass.

3.2 Sit a moment and discuss having a player drop back to play goalie when the ball comes near the goal. Consider having different players drop back based on the location of the ball on the field.

3.3 The person playing goalie should often step out of the goal toward the ball. This helps to decrease the size of the target for the person with the ball, making it harder to score.

3.4 Defenders, pressure the ball to make the attacker pass the ball. As the pass is made, one of the other defenders not putting pressure on the passer should try to intercept the pass.

3.5 Keep your passes short and quick. They will be harder for the defense to intercept.

3.6 Defenders, don't get too close to the ball. When you are very close, the passer can easily cut around you.

3.7 [Give the students the choice of adding a rule where they may kick for a goal after completing a designed number of consecutive passes. The number of passes required may vary with each group of students.]

SELF-ASSESSMENT: SOCCER PLAY

Circle the game play behaviors that you do consistently and almost automatically. Put a star in front of the behaviors you have improved compared to last year.

Name _____   Date _____

On Offense	On Defense
I cut to open spaces to create passing lanes.	I try to block the easiest passing lane.
I make crisp, short passes when possible.	I pressure the ball if I am nearest the ball.
I look for and pass to the most open receiver.	I use fakes and repositioning to confuse the offense.
I make quick decisions.	I communicate with teammates.
One other skill I do well is _____.	One other skill I do well is _____.

Unit 7

Place Hitting, Covering Bases, and Backing Up a Receiver

5 or 6 lessons

FOCUS Refining offensive and defensive strategies when place hitting, covering bases, and backing up a receiver

MOTOR CONTENT

Selected from Theme 7—Introduction to Complex Relationships

Relationships

Repositioning to cover a base when the baseman is pulled out of position; running quickly to get behind the receiver catching a batted or thrown ball; positioning for a relay throw from the outfield; and place hitting

OBJECTIVES

In this unit, students will (or should be willing to try to) meet these objectives:

- Cover a base when the baseman is pulled out of position (reflects National Standard in Physical Education 1).
- Reposition to back up the person fielding the ball or the person serving as a relay person for the throw into the infield (reflects National Standard in Physical Education 1).
- Understand and demonstrate that they should back up the receiver closest to them; to pull the ball to their left, they open the stance to contact the ball early out in front of the plate; close the stance and contact the ball late to hit to right field (reflects National Standards in Physical Education 1 and 2).
- Work as a team by calling for the ball when it comes in the middle of two playing areas and by hustling to make the catch and to back up the person calling for the ball (reflects National Standards in Physical Education 2, 5, and 7).

EQUIPMENT AND MATERIALS

For every 10 to 12 students in the class: One set of bases; one batting tee; one bat; one softball.

LEARNING EXPERIENCES

1.0 [Set up the bases, the batting tees, bats, and balls for each playing area ahead of time. (Batters hit more accurately when hitting from a batting tee.) Discuss and demonstrate the concepts of covering and backing up a play through the use of charts or by placing students in the backing-up positions as you discuss. Divide class into groups of 10 or 12. Eight play all positions in the field except pitcher. Two to four students will bat with one of them starting as a runner on first base to make the fielders consider throwing the ball to second base to get the runner out. This player starting on first will get a turn to bat after being batted home. Have the students take the field and practice backing up a throw, fielding, and covering bases with a runner on first base. See 4.0 for tasks and rotate them in to practice fielding and base running. Have extra students not on a team practice pitching and catching.]

1.1 There is a runner on first base. Batters, try to hit the ball between second and third base toward left field. If the shortstop or third baseman gets the ball, the throw goes immediately to second base. If the ball goes into left field, the shortstop will act as the relay person and throw to third base to keep the runner from advancing.

1.2 As soon as the throw to second is made, the runner who ran to second should return to the batting lineup. The player who batted takes the position of runner on first. The next batter puts the ball in play by hitting the ball to left field. [Procedures for rotating: Each batter has one turn at bat and one as the runner on first base. After the batting team has batted, outfielders and shortstop rotate to become the basemen and catcher. Basemen and catcher rotate to be the next four batters. Batters rotate to the outfield and shortstop positions. Repeat this rotation until everyone has had a turn at bat and has played the infield and outfield positions.]

1.3 All fielders, be on your toes ready to catch the ball, to cover a base, to back up another player, or to act as a relay person for a long throw from left field.

1.4 Batters, the minute you hit the ball, run as fast as you can to first base. If you get a real long hit, try for second base. Fielders, be alert. You may need to throw to third or to home to get the lead runner out.

1.5 If the ball is hit long into left field, the shortstop should run toward the fielder to act as the relay person and should be ready to throw to third base or home if the base runner advances.

1.6 Fielders, call for the ball when the ball is dropping between two of you. Also be ready to back each other up by positioning behind the receiver.

1.7 Let's play a softball game and see if the fielding team can remember where to go when the ball is hit into left field. Batters, try to hit the ball to left field. Continue rotating positions after each of the four batters has had a turn to bat. If you would like, record the runs that come in for every four batters.

2.0 This time, let's practice hitting [or throwing] the ball to right field with a runner on first base. [Organize in groups of 10 to 12 as in task 1.0.]

2.1 The minute the ball is hit, check who is receiving the ball, and the closest person to the receiver quickly move behind the receiver to back up the hit. If the ball goes deep into right field, the shortstop should cover second base while the second baseman acts as the relay person for the throw to second.

2.2 Every time a batter comes to the plate, you should all be on the balls of your feet in a crouched position, ready to charge the ball, to serve as cutoff or relay person for the throw to the base, or to run to back up a receiver.

2.3 Try to make your throws go straight, not arching up, to the baseman. The straighter the throw, the faster it gets to the base.

2.4 Runners, you can run past first base without worrying about being tagged if you turn to your right on the way back to base. If you turn left, you can be tagged out.

2.5 Shortstop, when the ball is hit to right field, cover second base as quickly as you can. On a force-out, you do not have to tag the runner—just step on the base.

2.6 Third basemen, keep your eyes on the ball and the lead runner. The throw can come to you if the runner rounds second.

2.7 When fielding grounders, make the catch and the throw one smooth motion by letting the give in the catch become the preparation for your throw.

2.8 Batters, change where you hit the ball. Fielders, think ahead where to throw the ball, depending on where runners are on the bases. Remember, always try to get the lead runner.

3.0 Batters, let's practice place hitting. Follow through with your bat toward the field where you intend the ball to go. Each time you come up to bat, try to place the ball to a different field.

3.1 Batters, tell the person who will bat next which field you intend to hit the ball to. Those waiting to bat, see if the batter sends the ball to the designated field.

3.2 Swing the bat level with the ground so you hit only line drives. Try not to hit under the ball, hitting pop flies that are easily caught.

3.3 See if you can select a field and place your hit into that field. If you bat right-handed, it will be easier for you to hit the ball into left field. Left-handed batters will be able to hit the ball into right field easier.

3.4 Some of you may need to choke up on the bat by three or four inches to give you more control in placing the ball.

3.5 In batting, your feet are usually parallel to the plate. [Demonstrate.] Right-handers, to send the ball into left field, pull your left foot back a little so you have opened your stance. Left-handers, you will pull your right foot back from the parallel line.

3.6 Be sure to complete your follow-through with your bat clear to your opposite shoulder. Let the bat come all the way around as you swing.

3.7 Now try to place the ball into the opposite field. Check your feet. Pull your right foot back when batting right-handed to send the ball into right field. Left handers, pull your left foot back to send the ball into left field.

3.8 Shorten your follow-through to help you hit the ball to the opposite field.

4.0 Let's add a pitcher to our games. Pitch the ball underhand with a nice, soft arc so the batter can hit the ball. [Let the batter choose to bat from a tee. This is recommended when pitching is inaccurate or if the batter has trouble hitting the ball.]

4.1 Pitchers, start with your feet together and take a step toward the plate as you toss the ball underhand to the batter. Be sure to arch your pitch to give batters more time to focus on the ball and swing.

4.2 Batters, try very hard to place the ball in the field where you want the ball to go. Don't be satisfied with just hitting the ball.

4.3 Pitchers, really try to place your pitch over the plate to give the batter confidence in batting and the fielders practice in fielding.

4.4 Make your throwing hand follow through to the plate at a level between the shoulders and knees of the batters.

4.5 Batters, don't watch the ball after it is hit. Look at first base and run like a sprinter.

Batters, each time you bat, try to place the ball to a different part of the field.

4.6 When you are running from first to second base, round second base by touching the inside corner and head for third. Don't pass second too far if you think you will need to make it back safely to second base if the ball is thrown to third.

4.7 Raise your hand if you want to work only on batting. [Place these students in groups of four: a batter, catcher, pitcher, and a fielder.]

4.8 Infielders, get your throws to the basemen as quickly as you can by straightening out the path of your throw.

4.9 Basemen, cover the space next to your base. When you know the ball isn't in your territory, run to cover your base if there is a base runner coming to your base.

4.10 If you are on a base, take a few steps toward the next base and watch to see if a fly ball is going to be caught. In case a fly ball is caught, return to your base quickly, otherwise run to the next base.

4.11 Fielders catching a fly ball, know which bases are filled and who might be running. As you catch, look and throw quickly to the relay person—unless you can throw low and hard to the base ahead of the runner to get the runner out. This is difficult—but it's exciting when you get the runner out.

Sixth Grade Gymnastics

Mounting, Dismounting, and Linking Movement on Apparatus

5 or 6 lessons

FOCUS Mounting and dismounting apparatus, linking one movement to another

MOTOR CONTENT

Selected from Theme 5—Introduction to Weight and Theme 6—Flow and Continuity in Movement

Effort

Force—selecting and controlling muscle tension
Flow—keeping the body moving from one movement to another and stopping intentionally

OBJECTIVES

In this unit, students will (or should be willing to try to) meet these objectives:

- Develop and refine movement sequences that include mounting and dismounting apparatus by controlling the flow of movement and muscle tension (reflects National Standard in Physical Education 1).
- Refine gymnastic sequences by controlling muscle tension and blending one movement into another to develop a feeling for performance posture and flow of movement (reflects National Standards in Physical Education 1 and 7).
- Understand that blending one part of a sequence with another and the quality of posture greatly affects the rating of a gymnastic performance (reflects National Standards in Physical Education 1 and 2).

EQUIPMENT AND MATERIALS

Several pieces of apparatus; sufficient mats to protect the landing surface. (If the number of mats available requires more than two or three to work at the same mat, divide the class in half, with half of the class working on the floor on a short sequence of step-like actions on their hands and feet while the other half works on the mats.)

LEARNING EXPERIENCES

1.0 What makes a shopper select one apple from another? You look for the kind you like, then you select them for their color and their firmness, rejecting those with bruises. If an Olympic gymnastic coach was here to select you, your gymnastic performances would all improve. What would you do to polish your performance? Right, you would try to look sharp and feel sharp. Everyone would strut like peacocks and would be saying 'look at me' with every fiber of their body. Let's start out doing a very simple, short series of three or four movements on the mat [floor]. Try extra hard to develop that feeling of greatness, that 'look-at-me' attitude that Olympic gymnasts have, by making your whole body look crisp and tight throughout your entire performance.

1.1 Really go for a lifted feeling in your body. Stretch and feel proud. Don't slump.

1.2 Take a moment and examine what you are including in your sequence. For now, select things you do best. Remember, shoppers don't always select expensive fruits and vegetables, but they always reject the ones that don't look crisp.

1.3 Make the flow of your movement clear and precise. Think about the order of the movements in your sequence before you repeat your sequence. You should now know exactly which parts of the sequence you are linking together. Make it clear when you intentionally plan to go from one movement right into another with no stops or when you make a definite planned pause.

1.4 Let's look at these short sequences and see how sharp simple movements look when you concentrate on blending one movement into the next and when you concentrate on *upness* and tightness in your body and don't sag. This half of the class sit down, and the other half, starting at the far end, take turns doing your best to make every movement look sharp. [After further practice, repeat this, changing roles.]

1.5 Create a new sequence combining two or three different balances and forms of traveling. [Repeat tasks 1.1 through 1.3 to refine the new sequence and then do 1.4 again.]

2.0 Arrange your apparatus to create an interesting floor pattern [not in straight lines] and arrange the mats to give you safe landing surfaces. Once you get the apparatus arranged, work on traveling onto and off your apparatus, selecting gymnastic movements that make you look and feel sharp. [Organizational tips: Try to allow the students two or more pieces of apparatus to include in their arrangement, keep the pathways of one group from crossing paths of another group, and check to be sure landing surfaces are protected with mats.]

2.1 Experiment with several ways to mount and dismount the apparatus. Include several of your most skillful ways of traveling when you are on the mats or on the floor between the mats.

2.2 Select some of your mounts, dismounts, and ways of traveling that make you feel like you can give your best performance. Repeat them in the same order each time it is your turn.

2.3 Take time to think about your approach to each piece of apparatus. Mount the apparatus lightly from a nice, springy takeoff. Remember, if you are doing a running approach, lengthen the size of your stride as you near the apparatus and plant your feet very close to the apparatus for the takeoff.

2.4 Somewhere in your work on the apparatus, see if you can mount the apparatus and go immediately into a balance when first landing on the apparatus. You might take off from the floor and make a half-turn in the air, land on your seat on the apparatus, and go into a V-sit by balancing just on your seat, or you might pop right up on the apparatus into a headstand. You might land on one foot on the apparatus and go into a scale with your arms out to your sides.

STRENGTH

Remember relative strength? It is important to know your capabilities and limits. It takes relative strength to do a headstand or a handstand. If someone doesn't have adequate relative strength, that person needs to choose a balance within that person's relative strength. It is necessary and okay to make this adjustment.

You might do a headstand on the apparatus.

You make your own choices—but land carefully and softly. See if you can select different landings and dismounts using all of the apparatus in your working area.

2.5 I've noticed some of you are taking unnecessary steps sometimes, while others adjust their position once they land on the apparatus before going into the balance. These unplanned movements spoil your performance a bit. Take time to share your sequence with each other at your apparatus. Try to critique [help] each other. Look for the little things each of you do that aren't planned. Identify the unplanned parts for each other and work to remove them.

2.6 From the moment you pause to start your turn, think about extending your free body parts and do your best work to impress the Olympic coach. Maintain that performance attitude throughout your whole trip. Make every little thing you do a beautiful, planned part of your sequence. Go for the gold!

3.0 Let's add some very unexpected moments to your sequence. Most of you have been doing the usual: mounting the apparatus, dismounting it, and moving on. Instead of dismounting and moving on, see if you can remount the same piece of apparatus, creating a special moment before traveling on. [Caution students to wait until the person ahead of them has completed their sequence before they start.]

3.1 These additional moments you have added on the apparatus are looking sharp! Now add more variety to your special moments. You can achieve variety by sometimes pausing on the apparatus to balance and sometimes vaulting over the apparatus. Changing what you do makes your performance much more interesting to the observer and more challenging to you.

3.2 Watch your landings as you dismount. Make them light and springy to help you pop right back up onto the apparatus without hesitating.

3.3 Don't overlook the mat and floor work. Be sure to include both rolling and step-like actions. As you do, remember to get full extension in your whole body and legs and keep that tight, compact feeling.

3.4 You could add even more interest in your floor work by reversing your direction, going into an unexpected balance, or drastically changing your speed. Choose a couple of ideas for adding greater interest to your work on the floor or mat.

3.5 Begin to settle on all of the things you want to include in your sequence. Select your favorites and practice them in the same order so you can focus your attention on refining your muscle tension and your body extension as you repeat them.

3.6 As you repeat your sequence, begin to exaggerate the special features that are unique to your sequence so they stand out and wow the Olympic coach.

3.7 Think of the care you are taking to blend one phase of your sequence into another. This is the part which makes your whole sequence look and feel smooth. Plan your pauses and plan those moments that give you a nice, ongoing feeling and make them all blend into one performance. Don't forget to hold a lifted, standing position at the end to tell the judges you have finished your routine.

3.8 Work hard on getting rid of the little things you helped others see in their performances that took away from their sequences. Work to make every little movement you do be a genuine part of your routine.

3.9 You people have put together some exciting work. Sit so you can see, and let's take pride in each other's accomplishments. As we observe, look for the special performance attitude that you have developed through concentrating on muscle tension, extension, and that special feeling for ongoing movement punctuated by planned moments of hesitation or balances (Be sure to work this task in as part of several lessons, inserting the specific content of the day's lesson.)

Unit 2

Counterbalance and Countertension

3 to 6 lessons

FOCUS Practicing counterbalance and countertension with a partner

MOTOR CONTENT

Theme 7—Relationships to Others

Body

Activities of the body—countertension, counterbalance

Relationships

Of individuals and small groups—supporting and being supported; student-selected relationships, such as following, copying, and contrasting

OBJECTIVES

In this unit, students will (or should be willing to try to) meet these objectives:

- Develop and refine a sequence of movement accommodating the skills of others while traveling in and out of countertension and counterbalance positions in a variety of ways with apparatus or others (reflects National Standards in Physical Education 1 and 6).
- Remember to achieve counterbalance they lean toward another person and in countertension they lean away (reflects National Standard in Physical Education 2).
- Accept responsibility for the safety of themselves and others when moving into and out of mutually formed balances by planning the next move with others in the group before releasing their hold (reflects National Standard in Physical Education 5).
- Select balances, activities, and positions that each member of their group can perform successfully and reserve options which are difficult for others for times when they are working or moving independently (reflects National Standards in Physical Education 6 and 7).

EQUIPMENT AND MATERIALS

Selection of apparatus may include the following: Vaulting boxes; benches; stools; platforms; tumbling and landing mats.

LEARNING EXPERIENCES

[While you may teach the unit without apparatus, the content requires that all tasks be performed with at least one other person. Usually students work more productively in small groups after experiencing success in countertension and counterbalance with a partner.]

1.0 Today, let's remember to be very careful of one another when working on countertension or counterbalance. Be sure both people know when to move out of your balance to change your base of support. Remember, to develop countertension, you place your base of support very close to your partner's base of support or to the apparatus and lean away until your balance depends on your partner or the apparatus. Let's see how carefully you can hold on to someone, place your base of support close to each other, and gently lean away until you are forming one balance, each dependent upon the other for balance. Select someone about the same height and weight as you, a place where you can work safely, and begin.

1.1 First, try to feel the countertension developing as you lean away from your partner. When both of you sense you are mutually supported by your partner, carefully plan the body part that is going to receive your weight after you release your hold and begin to travel independently out of your partner balance.

1.2 [In the first two or three lessons, focus on tasks that encourage the students to experiment with a variety of bases of support, levels, and body parts contacting the partner.] Hold or hook on to your partner with a different body part. Feel that new countertension develop as you lean away. Plan your next base and, keeping your performance posture, travel out of your balance.

1.3 Each time as you and your partner travel out of your countertension balance, really make your body lines sharp and clear by maintaining the upness and alertness in all parts of your body. Each of you arrive carefully into a balance you can hold for a moment alone. Then start over again and make a new countertension balance.

1.4 Holding your own balance away from your partner, devise a gymnastic way to travel right back into countertension, making each moment and each movement demonstrate your very best gymnastic posture and performance.

1.5 [Choose and prearrange the apparatus or allow the students to select and arrange the apparatus safely if they have become disciplined in making reasoned and wise choices.] Some of you might like to begin your work by creating a balance showing countertension with you and your partner balancing on top of or holding on to a piece of apparatus. Take extra care as you release your partner because you both must be very ready to care for your own weight while traveling onto a new base. This may mean you have to prepare to land on the mat or floor as you travel off the apparatus.

2.0 [Repeat 1.0 through 1.5, inserting "counterbalance" for "countertension." In creating counterbalance, the students may need reminding to place their bases away from their partners or their apparatus because they must lean toward the person or apparatus to create and maintain counterbalance.]

3.0 Let's begin to pay closer attention to what you choose to do and how you perform as you come out of your partner balances. Make your individual

ENDURANCE

If a partner slumps or looks tired, it may be that he or she does not have enough endurance. Partners need to encourage each other to jog at home to increase endurance so they can improve performance in gymnastics.

movement also represent your best gymnastic talent. Think performance all the time. Decide with your partner whether you will start in counterbalance or countertension and begin.

3.1 Begin away from your partner [and apparatus]. Plan how you are going to travel to your partner or onto the apparatus. Perfect your movement! Look like a performer all the time by thinking, feeling, and lifting body parts upward as you travel. Then, with as few movements as possible, go into your countertension or counterbalance partner balance.

3.2 Discuss and decide when and how you and your partner can leave each other and arrive back together to create a different partner balance. If the first balance showed counterbalance, make the second one show countertension and vice versa.

3.3 Watch each other as you perform your sequence. Show each other that constant, caring, performance attitude all of the time. Remember the two of you are performing as a unit to create a skillful, smooth-flowing gymnastic sequence.

3.4 [After working with a partner to perfect their sequence, have them join another pair and give their performances for each other.] Think about what your partner is doing as you travel away or toward each other. Intentionally begin to think of your movement in relation to your partner's. Are you copying, matching, contrasting? You can contrast, copy, or match the speed, level, direction, and type of movement you select.

3.5 Make your selection of relationships very clear. If you are copying or matching, remember to perform exactly the same as your partner, including the speed of your movement, the space you use, as well as what every part of your body does.

4.0 If you have felt good upness in your work and you think you can increase the length of your sequence without losing your performance attitude or reducing the quality of your work, include at least three different partner balances in your sequence, having at least one counterbalance in it. Stick with your present length if your sequence needs more work on quality.

4.1 See if you can add a little variety in the way you are traveling away from and back to your partner. Some of you are doing all rolls [name the activity observed most].

4.2 [Observe and determine whether space, speed, or both need to be called to their attention. Usually it is best to have them focus on one of these at a time.] Take care and watch the space you use as you travel away from and toward your partner so you can duplicate your performance each time you repeat it.

4.3 Begin to check where your eyes focus. Make your posture really alert and lifted before you start your sequence and don't forget to hold your ending for a few seconds.

5.0 If you are feeling in control while moving in and out of partner balances, join with one or two other pairs and see if the four or six of you can synchronize creating and moving out of balances showing countertension and counterbalance. Change partners for different balances. Show countertension or counterbalance in groups of three or more for one of your balances.

5.1 [Observe their performances and repeat needed tasks from among 3.0–4.3 working in these larger groups.]

5.2 You should be pleased with your performance. Everyone except [name two or three pairs or groups who will share first] come over and have a seat with me. Let's all take turns showing the results of dedicated work. We observers will really watch how performers synchronize joining to balance and how carefully they leave their group balances.

ASSESSING COUNTERBALANCE AND COUNTERTENSION				
Class list	**Shares responsibility for safety of self and others.** (scale, date)	**Provides input for creating partner/ group balances.** (scale, date)	**Creates balances showing counterbalance and countertension in harmony with others.** (scale, date)	**Performs a sequence of four or more balances with a partner or small group.** (scale, date)
Gott, Minch	3 4/26	3 4/26	3 4/27	3 4/26
Nadda, Tobin	2 4/25	3 4/25	4 4/25	3 1/26

Scale: 5 = *Performs skillfully and contributes to the success of others* 4 = *Works to achieve success* 3 = Shows progress 2 = Contributes and performs reluctantly 1 = Deters success of partner and group*

Unit 3

Matching, Cannoning, Supporting, and Being Supported

4 or 5 lessons

FOCUS Developing a gymnastic sequence, emphasizing matching, cannoning, supporting, and being supported

MOTOR CONTENT

Selected from Theme 6—Flow and Continuity in Movement and Theme 7—Relationships to Others

Effort

Flow—transitional movements performed to develop continuity in linking two movements together

Relationships

Of individuals and groups—cannoning, matching, supporting, and being supported

OBJECTIVES

In this unit, students will (or should be willing to try to) meet these objectives:

- Develop a gymnastic sequence containing balances, rolls, step-like actions, and flight, demonstrating flow and continuity while matching, cannoning, supporting, and being supported (reflects National Standard in Physical Education 1).
- Understand that mutual trust must exist to engage safely in creating and moving out of group balances (reflects National Standards in Physical Education 2 and 5).
- Recall that cannoning requires one or more performers to copy the work of another, following one right after the other, and matching occurs when two or more performers make the same movements simultaneously (reflects National Standard in Physical Education 2).
- Work seriously to bring out the best performance from every member of the group (reflects National Standard in Physical Education 2).
- Remember the safety of themselves and others when supporting others by carefully lowering or releasing the one being supported, staying mindful of the extra strain their weight places on the person serving as the base (reflects National Standard in Physical Education 5).

- Gain satisfaction in interacting with others by refining their individual techniques for the purpose of improving the performance of their group (reflects National Standards in Physical Education 5 and 7).

EQUIPMENT AND MATERIALS

One to three mats for every four to six students.

LEARNING EXPERIENCES

1.0 Have you heard the saying, 'Anything you can do, I can do better?' I think you might find it fun to start this gymnastic unit with that saying in mind. One person will start by doing a simple roll, a balance, or step-like action on hands and feet. The partner observing the performance, duplicates what was observed and, without stopping, goes right into a movement of their own choice. Think carefully about selecting someone with whom you can work seriously. One of you tell the first gymnastic 'story' while your partner observes, duplicates it, and adds something on to it. [If the class has an odd number, have one group rotate roles among three people.]

1.1 Take care and make your first choices rather simple so you can keep building a long series of gymnastic stunts or movements. Those of you who go first, don't forget you always go back to the very first thing you did and repeat exactly everything you and your partner have done up before adding something new.

1.2 Be sure to duplicate each other's work precisely. You have to copy what your partner does, but also their speed and the amount of space used to make everything the same.

1.3 Each time you add something, try to include all necessary movements needed to make your partner's last contribution blend right into your new addition.

1.4 Find unique ways to give continuity to your sequence. For example, move away from and back to the mat again and again, add a change in direction, or use the floor space by taking weight on hands.

1.5 When your memory fails you, the sequence becomes too complicated, or your work gets sloppy, start again, letting the other [or a new] person start building a different sequence.

2.0 You have been doing a tremendous job of observing and copying a gymnastic performance. One person develops a sequence involving a nice, tall starting position, traveling into a balance, balancing, and traveling out of the balance, ending with the same tall starting position. The second person [or others] observes and copies the sequence. Leaders, repeat the sequence several times to give copiers practice copying.

2.1 Once each of you knows the sequence, see if you both can perform the sequence at exactly the same time in exactly the same way so all of you look alike.

2.2 Cue each other when to come out of the balance so everyone comes out of it at the exact same moment.

2.3 Find another pair near you [at the same mat, if there is more than one pair per mat] and watch each other perform your matching sequences. Observers, watch the little parts of the sequence and see if the performers truly match each other. Tell them which parts are matched very well, which parts need more work, and how they may be corrected. Once you have critiqued [discussed] the degree of matching in each other's sequence, work on your problem areas.

2.4 [Observe groups for those who might be able to join with another group and still be able to perform a matching sequence. Suggest both groups show their sequences and then select the easiest sequence for all to perform together. The mats may need rearranging to accommodate the larger group.]

3.0 Do you remember when we worked on counterbalance and countertension how you had to be very careful for the safety of each other while moving out of the balances? Caring for each other's safety is very essential. You need to be extra sensitive and take responsibility for each other's safety going into and out of partner balances. We are going to create partner balances with one person safely supporting the other person. [Be sure students select partners of similar height and weight.]

3.1 The person playing the supporting role, experiment with several starting positions. Some supporting positions are standing up with your knees bent slightly so your partner can stand on your knees, getting down on your hands and knees so your partner can do an inverted balance on your back, or lying on your back on the floor with your knees bent and your feet flat on the floor. For the person on top to achieve a balance, they will need to hold on to you or you will need to hold on to them. In some balances, you both will have to hold onto each other.

3.2 Be sure you both work to protect each other. If you are supporting a partner, make your muscles firm and your base of support steady and strong.

3.3 Each time the two of you achieve a partner balance, the top person must safely travel out of the balance doing some form of gymnastic movement. It may need to be a landing and a roll or you may create an independent balance.

3.4 Practice coming out of your partner balances in different ways to see which way feels best and is safest for both people.

3.5 People performing the supporting role, once you are sure your partner has left your partner balance safely and is on their own, see if you can travel smoothly into your own balance.

Two must work carefully together to create partner balances.

3.6 To improve your performance, make the transition from the partner balance to your individual work as smooth as possible. Move into the next part of your own act with as few motions as possible.

3.7 Start your partner balance away from each other. Plan every movement needed to go into the partner balance. You might match each other and travel at the same time or you could perform a two-part canon with one person traveling to a spot, then the other person follows, repeating the traveling action.

3.8 Some of you may be ready to try two or more partner balances, working to put them into a sequence by thoughtfully adding the matching or cannoning traveling to and from each balance.

3.9 [Students working safely and successfully in achieving variety in their partner balances may be up to the challenge of group balances working in threes or fours.]

4.0 Let's build another long sequence one segment at a time. Work on a short matching sequence the two [three or four] of you can do like pros, trying your best to match every movement in the size of steps, placement of hands, relationship of legs—everything.

4.1 Check your selections. Add a bit more variety to give you more satisfaction and quality in your sequence. Some things to consider to achieve greater variety are to change your starting level, direction, speed, and/or relationships of various body parts.

4.2 Now repeat your new matching sequence performing it in a two-part [or three- or four-part] canon-style with each gymnast performing the sequence alone. When you are not performing the sequence, be sure to hold a nice, lifted ending position and look like a gymnast ready to spring into action because you are still very much a part of the performance.

4.3 Repeat the sequence twice. First perform the sequence matching each other. Repeat the same movement immediately by cannoning one at a time. Go from your matching sequence to your cannoning sequence without pausing so the two sequences become one.

4.4 Now recall two or three of your partner [small group] balances and add them to your matching and cannoning performance.

4.5 [Refining tasks to match your students' needs may be selected from among the following: As you add to your sequence, work to figure out a way to blend the new material with the old by eliminating any unnecessary movement to get into position. Select your new base of support and then plan how to place that new body part so you move onto it immediately.] Continue to be very careful of each other in your balances, making sure you know exactly when and how each of you move into and out of them. Remember you might have to cue [signal] each other to synchronize your next move. Work to eliminate talking to each other by trying to develop more subtle, nonverbal cues with your eyes or a gentle squeeze or tap if you are holding on to each other in your balances so observers don't know you are giving each other cues. Try to make sure each action and each body part is well-timed and covering the exact same amount of space as your partner.

4.6 Begin to polish your sequence. Assume and maintain that sharp, lifted, proud posture throughout your sequence. Make each phase of the sequence blend together to form one lovely continuous performance.

4.7 Let's share some of our work. Which three sets of partners [groups] wish to go first? Observers, join me and truly enjoy this lovely show I have been seeing throughout the unit.

Unit 4 — Rolling and Initiating Momentum

6 or 7 lessons

FOCUS Rolling onto a wide variety of body surfaces, emphasizing twisting and turning actions initiating momentum

MOTOR CONTENT

Selected from Theme 3—Introduction to Time and Theme 6—Flow and Continuity in Movement

Body

Locomotor activities—rolling
Nonlocomotor activities—twisting, turning, balancing

Effort

Flow—bound, free
Time—acceleration, deceleration

OBJECTIVES

In this unit, students will (or should be willing to try to) meet these objectives:

- Achieve clear body shapes to help maintain control of the whole body when traveling or when holding a balance (reflects National Standard in Physical Education 1).
- Select the appropriate amount of acceleration to accomplish a particular goal and purposefully arrest momentum to achieve balances on unusual body parts (reflects National Standard in Physical Education 1).
- Work to refine arriving in a balance on shoulders, arms, shins, and the side of the face (reflects National Standard in Physical Education 1).
- Understand that they may twist body parts to help generate momentum for turning or traveling actions, and when they allow the momentum to determine the direction, they will move more freely, making the sequence flow more smoothly (reflects National Standard in Physical Education 2).
- Select and refine a series of movements into a short sequence, demonstrating variety, quality performance, and smoothness in linking the movements together (reflects National Standard in Physical Education 1).
- Feel the satisfaction of achieving something that is both new and challenging, taking pride in their own work and their classmates' work (reflects National Standard in Physical Education 7).

EQUIPMENT AND MATERIALS

Mats; benches; vaulting boxes. (Most of the unit is planned for the floor; however, students should have the opportunity to roll and balance on equipment that has surfaces to grip to create even greater opportunity for success.)

LEARNING EXPERIENCES

1.0 Let's start today by getting your bodies and minds thinking about twisting and letting twisting actions lead you to new bases of support. Start by getting down on two hands and two feet with your hips high in the air and chin away from your chest. On your own, carefully lift one hand and slowly and smoothly take it back as far as you can without losing your balance. Follow that hand with your eyes.

1.1 [Repeat with the other arm and each leg two or three times. Encourage students to rotate farther and farther, increasing the flexibility in their backs and shoulders. Eventually they will be able to rotate into a back bridge or back bend as they transfer part of their weight onto their leading hand or foot.]

1.2 Feel a stretching and reaching in your arm and upper part of your body.

1.3 Keep returning to your beginning position. Each time you lift one hand, try to reach your arm farther away from the side of your body.

1.4 As you pick up your hand, feel your weight shift over to your other hand and your feet. Work on keeping your weight equally spread over all parts of your base of support.

1.5 Your arm should be leading you into a twisted shape when you are rotating your trunk [define]. Try to twist farther and farther each time.

1.6 Keep your hips high and twist them upward toward the ceiling. See if you can make the whole front surface of your trunk face upward.

2.0 [Have students take the same beginning position as in 1.0 or they can balance on hands and knees or shins.] Take one hand and arm and reach through the space between your other hand and your foot or shin, letting your head follow. Find ways to reach through that space until you are rolling across your shoulders in a straight line.

2.1 Try stopping the shoulder roll by extending and straightening your back and legs upward into a shoulder stand until you feel yourself balanced equally on your shoulders, the back of your head, and both arms.

2.2 Transfer your weight very slowly so you can feel your weight gradually moving from one body part to the next.

2.3 As you reach through and place your shoulder down to go into a shoulder stand, you will have to keep your hips high above your shoulders or they will cause you to get off-balance and roll down your back.

2.4 Work on traveling in a straight pathway across the mat as you roll from one shoulder across to the other. Twist your hips or your trunk to help you place your knee on your straight pathway as you transfer your weight from one shoulder to the other.

2.5 Stretch your arm through as far as you can and place your arm and shoulder on the mat to form a long, firm base with your shoulder and arm, moving your hips into a position ready to be lifted up over your shoulder. Then push with your knee and foot to help move your hips over and above your shoulders.

FLEXIBILITY

Stretching is fun.
Lie down at home
and stretch your
body, all parts, as
far as you can. Hold
this while you and
an adult count
slowly to five. Each
day, try to count to
a larger number
when you stretch.
Remember that
stretching should
never hurt.

2.6 As you work, keep shifting your weight by letting your knee lead your hips gradually to take your weight from one shoulder to the other shoulder. Resolve [finish] your movement by transferring your weight onto one knee and shin. [Encourage the students to stretch all free body parts upward, away from the knee and shin.]

2.7 [Repeat 2.0 through 2.6, having them take the opposite arm through the space on the opposite side of the body. Make sure they learn to arrive into a shoulder stand reaching through with either arm to develop versatility. Tasks 2.0 through 2.7 present a challenge closely associated with skills developed in wrestling. Many of the students may enjoy experiencing this rolling action, traveling from one end of a low vaulting box to the other end. If so, repeat 2.0 through 2.6, having them start on one knee at the end of the box. The students can grip the sides of the box to give them more stability; let them pull with their arms to lift their hips over their shoulders.]

3.0 Find ways to arrive in a front shoulder stand, balancing on one shoulder, the side of your face, and your hands, making up the base of support and resolve [come out of] it maintaining a performance posture.

3.1 Try placing your new base and lifting your hips and legs as you tighten your back and arrive in a front shoulder balance.

3.2 Begin to rock back and forth on the front surface of your body from the side of your face to your knees and shins. Try to create enough momentum to roll into a front shoulder balance.

3.3 The placement of each part of your base, especially your arms and hands, is very important. As you work, you must time exactly when each part pushes and where each part must be placed in order to arrive into and hold a new balance.

3.4 Once you are in your balance, see if you can go from having your back extended to flexing your back and rolling onto your shoulder and down your curved back.

Find ways to arrive in and resolve a front shoulder stand.

4.0 Starting in a shoulder stand, twist your hips and take one of your legs across your body as far as you can. Then let your legs go to resolve your balance any way you can, still looking like a gymnast as you come out of your balance. Stay in control so you can end up in a nice, firmly held position.

4.1 Try taking your legs apart as you twist them across your body. Twist tightly and let it go. Don't stop the natural flow of energy as you release the twist. Wind up so far and tight that when you release and twist in the opposite direction, you spin off your old base onto a new one.

4.2 The tighter you twist, the more momentum you will generate. Keep repeating, twisting tightly to feel your weight being carried to different bases of support.

4.3 The level that you rotate your legs to twist will cause different actions. If you want to go high over your shoulder into a front chest roll, you must keep your hips and legs high as they wind up and lift the weight onto one shoulder.

5.0 We have worked on isolated actions where twisting, rolling, and balancing on your shoulders vary deliberately. When doing deliberate, stoppable movement, you are able to stop at any time. You have also performed free, accelerating actions which are extremely difficult to stop. Select two or three of your favorite actions and link them together. Make sure you end holding your balance [shoulder stand] momentarily. [A sequence might be shoulders, twist, untwist, roll, roll, and roll, spinning back to a shoulder stand. If students hesitate to start, you may need to start them out by having them try this sequence or one you design.]

5.1 Link your actions smoothly into one continuous movement with your only stops being your planned balances.

5.2 Think of where you are going on the floor or on the mat. Remember to twist within the roll if you need to change direction for your next movement.

5.3 Keep practicing until you have eliminated any unplanned movements.

5.4 Once you begin your sequence, you must maintain a degree of muscle tension to hold your body firm. A tight, firm body is easier moved than one that is relaxed.

5.5 Try to helpfully critique each other's sequences. Point out their good points and give them hints on how they can improve, such as twisting a little further, stretching ankles and toes, and getting rid of unplanned movements.

5.6 I can tell you have been challenged and have enjoyed the free flow and letting the energy go by your nonstop work and the way you have helped each other. You have learned many new ways to move and balance as you experimented with generating power or momentum, using the momentum developed from one action to take you directly into the next to link your movements together into a sequence. Let's take turns sharing each sequence. Perhaps there will be time to try some of the ideas you see others doing after everyone has shared.

ASSESSING ROLLING AND TWISTING

Work with the art instructor in your school to have your sixth grade classes sketch and draw their representations of various balances or twisted shapes. Use their artwork to celebrate this unit as well as to analyze the quality of their balances in relation to their understanding of the principles of balance.

Unit 5 — Creating Shapes and Vaulting Partner Balances

6 to 8 lessons

FOCUS — Developing short gymnastic sequences, emphasizing creating shapes and vaulting over or going under balances held by a partner

MOTOR CONTENT

Selected from Theme 7—Relationships to Others

Relationships

Of individuals and groups—changing relationships with partner; over and under

OBJECTIVES

In this unit, students will (or should be willing to try to) meet these objectives:

- Experiment with a wide variety of body shapes they can hold in a balance for their partner to travel over or under (reflects National Standard in Physical Education 1).
- Select and perform safely a variety of gymnastic forms of traveling, executing each safely when traveling over or under balances held by a partner (reflects National Standards in Physical Education 1 and 5).
- Understand that the safety of one partner depends upon the caring work of the other (reflects National Standard in Physical Education 5).
- Discover and enjoy gymnastic experiences that are impossible to do alone (reflects National Standards in Physical Education 5 and 7).
- Be satisfied when interacting with others and take responsibility for challenging others by striving to do their best (reflects National Standard in Physical Education 7).

EQUIPMENT AND MATERIALS

Mats. *Optional:* Other equipment such as vaulting boxes, benches, stools, platforms.

LEARNING EXPERIENCES

1.0 Select a partner, and one of you make and hold a shape very still that your partner can travel over safely without touching or making contact with you. Start at the end of your mat. Let your partner practice going over your shape three or four times before you change places. [If students need ideas, suggest shapes such as curled, long and narrow, and low and twisted. If the class has an odd number, group three together.]

1.1 Those of you who are traveling over the shape, think how you can travel safely, always looking like a gymnast.

1.2 Remember to hold your shape very still in a firm balance so your partner can make an accurate judgment in selecting their takeoff point and know exactly what part of your body they will go over.

1.3 Those of you responsible for making the shape for your partner, vary your shape by changing your base of support.

1.4 This time, after the first person travels over the partner, they will travel quickly and take a shape. Then the second person will travel over the first. Both partners decide on an ending and hold it very still.

1.5 If you are traveling or balancing, don't let your work get careless. Be serious about your work and be sure you make no contact with your partner.

1.6 Some of you may be able to take turns with each of you forming two or three shapes before you go into your ending. If you choose to lengthen your sequence, include different balanced shapes and different ways of traveling.

2.0 This time, one person will work and make a shape that is wide or arched. Your partner should think for a moment before choosing whether to travel under, over, or through the shape.

2.1 Hold your shape as steady as a piece of apparatus, gripping firmly to the ground and stretching away from your base of support. Partners moving, make sure you make no contact with your partner while traveling under, over, or through the shape.

2.2 As soon as you have negotiated [traveled under, over, or through] the shape made by your partner, immediately make a shape for your partner to go over, under, or through. Both of you carefully try to change these two roles continuously, taking your time so you are both safe and both looking like gymnasts.

2.3 Each time you make a balance for your partner, make each shape different by changing the body parts serving as your firm base, being sure to hold very still.

3.0 [In rolling, it is essential to use arms and hands to take the force off the moving body and absorb the force smoothly on curved large body parts. No large weight or direct force can occur on the neck or high back area. For this reason, many children without such strength or confidence in their strength should *not* even consider a backward roll or a dive roll.] Let's all work for a few minutes on acting like you are going to do a forward roll and, instead, go right into a shoulder stand with your legs spread far apart.

3.1 As you place your shoulders on the mat, you must slow down the action of your legs by keeping the top of your back firm and on the mat and by tightening your stomach muscles to prevent you from rolling down your spine.

3.2 Begin the roll by tucking your head and placing your arms and hands flat on the mat to help form the base, then raise your legs high in the air, stretched far apart.

3.3 Practice this several times until you can roll directly into a shoulder stand and hold your balance very still.

4.0 Once you are able to roll into a *set* [still] shoulder stand, you might want to try this task. First person will roll into a shoulder stand with legs apart. The second person will travel through the gap between the legs by performing a movement that leads them into a curled position on the mat, ready for the first person to go over.

4.1 Each of you will have to work on your timing so you can create continuous movement. One of you should be on the move all of the time. Each must be ready to travel out of your balance as soon as your partner has traveled over it.

4.2 Take turns being the person who goes first, so you each feel and appreciate the importance of both roles.

5.0 Begin to experiment with other balances or shapes that can be negotiated by your partner without contact.

5.1 Select different bases of support. Create some for your partner to move through and others to go over.

5.2 Working together, develop a sequence that focuses on preciseness in timing as you come out of your balances. Keep your sequence short so you can work on refining the timing necessary to make your sequence exciting to watch and fun to do.

5.3 Both of you vary your balances and your forms of traveling. Include both rolling and stepping actions on your hands and feet.

5.4 Take care and plan how you will come out of your balances. Make your body shapes when balancing clear, holding them very still so your partner can negotiate them safely.

5.5 [Have three to five sets share at a time. As you observe, look for something to add to your sequence.]

5.6 Both of you try your best to rid your sequence of unnecessary, unplanned movements.

5.7 When you both have ended going over or under the last balanced shape, both end your sequence in a very controlled position and hold it, focusing your eyes on a fixed spot.

ASSESSING SHORT PARTNER SEQUENCES

Videotape at least one whole sequence for each set of partners and record the time for each group. Partners observe and analyze their own sequence, including variety of stationary balances used, safe flight over stationary shapes, quality of movement, and linking of movements into smooth sequences. Analysis could be recorded as part of their physical education "analysis log."

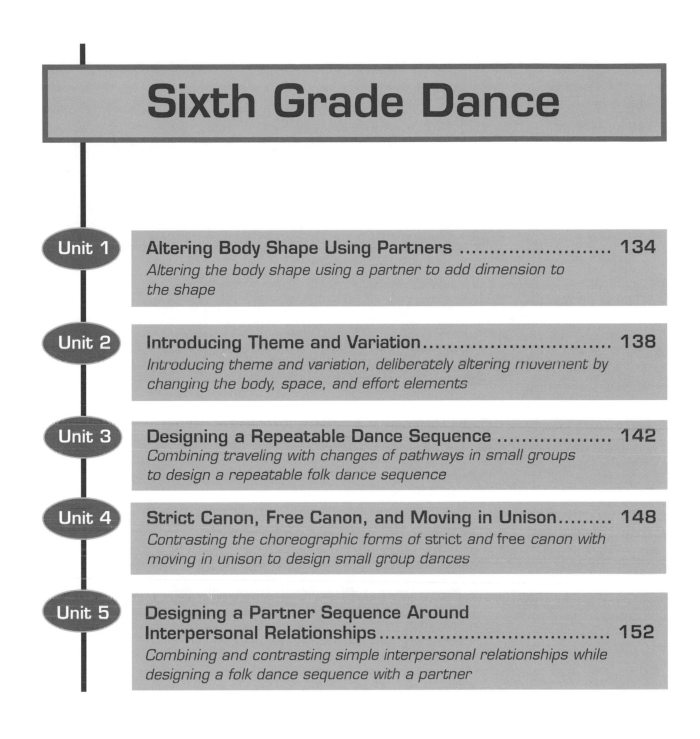

Sixth Grade Dance

Unit 1 — Altering Body Shape Using Partners

3 or 4 lessons

FOCUS Altering the body shape using a partner to add dimension to the shape

MOTOR CONTENT

Selected from Theme 5—Introduction to Relationships; Theme 9—Awareness of Shape in Movement

Body

Shapes of the body—curved (round), straight (narrow, angular), wide (spread), twisted
Nonlocomotor—counterbalance, countertension

Relationships

Interpersonal—individual to individual: apart, together; above, below; in front of, behind, at the side of; over, under

OBJECTIVES

In this unit, students will (or should be willing to try to) meet these objectives:

- Make a variety of different body shapes with a partner for the purpose of changing the dimension and pattern of mutually formed shapes, demonstrate their most interesting shapes, and discuss the reasons for their choices (reflects National Standard in Dance 4a).
- Understand and demonstrate underlying principles of alignment, balance, and weight shift (reflects National Standard in Dance 1a).
- Use countertension and counterbalance to invent sequences with a partner, clearly demonstrating the principle of transition (reflects National Standard in Dance 2a).
- Explain and demonstrate examples of concepts used in dance and disciplines outside the arts (reflects National Standard in Dance 7b).
- Work safely and cooperatively with a partner by forming shapes and balances that are challenging, visually interesting, and controlled (reflects National Standard in Dance 2e).

EQUIPMENT AND MATERIALS

One drum; musical selections that are quiet and not identified by a strong beat, such as New Age music, e.g., Kitaro's *Silk Road*; Nakai's *Desert Dance*; or Winston's *Forest*; or classical music set to sounds in nature.

LEARNING EXPERIENCES

1.0 [Accompany work with quiet music.] Start with an opening body shape in which you and your partner are joined or connected by your hands [or hands to wrists]. Keep changing your shape by making it wider, narrower, more angular, or more curved. Find a partner and begin. [See photo on p. 136.]

1.1 Quietly share ideas with your partner and work cooperatively. Make each shape a joint effort rather than a performance of two soloists.

1.2 What other body parts could you link or join together to create a mutual shape? As you connect to your partner with a variety of body parts, change your level to achieve new, interesting shapes.

1.3 Make up a sequence with your partner, beginning with a straight, narrow shape, changing to a wide, spread shape, and ending with an angular body shape you both can hold. Work to make the transition from one shape into the next very smooth.

1.4 [Tap a slow, steady beat on the drum.] Gradually change your shape on taps one, two, and three, then freeze on the fourth tap. Think of some gelatinous or amoeba-like substance that changes slowly as you change the mutual shape. Take a beginning pose. '[Tap:] Change, [tap] change, [tap] change and [tap] hold; and change, 2, 3, and freeze [4].' [Repeat.]

1.5 Improvise some new body shapes with your partner. As I tap the drum [slow, steady pace], quickly make a shape on the first tap and hold it during the next three taps. Then both make a sudden change and hold that shape. 'Shape number 1, hold 2, hold 3, hold 4; now a different shape, hold 2, hold 3, hold 4.' [Repeat several times.]

1.6 Remember to change your level and the body parts you join together. Make each shape look new and different. Challenge yourselves, but make sure you can hold each shape. [Practice without the drum to give students time to explore multiple solutions and select and order new shapes. Then have students perform partner sequences with the drum.]

1.7 Anticipate each change and make your transitions sudden, clear, and purposeful.

2.0 In dance, one individual can relate to another individual by positioning themselves above, below, in front of, behind, over, under, or alongside. With a partner, demonstrate a variety of different spatial relationships as you create combined shapes. Rather than being face to face all the time, change your relationship to your partner, still maintaining a physical connection. [Provide time to experiment.]

2.1 Show a variety of shapes where you are back to back with your partner. Try to mutually lean your bodies against each other while your feet form a wide base to achieve counterbalance.

2.2 Remember to work safely with your partner by selecting shapes or balances that both of you can hold. What body parts can lean toward each other and connect to hold firm, strong shapes?

2.3 [Tap a drum at a slow, steady pace.] Change your spatial relationship to your partner every four counts and name aloud the relationship you are making with your partner. 'Take your first position [above or below], 2, 3, 4; now change [behind], 2, 3, 4.' [Repeat many times.]

2.4 [Accompany work with a quiet selection of music.] This time, design a short sequence that changes your spatial relationship to a partner. Take an

STRENGTH

Two kinds of strength affect our work in this unit. Gross strength is the total amount of strength you have to lift or support something heavy. Relative strength is how much strength you have for your own body—when climbing easily, supporting your weight on bars, or during floor work for a long time, and when doing many pull-ups. How do these ideas apply to our work with partners in this unit?

opening shape with your partner and gradually alter the shape four different ways by changing your positioning. As you plan and perform your shapes, make the entire dance flow from one shape into the next with smooth transitions.

2.5 This half of the class, quickly take a seat and watch the other half perform their sequences. Observe one set of partners. Do they clearly demonstrate four different spatial relationships? [After several tries, have groups reverse roles.]

3.0 Let's review what we have learned about spatial relationships. Carefully lean or push against your partner and try to maintain your balance by creating counterbalance. [Have two students demonstrate.] Find a partner, an open space, and begin.

3.1 As you lean or push gently against your partner, change your levels and bases of support. Exactly how much muscle tension do you need to move into and hold each shape? To move smoothly out of each shape?

3.2 Remember to maintain wide bases of support in each position of counterbalance. Work with the weight of your partner to feel the balance.

3.3 To feel the difference between counterbalance and countertension, let's experiment with positions of countertension. Stand very close and hold on to your partner, then gradually lean away. Remember, the only way to achieve countertension is by mutually pulling away so both partners are responsible for each other's balance.

3.4 Select positions of counterbalance and countertension and alternate them. Work hard to make the transitions between these positions smooth—no unnecessary movements.

Try to lean toward (or push against) your partner to create a shape that both of you can hold. This is counterbalance.

3.5 Experiment with a variety of spatial relationships as you demonstrate counterbalance and countertension. Side by side? In front of, behind? Close together? Far apart? Above, below? Over, under, on? Pull away from your partner or lean against them to achieve different relationships.

3.6 Design a short sequence of counterbalances and/or positions of countertension that clearly demonstrates changes in spatial relationships.

3.7 [Play quiet music to accompany work time.] As you design your sequence, allow the musical phrasing to sometimes determine when you alter your shape. The music will serve as the impetus for making the changes.

4.0 Beginning in several different places away from your partner, travel toward and connect momentarily in passing with your partner. [Use the term "connect" interchangeably with "join," "link," and "bond."]

4.1 Each time you join with your partner, make a slightly different shape. At first, you are creating only brief, momentary connections with your partner.

4.2 Consider changing your connecting body parts, your spatial relationships, and your bases of support each time you meet your partner.

4.3 With each contact, stay awhile longer, so each relationship with your partner lingers a little longer. A temporal relationship means the time spent with a partner.

4.4 Don't be in such a hurry to rush off; stay with your partner. Take longer to form your new shapes but don't lose your performance attitude. Keep alert and focused on creating shapes but ready to move on.

4.5 [Provide music for work time.] Design a sequence where you travel together [in unison], separate to travel alone, then meet and stay for a longer relationship as you change your shape with your partner on the spot.

4.6 In your dances, be prepared to say how your relationships with your partner are changing. Combine at least two spatial and two temporal relationship changes. Remember, a temporal relationship involves the amount of time you spend with your partner.

4.7 Show a clear change in the amount of time you spend with your partner. Stay with the partner a long time, then the next time linger just a moment.

4.8 [Provide music to accompany dances.] Let's see your dances in groups of four or five partners. Hold your opening position until you hear the music, then begin. Remember to travel into the empty spaces during your traveling parts and be aware of those dancers changing their shapes on the spot. Hold very still at the end of your dance until the music is turned off.

ASSESSMENT: ACROSS DISCIPLINES (ENRICHMENT PROJECT FOR INDIVIDUALS OR GROUPS)

Structure several assessment contexts, including "orchestrating a dance showing different connecting/bonding patterns" (Armstrong 1994, p. 124), to reflect student understanding of this concept and their actual skill competency. Coordinate your efforts with the classroom teachers.

Unit 2 — Introducing Theme and Variation

3 to 4 lessons

FOCUS — Introducing theme and variation, deliberately altering movement by changing the body, space, and effort elements

MOTOR CONTENT

Selected from Theme 3—Introduction to Space; Theme 5—Introduction to Relationships; Theme 6—Instrumental Use of the Body; and Theme 10—Transitions Between Basic Effort Actions

Body

Locomotor activities—traveling, walking, jumping, turning
Nonlocomotor activities—curling, stretching, twisting
Actions of body parts—supporting, transferring weight

Effort

Altering one, two, or three motion factors (weight, time, space)

Space

Directions—forward, backward, sideways
Levels—high, middle, low (deep)

Relationships

Interpersonal—individuals, group: mirroring, leading, following; contrasting, alternating, successive, in unison

OBJECTIVES

In this unit, students will (or should be willing to try to) meet these objectives:

- Demonstrate increasing kinesthetic awareness, concentration, and focus in performing movement skillfully (reflects National Standard in Dance 1f).
- Deliberately change the body, space, and effort elements of a movement for the purpose of designing variations: Explore multiple solutions, select and demonstrate the most interesting variations, and discuss reasons for choices (reflects National Standard in Dance 4a).
- Share movement ideas during improvisations and performances; observe and describe elements of the dance, using appropriate movement and dance vocabulary; and identify aesthetic criteria for evaluating dance (reflects National Standards in Dance 1h and 4d).

- Understand that theme and variation is a way to achieve variety and contrast in movement by changing the main movement idea (theme) in a variety of ways (variations), i.e., altering the tempo, tension, direction, level, body parts supporting the weight, or body actions.
- Demonstrate appropriate audience behavior, offering opinions in supportive, constructive ways (reflects National Standard in Dance 4b).

EQUIPMENT AND MATERIALS

"Theme" and "variation" compositions, such as Johann Sebastian Bach's *Goldberg Variations*, Ludwig Van Beethoven's *Eroica* Variations, Johannes Brahm's "Variations on a Theme by Handel," Arnold Schoenberg's *Variations for Orchestra*, and the like.

LEARNING EXPERIENCES

1.0 [Demonstrate a very simple movement plus two or three variations for the class.] Watch as I demonstrate this movement and then be ready to say how I change it. Theme: 'Walk forward, 2, 3, 4, 5, 6, 7, 8.' Now watch how I change it. First variation: 'Walk sideways, 2 . . . 8.' Here is another variation. Second variation: 'Walk forward, 2, 3, turn around [4], walk backward [5], 6, 7, 8.' Notice the main movement idea was simply walking forward. How did I vary my idea? Yes, the first variation changed the direction; the second variation added a turn as well as a change of direction. As I demonstrate simple movement ideas [body actions, locomotor, or nonlocomotor activities], change either the *direction* or the *body action* used to perform the movement theme. [Perform several simple movement ideas for the class to vary, then select a student to lead.]

1.1 We can also deliberately change the *tempo* to vary a movement theme. We can make the movement fast or slow. Watch [Kevin] demonstrate a movement idea in slow motion, then change the tempo by performing the same actions very fast. [Repeat, with other students leading.]

1.2 This time let's vary the *level* of the movement idea or theme. This may require changing the supporting body parts as you design your variation. After you perform each movement idea [have different students demonstrate themes], change the level in each variation. [E.g., Make a huge body circle while standing; vary it by making a small upper torso circle while seated or kneeling.]

1.3 Sometimes when you vary the level or body parts used, the *size* of the movement changes, too. Everyone, make a small, lifting, circling motion with one arm; now vary the size of the movement idea by translating your small movement into a whole body action. Make a big, turning jump! What *pathway* is drawn in the air?

1.4 [Select five or six students to lead different groups of students.] This time your leaders will demonstrate very simple movements for you to vary. Choose whether to change the *direction*, *tempo*, *level*, or *pathway* of the original theme. Leaders, wait until all members of your group have completed their variation before demonstrating the next theme. Find a group of five or six people and begin.

1.5 In your groups, show two completely different variations for each movement theme. Remember to closely observe your leader's movement idea, then design two variations. [Practice awhile, then have groups demonstrate.]

1.6 Select your own movement idea and vary the *direction*, *speed*, *level*, or *pathway* of the movement. Select a movement you can do in a phrase of eight counts. 'Your idea, 2, 3, 4, 5, 6, 7, 8.' Now design your first variation, '2, 3, 4, 5, 6, 7, 8'; now your second variation, '2, 3, 4, 5, 6, 7, 8.'

1.7 Let's try this again and add four counts of complete stillness between the theme and each variation. This will help the audience clearly recognize when each variation starts and stops.

2.0 Make up a short, simple movement idea of your own, then change it in some way two times. Try to change the direction or speed of the movement, the body parts supporting you [level], or the pathway the movement draws in the air or on the floor. Pause for two or three seconds between the main theme and each variation to show that one idea is completely finished.

2.1 This time your group leader will demonstrate a movement idea and, after each of you design two variations, 'pass the leadership' to the next person. Each new movement idea will be introduced by a different classmate in your group. Find groups of four or five. Decide who leads first, what the order should be, and begin. Each new leader must be sure to wait until the entire group has performed two variations before introducing her [or his] new movement theme.

2.2 This time, the leader presents a movement idea, then follower #1 designs a variation, and follower #2 designs a completely different variation. Each person in the group, in their turn, designs a different variation. When all followers have presented a variation, the leader becomes the last follower and all followers move up one, with the leadership role passed on to follower #1. [Walk one group through rotation to demonstrate.]

2.3 On your own now, each of you design your very own movement ideas for two variations, each lasting eight counts. Include a pause of four counts between each variation. Your dance has one theme and two variations. Our dances will last 36 counts. [Main theme for eight counts, pause four; variation #1 for eight counts, pause four; variation #2 for eight counts, pause four (to finish).]

2.4 I'm going to teach you a short movement phrase of 16 counts. This will be theme A, and we will perform it together [in unison]. Here we go. Theme: 'Run, run, run, run [counts 1 through 4]; stamp, stamp, stamp, jump-clap [counts 5 through 8]; sink, sink, sink, sink [9 through 12]; roll, rise, stretch, stretch [13 through 16].' Try to stay right with me. On your own now, develop a 16-count variation. [Continue to verbalize the movement theme as written and count the 16 beats for the variation.]

2.5 Let's design a second variation of our main theme. Try something different with either the *body parts used* or the *direction*, *tempo*, *level*, or *pathway* of movement. What other element could be changed? Yes, *force* of the movement! You could show stronger or lighter tension. [Have students work on their own time, exploring solutions.]

2.6 Now, let's take it from the top with the theme, then your first, and finally your second variation. In unison, 'Main theme 1, 2 . . . 16; variation #1, 2 . . . 16; variation #2, 2, 3 . . . 16. *End*.'

3.0 [The structure of this task follows the same format as 2.4 through 2.6. Accompany this section with music.] Let's design a short group dance that

AEROBIC ACTIVITY

Besides dancing, activities that help you improve your aerobic heart endurance are exercise walking, hiking, running, swimming, ice skating, rollerblading, and biking for 20 minutes or more while your heart is exercising at a medium rate.

ASSESSMENT: SELF-EVALUATION AND REFLECTION

Discuss criteria for selecting a main theme: simplicity or clarity of gestures, actions, and activities; originality of movements; and variety and interest, using a combination of curved, straight, and twisted movements. Provide time for small groups of students to design movement ideas. Have entire class evaluate and select a main theme A.

clearly shows a main theme and three variations. [Perform a simple 16-count movement idea for the class to learn or have students design this main theme (see assessment).]

3.1 As you refine the main theme, concentrate on some of its *identifying* features, for example, 'swinging, falling, and rising; or reaching, turning, and jumping.' Let's practice our movements together. [Repeat theme A several times.]

3.2 As your group designs your three variations, remember the many elements that are easy to change. We can change the *body actions* or *body parts* that support our weight. We can change our *direction*, *level*, or *pathway*. We can change the *tempo* by performing movements faster or slower or vary the *force* by using a lot of muscle tension or just a little. [Provide time to explore several possible solutions; let groups select their most interesting variations.]

3.3 We're ready to combine the main theme A with our three variations. This dance has four parts. When you are finished, hold your ending position very still. [Rehearse and perform dances in groups of four or five students. Observers identify and discuss dance elements. Performers explain reasons for their choices.]

3.4 [Do another day.] Let's restructure the design of our dance. This third of the class, design a variation on the *tempo* of the main theme. The group over here, design a variation on the *directions* and *pathways* of the theme. This third group, design a variation that features changes in *body parts* used to support the weight. Each variation takes 16 counts and requires a group collaborative and cooperative effort.

3.5 Now we'll combine our three group variations into a format. Everyone in unison perform the main theme A. Hold as group 1 performs variation #1 in 16 counts. Hold as group 2 performs variation #2 in 16 counts. Hold as group 3 performs variation #3 for 16 counts. Finish the dance with everyone moving again in unison to theme A.

3.6 This time when you are waiting to perform your section, hold completely still and don't even move your eyes so nothing distracts from the performance. Count the beats without moving your lips and be ready to move. [Count and cue groups for performance. Observe for stillness, concentration, and focus.]

3.7 As we perform this dance in two groups [have half of each variation group demonstrate at a time], audience, be ready to explain how the groups have varied theme A. How does each variation add interest to the dance? [Encourage and compliment students as they offer their opinions in supportive, constructive ways.]

Designing a Repeatable Dance Sequence

4 or 5 lessons

FOCUS Combining traveling with changes of pathways in small groups to design a repeatable folk dance sequence

MOTOR CONTENT

Selected from Theme 6—Instrumental Use of the Body; Theme 8—Occupational and Everyday Rhythms; and Theme 9—Awareness of Shape in Movement

Body

Locomotion—running, prancing

Effort

Metric rhythm—folkdance based on work actions and song

Space

Floor patterns (pathways)—straight lines, zigzags, curved lines, circles

OBJECTIVES

In this unit, students will (or should be willing to try to) meet these objectives:

* Design and demonstrate a repeatable dance sequence with three others (trio formation); competently perform the basic steps and style of the folkdance "Troika" (reflects National Standards in Dance 1g, 5a, and 5b).
* Demonstrate variations on the dance "Troika" by selecting and performing a variety of floor patterns (straight lines, zigzags, circles) in time with 2/4 music (reflects National Standard in Dance 1c).

EQUIPMENT AND MATERIALS

One drum; recording or piano music of "Troika" (see p. 143). *Optional:* Two bandannas or ribbons for *every* trio.

LEARNING EXPERIENCES

1.0 [Tap a steady jogging pace on a drum.] As I tap the drum, travel throughout the space, taking one running step per beat and avoiding others. Stop quickly when I say, 'And stop.' Ready and, 'Travel with running steps . . . travel . . .

Troika

travel . . . and stop!' [Repeat many times, reinforcing spatial awareness and even spacing.]

1.1 Take one step with each tap of the drum. The speed of the drum tells you how fast to run. [Play steady beats, gradually increasing speed as students show safe traveling and moving in time with the drum.]

FLEXIBILITY

Stretch the upper and lower leg, especially your quadriceps (touch the front of your thigh) and Achilles tendons (touch tendon above heels). [Demonstrate.] When you stretch before or after vigorous activity, holding a stretch for 10 or more seconds can help increase your muscles' flexibility. Not only is stretching a good warm-up, it can also be a way to maintain or improve your flexibility.

1.2 As you travel, make your knees important. Lift or thrust your knees upward, accenting your running steps! Feel a slight lift of your whole body with each step.

1.3 Let's take it a little faster now. Keep your stepping sharp, light, and precisely with the drumbeat. [Play the drum twice as fast as the underlying beat of the music "Troika," on page 143. A fast running (prancing) step is used throughout the dance, two steps to each musical beat. Musicians count, "One and two and three and four and," whereas dancers often count, "One, two, three, four," and group movements into four- and eight-count phrases.]

1.4 Let's travel forward in a straight pathway for eight counts, then change directions and travel again. Ready and, 'Travel, 2, 3, 4, 5, 6, 7, 8; change directions and travel again . . . 8; . . . .' [Repeat phrases many times without, then with, the music.] Your quick running steps can take you forward, backward, sideways! Keep moving into empty spaces in straight pathways. Then run in place momentarily, let others pass by.

1.5 Draw a zigzag pattern on the floor with your finger . . . no curved lines, only straight pathways with sharp corners or angles! Let's run this pattern, putting a sharp zig or zag in your pathway every four beats. Ready and, 'Run, 2, 3, 4; change, 2, 3, 4; zig, 2, 3, 4; zag, 2, 3, 4 . . . .' [Repeat several times without stopping, accompanying on the drum. Eliminate counting, but cue changes in pathway.]

1.6 Try hard to make your changes of direction and pathways very clear by turning sharply and maintaining the same body part leading. Iron out all the curved, rounded edges. What body parts can lead you sideways [forward, backward]? Show us!

1.7 Let's try traveling [running] quickly for 16 counts, combining a straight pathway with a zigzag in groups of three. Find two others and a working space. Your trio will face the same direction, staying side by side as you travel, no one ever leading. You are all equally important! Decide when to zig or zag and when to travel straight, then begin. [Tap the drum up to tempo with the music.]

1.8 As you practice your traveling sequence, remember within 16 counts [running steps] we want to see both straight and zigzag floor patterns. Ready and, 'Travel, 2, 3, 4 . . . 16.' [Add music, still tapping the drum; on piano arrangement, play measures one through four.]

1.9 See if your shoulders can almost touch as you travel—align your trio. All of you, lift your knees at exactly the same time . . . step sharply, precisely with the drumbeat. Feel a rhythmical motion or cadence! (See photo p. 145.)

1.10 We'll have four groups at a time demonstrate their running sequence, or part A of our dance. Observers, we are looking for a trio moving as one unit, traveling together, stepping on the beat, and changing direction and pathways sharply. [Accompany with music, giving cues as needed.]

2.0 In your groups of three aligned dancers, change places with each other while running, keeping the beat in your feet. Watch as this trio [select a group] demonstrates one possible way. Outside people on the right and left sides run four steps clockwise around the middle person to exchange places. Next, the middle person runs four steps in place, turning around in a half-circle. Ready and, 'Outside dancers exchange places, 2, 3, 4; middle person turns in place, 2, 3, 4 . . . .' Repeat this eight-count phrase again to return to your home position. [Walk out a 16-count phrase (part B), talking dancers through changes of position.]

Lift your knees at exactly the same time . . . step sharply, precisely with the drumbeat.

2.1 It's important to stay close together and move as a set of three. Your trio could lightly hold inside hands or the middle person could hold a bandanna [ribbon] in each hand for the outside people to grasp. Decide what's best for your group and practice this 16-count phrase. [Play drum up to tempo with the music; then add "Troika," measures five through eight (16 running steps).]

2.2 Listen carefully to the musical phrases. Begin each exchange of positions on a new phrase of eight counts. Work to keep your running in time with the music! [Play music and count aloud the phrases of eight. Repeat several times.]

2.3 Remember to keep your grasp loose so your classmate's hand can turn easily in yours and run or prance at a steady pace to the music.

2.4 Let's combine parts A and B of our dance: traveling in straight lines and zigzag pathways for 16 counts [part A]; exchanging places twice for 16 counts [part B]. All trios ready? [Tap the drum up to tempo while talking students through the sequence.] And, 'Travel, 2, 3, 4, 5, 6, 7, 8; travel again . . . 8; exchange places . . . 8; trade places again . . . 8 . . . .'

2.5 As you perform both parts, see if you can stay close together and keep the motion going. Be a team in synchrony, working together.

2.6 Let's take it again. Reduce the size of your steps and exaggerate the lifting of your knees. Work to achieve a proud, spirited running [prancing] step with chests lifted and heads held high.

3.0 [Accompany student's work by tapping a steady pace on the drum.] Remember a curved pathway has no straight lines. Draw with your finger circular floor patterns—curving, circling, spiraling around. Now follow the patterns as you travel, creating a variety of curved pathways. When I say, 'Stop,' hold a position of stillness. Ready and, 'Travel . . . travel . . . in curved pathways . . . and stop.'

3.1 If you had chalk dust on your feet, the path of your footprints would make curved or circular patterns and designs. Dance out your favorite patterns using a variety of quick steps—running, stepping turns, jumps.

3.2 Let's travel in curved pathways for 12 counts, *stamp* three times and pause. Ready and, 'Travel . . . 12, *stamp, stamp, stamp,* hold 16!' Take it again, trying to vary your direction and pathways. [Repeat several times, gradually increasing the tempo. Add music.]

3.3 Form a small circle with your trio, facing in, and practice running together, circling to the left and to the right. Decide with your group which foot to start on.

3.4 Can you hold hands [or opposite ends of bandannas or ribbons] lightly and keep your circling pattern flowing? Lift knees high and work together to achieve a cadence.

3.5 Let's try circling clockwise with our trio for 12 running steps, then *stamp* three times and pause. Ready and, 'Circle . . . 12; *stamp, stamp, stamp,* hold [16]!' [Play "Troika" measures 9 through 12.] Now repeat this 16-count phrase, circling to the right or counterclockwise [measures 13 through 16]. You have just learned all of part C! [See below.] Let's try Part C again with the music.

[*Optional variations:* Instead of "Circling" on the last four measures of the dance (measures 13 through 16), you may substitute either of the following variations for greater variety and interest:]

- Run under an arch, tracing circular and spiral floor patterns with your feet—start by aligning your trio and lightly hold inside hands [or bandannas or ribbons]. Person on the right [outside] runs forward, going around the middle person and under an arch formed by the left and middle persons. Then, the middle person follows along under the arch and the left person simply turns once [spirals] in place. Try the same steps to the other side with the left [outside] person leading the traveling under an arch formed by the middle and right persons.
- Improvise your own curved floor pattern as a trio—see how many different ways you can travel together, circling, curving, spiraling. Show your best running and prancing, stepping turns, and jump. Use the jump as a surprise moment in your dance.

4.0 Let's combine all parts of the dance—traveling in straight and zigzag pathways [part A]; exchanging places twice [part B]; and circling as a trio [part C]:

Part A [measures 1 through 4, 16 running steps] 'Travel in straight and zigzag pathways . . . 8; sharp, light, precise steps . . . 8.'

Part B [measures 5 through 8, 16 running steps] 'Outside dancers exchange places . . . 8; repeat, trading places again . . . 8.'

Part C [measures 9 through 16] 'Circle left for 12 running steps . . . 12, *stamp, stamp, stamp,* hold [16]; now reverse directions and repeat circling right . . . 12, *stamp, stamp, stamp,* hold [16].'

4.1 As you travel, work hard to take one step per drumbeat [two steps per musical beat or double time]. Remember, in part C, decide with your group which foot to start traveling on so you synchronize your movements.

4.2 As you practice your dances with your group, work on refining your curved pathways and straight pathways. Really show us the difference between straight, zigzag, and curved floor patterns. What do you need to do with your torso to show a sharp change of direction? Right! Align your shoulders over your hips and 'squarely' face that direction.

4.3 Let's watch our dances [divide class in half to observe]. Remember to always move with your partners into the empty spaces as you travel, demonstrating three different floor patterns. [Accompany performance with music.]

5.0 *Optional enrichment project:* [Learn the traditional steps and style of "Troika," a Russian folkdance imitating "sleighs drawn by spirited, prancing ponies." See Van Hagan, Dexter, and Williams 1951.] Begin in trios in a large circle facing clockwise with the person on the right being nearest the center of the circle. [*Note.* This dance calls for a fast prancing step throughout, *two* steps to each beat.]

Measures 1 through 4: Starting with the right foot, and holding inside hands lightly, all trios take 16 running steps forward, two steps to each beat.

Measures 5 through 8: Outside [left] person of trio, still holding inside hands, takes 16 prancing steps around the other two [middle and right] dancers while they prance in place.

Measures 9 through 12: Outside dancers [left and right] now join their free hands to form small circles of three. All take 14 prancing steps, circling around to their left and *stamp, stamp.*

Measures 13 through 14: All [trios] take eight running steps, circling around to the right.

Measures 15 through 16: The outside dancers [left and right] now raise their joined hands, forming an arch, and 'shoo' the middle person under their arch.

[Rehearse "Troika" and perform the dance for a primary grade class. Explain how the middle person represents the driver of the coach, while the outside dancers play the role of beautifully groomed ponies, proudly pulling a sleigh.]

Unit 4

Strict Canon, Free Canon, and Moving in Unison

3 or 4 lessons

FOCUS Contrasting the choreographic forms of *strict* and *free* canon with moving in unison to design small group dances

MOTOR CONTENT

Selected from Theme 5—Introduction to Relationships and Theme 6—Instrumental Use of the Body

Body

Combinations of activities—gesturing while stepping, weight transference during walking, stepping during turns; turns with gestures; sequences of activities

Relationships

Interpersonal—canon forms, strict and free

OBJECTIVES

In this unit, students will (or should be willing to try to) meet these objectives:

- Work cooperatively within a small group to design and perform a group dance, developing an appreciation for the choreographic tool of the canon (reflects National Standards in Dance 2c and 2d).
- Demonstrate a "performance attitude" by concentrating and focusing on their movement as it is being performed without being distracted by others (reflects National Standard in Dance 1f).
- Understand the difference between a *strict* and a *free* canon.
- As an observer, develop an appreciation and respect for the movement ideas and designs of others by recognizing canon as a choreographic form and thoughtfully discussing their reactions and opinions (reflects National Standard in Dance 4b).
- Create their own warm-up and discuss its benefits (reflects National Standard in Dance 6c).

EQUIPMENT AND MATERIALS

One drum; musical selections with a steady beat, such as Johann Sebastian Bach's "Fugue" in G minor or "Jesu, Joy of Man's Desiring"; Aaron Copeland's "Hoe Down" from *Rodeo—Four Dance Episodes*; Respighi's "Danza" from *Brazilian Impressions*.

LEARNING EXPERIENCES

1.0 [Demonstrate a simple two-voice-two-dancer canon.] Copy the movement I make four counts after me. [For example, "I walk forward, 2, 3, 4 while you (all students) *wait*; then you walk forward, 2, 3, 4."] This is a two-voice-two-dancer canon. I am one voice and you as the class are the second voice, joining in after an interval of time following the first voice. Let's try this two-voice canon several times, adding more movement to our sequence. [Demonstrate the first voice; the class moves as the second voice.] [Teacher's "voice":] 'Walk, 2, 3, 4; reach, 2, 3, 4; sink, 2, 3, 4; rise, 2, 3, 4.' [Students' "voice":] '*Wait*, 2, 3, 4; walk, 2, 3, 4; reach, 2, 3, 4; sink, 2, 3, 4; rise, 2, 3, 4.' [Continue demonstrating and leading as the first voice and dancer or select two or three reliable students to lead half or a third of the class.] All leaders [first voices] need to select very simple movements with few gestures that are easy to copy exactly.

1.1 As the dancer [first voice] moves, the second dancer [second voice] must observe closely to know what will come next in the sequence. Concentrate only on how the first voice moves. [Practice 1.0.]

1.2 [Demonstrate this task initially with students following as the second voice.] As we expand the length of our canon, watch how we can design moments of moving as one voice in unison. Start from a low level. First voice: 'rise, 2, 3, 4; walk, 2, 3, 4; *walk, 2, 3, 4*; sink.' Second voice: '*Wait*, 2, 3, 4; rise, 2, 3, 4; *walk, 2, 3, 4*; walk, 2, 3, 4; sink.' Notice there is one section (underlined) when both voices are performing the same movement idea in unison [at the same time].

1.3 Continue to work in a two-voice canon, but in groups of four or five. The first volunteer leader in each group will lead first, then rotate leaders. You will all have a chance to be the first voice and the second voice.

1.4 Leaders, as you select movement ideas for the second voice to copy, try to consciously include changes in levels by using rising and sinking, carefully executed walking turns, or very simple gesturing movements with your arms. Remember that the actions of the first voice must always remain visible to the second voice so the second voice will know exactly what to do.

1.5 [Demonstrate a change of direction and change of leader with two to four students.] This time find a way to trade off the leadership role without the audience seeing the change. When the current leader [first voice] changes directions so that a new person in the group is in front, that person is now the new leader. Whoever is farthest in front leads. You need to watch as you move. If no one is in front of you, you are the leader! First voice: 'Walk, 2, 3, 4; sink, 2, 3, 4; rise, 2, 3, 4; turn, pause, pause, pause.' Second voice: '*Wait* . . . ; walk, 2, 3, 4; sink, 2, 3, 4; rise, 2, 3, 4; turn 2, 3, 4; and become the leader [first voice].' Notice that we are still working in strict canon form, copying the movement of the leader exactly, and the first voice pauses four counts during the transition to give the new leader time to start to lead. Decide in advance how many counts the first voice will lead. As you work, I will tap a drum and say the counts aloud.

2.0 [Demonstrate a strict three-voice canon with two students.] Watch as we demonstrate a three-voice canon with three dancers. Notice that the first voice leads, the second voice joins in after an interval of time, and the third voice starts to move an interval after the second voice. All the voices copy exactly the movement of the first voice. Here is a three-voice canon with a four-beat interval. First voice: 'Walk, 2, 3, 4; sink, 2, 3, 4; rise, 2, 3, 4; walk, 2, 3, 4; hold 2, 3, 4.' Second voice: '*Wait* . . . ; walk, 2, 3, 4; sink, 2, 3, 4; rise, 2, 3, 4; walk, 2, 3, 4; hold.' Third voice: '*Wait* . . . ; *wait* . . . ; walk, 2, 3, 4; sink, 2, 3, 4; rise, 2, 3, 4; walk, 2, 3, 4; hold.' Notice that the third voice [dancer] waits for a full eight counts before starting the sequence. Find groups of three, choose who is to be your first, second, and third voices, and take a position to begin. [Tap a drum softly and say the counts aloud, "One, 2, 3, 4; one, 2, 3, 4." If groups have four students, have the third and fourth students perform the third voice in unison. Repeat enough times to allow every student to experience each voice.]

2.1 The third voice dancer may find it easier to watch only the second voice. For this reason, it is very important that the second voice copies the movement of the first voice exactly and that the first voice moves with simple, clear ideas.

2.2 It is also possible to have a moment with all three voices moving in unison. Watch as I demonstrate with two students. First voice: 'Walk, 2, 3, 4; sink, 2, 3, 4; rise, 2, 3, 4; walk, 2, 3, 4; walk, 2, 3, 4; *walk*, 2, 3, 4.' Second voice: 'Wait . . . ; walk . . . ; sink . . . ; rise . . . ; walk . . . ; *walk* . . . ; walk . . . .' Third voice: '*Wait* . . . ; *wait* . . . ; walk . . . ; sink . . . ; rise . . . ; *walk* . . . ; walk . . . ; walk . . . .' Remember when there are three voices, in order to have a period of movement in unison, the first voice needs to do one of the movement ideas three times, or 12 beats if you're performing a four-beat canon.

2.3 Although we have been canoning in four beats, any interval of time between voices is possible. Let's change the interval of time between voices. Instead of moving with four-beat intervals between voices, let's lengthen our canon phrases to eight beats. The first voice continues the same movement idea for a full eight beats, then the second voice joins in and, after eight beats, the third voice begins moving. First voice: 'Walk, 2, 3, 4, 5, 6, 7, 8; sink . . . 8; rise . . . 8; turn . . . 8; walk . . . 8; sink . . . 8.' Second voice: 'Wait . . . 8; walk . . . 8; sink . . . 8; rise . . . 8; turn . . . 8; walk . . . 8; sink . . . 8.' Third voice: 'Wait . . . 8; wait . . . 8; walk . . . 8; sink . . . 8; rise . . . 8; turn . . . 8; walk . . . 8; sink . . . 8.'

2.4 The interval of time can also be reduced. Try a two-beat canon. First voice: 'Walk 2; sink 2; rise 2.' Second voice: 'Wait 2, walk 2, sink 2, rise 2.' Third voice: 'Wait 2, wait 2, walk 2, [and so on].' [Accompany work with a drum, counting, "1, 2; 1, 2." Keep repeating the first voice sequence.]

2.5 It is absolutely critical to focus on the person ahead of you in the canon and concentrate on how you are moving. Remember we are very proud, professional dancers. Lift through the chest as you walk. Maintain an alert, aligned posture, and keep your attention focused on the movement. [Observe for concentration and focus as students repeat and refine their sequences.]

2.6 Work toward achieving a performance attitude. Let your 'walking, sinking, rising' flow, one movement into the next. Begin to project outward, beyond the person in front of you and into space. Show your presence!

2.7 Let's perform our dances in canon for the class. Two groups at a time share the space as we in the audience observe how each group has structured their strict three-voice canons. Performers, try to stay on-beat because we are looking for simple movement ideas, copied exactly in the three voices with moments of moving in unison. [Accompany performances with one or two selections of moderate tempo musical selections in 4/4 time.]

3.0 So far we have been working in strict canon with each voice exactly copying the movements of the first voice. Another type of canon is the *free* canon in which the original movement of the first voice is changed slightly by the next voice or voices. Watch as we demonstrate a two-voice free canon. [Ask a student to be the leader (first voice); teacher performs the second voice.] [Student (first voice):] 'Walk slowly, 2, 3, 4; sink to the floor . . . reach arms to the ceiling . . . .' [Teacher (second voice):] 'Wait . . . ; walk quickly . . . [to 8 counts]; sink to floor . . . ; rise.' Notice how the second voice changes the length of time of the movement or the movement itself in some way. Try this with a partner and, after a bit of time, change voices.

3.1 As you work in a two-voice free canon, change only the traveling phrases. Maintain a strict canon for all nontraveling phrases, copying exactly the action of first voice.

3.2 When working in free canon, the second voice has to not only observe the movement of the first voice but also make some quick decisions about how to change the original movement idea. Think as you move.

3.3 Continue the free canon and add a third voice. The third voice has the option of changing the movement of the first voice or the second voice or both voices. Since this is a difficult role to assume, it may be easier if the third voice concentrates only on what the second voice does and alters only that movement.

3.4 Try working in a three-voice free canon with four, five, or six people in each group. One person will lead the rest of the group. Each one of you is free to interpret and change the movement of the first voice or the voice ahead of you.

3.5 Keep your improvised movement simple and highly visible, especially if you include gestures or turns while stepping.

3.6 Remember, in a free canon, the movement may not be copied exactly, but may take a longer or shorter length of time. It is challenging because you need to keep an eye on the leader for the next movement idea, then improvise on it.

3.7 Let's perform our free canons for the class. Audience members, be alert for those special moments of moving in unison that may happen. These moments provide contrast. Pay attention to how each voice alters the original movement idea. [After all groups have performed, discuss students' observations and opinions. Provide musical selections for performing groups.

Note. You may want to organize a large group dance involving the entire class in strict canon. Organize the class in three groups (a three-voice canon) and either teach a simple movement sequence or allow the first voice dancers to choreograph their own sequence.]

Designing a Partner Sequence Around Interpersonal Relationships

3 or 4 lessons

FOCUS Combining and contrasting simple interpersonal relationships while designing a folk dance sequence with a partner

MOTOR CONTENT

Selected from Theme 5—Introduction to Relationships and Theme 8—Occupational and Everyday Rhythms

Effort

Rhythms—folkdances based upon work dances

Relationships

Interpersonal—meeting, parting; leading, following; mirroring

OBJECTIVES

In this unit, students will (or should be willing to try to) meet these objectives:

- Combine and refine a variety of simple interpersonal relationships with a partner to form repeatable dance sequences, competently performing simple country dance steps and styles from various periods (reflects National Standards in Dance 1g, 5a, and 5b).
- As a leader, select movements that are enjoyable and challenging for the follower to perform; as a follower, work to mirror the leader's movement while performing a dance with two parts, AB form (reflects National Standards in Dance 2c and 2e).
- Recall the definition of mirroring (reflects National Standard in Dance 2e).

EQUIPMENT AND MATERIALS

One drum; recording of a simple country or folkdance with a two-part (AB) structure, such as "The Black Nag," on page 153, or "Heartsease" or "Cuckolds All A-row." *Enrichment:* More complicated formations may be introduced as students learn traditional steps and styles of Country folk dances, including "The Black Nag," "Greensleeves," "Picking of Sticks," or "Oranges and Lemons." (See Millar, 1985).

The Black Nag

"The Black Nag," selected by John Fitzhugh Millar, 1985, *Elizabethan Country Dances*, p. 32. © 1985 by Thirteen Colonies Press.

LEARNING EXPERIENCES

FLEXIBILITY AND WARM-UP

Stretch main muscle groups, especially upper and lower legs. Don't strain your muscles. You can become more flexibile safely by stretching often over many months and by performing stretches correctly. Stretch each muscle group (without bouncing) for 10 or more seconds.

1.0 Face your partner, standing five or six steps away. Travel to meet your partner, then separate. 'Travel, 2, 3, 4, and separate, 2, 3, 4; travel to meet, 2, 3, 4, and part, 2, 3, 4.' [Tap a steady rhythmic pattern on a drum and talk students through the sequence, saying counts aloud; repeat many times.]

1.1 See if you can pace yourself to allow for continuous travel through all the beats. If you find one of you is arriving too soon and waiting around, ask yourself, 'How do I need to adjust my space and size of step?'

1.2 This time, start quite a distance from your partner so you both need to burn up the miles as you travel.

1.3 Show that you have actually met your partner by clapping each other's hands, shaking hands, or saluting to greet each time you meet.

1.4 In dance, we often want to express feelings. Show us in your body posture and facial expression how pleased you are to see your classmate.

1.5 Travel to greet a different classmate during each meeting phrase. I'll call it: 'Travel, 2, 3, 4, and part, 2, 3, 4; and find a new classmate, 2, 3, 4, and part, 2, 3, 4; and on to the next, 2, 3, 4, and separate, 2, 3, 4.' [Tap the drum to accompany; repeat many times.]

1.6 Every time you meet and part, change how you travel. So far, I've seen magnificent marching, gourmet galloping, sophisticated skipping, and jolly jogging. Everyone travel in different ways.

1.7 [Accompany this task with suggested music. If using "The Black Nag," this material will accompany the first melody or theme A, which consists of 16 counts.] Design a repeatable sequence of meeting and parting that you can do the same way every time with your partner. After we design and practice our phrases, we will watch them. Remember, we meet four counts and part four counts, then repeat the meeting and parting actions. 'Meet, 2, 3, 4, and part, 2, 3, 4; meet again, 2, 3, 4, and part, 2, 3, 4.' [Repeat many times, saying actions and counts aloud until students understand and follow the sequence without verbal cues.]

2.0 In your own space, face your partner, and let's have the younger person be our first leader as we work on mirroring actions. Leaders, it takes time and practice to become skillful at mirroring, so begin with very simple movements repeated many times at a slow tempo. This will really help your partner become good at mirroring.

2.1 Remember followers, when mirroring you do the same movements at the same time, but you do your movements with the opposite side of the body than your partner. [Have leaders and followers change roles every few minutes.]

2.2 Some of you are ready to travel as you mirror one another. Remember to travel slowly, with simple locomotor movements [step, jump, hop, slide, gallop, skip], and be aware of other people as you travel into empty spaces. [Post a list of locomotor movements for students to choose from.]

2.3 Work harder on changing levels as you mirror. Followers, watch closely and give each movement your best attempt.

2.4 [Tap a drum at the same tempo as the music.] Many of you are ready to travel at a livelier, quicker pace. This time leaders, do your best to move your partner quickly and safely through the empty space.

2.5 [Accompany this task with suggested music. If using "The Black Nag," this will be theme B which consists of 32 counts (eight sets of four counts).] Let's combine traveling with changes of directions as we mirror our partner. Remember, if the leader moves backward, the follower also moves backward. 'Travel, 2, 3, 4; change direction, 2, 3, 4; change again, 2, 3, 4; and bow to your partner, 2, 3, 4 [16 counts].' Repeat this with the other person leading. [Give verbal cues as the music plays until the students understand the sequence.]

3.0 Begin fairly close, standing face to face with your partner. As I tap the first four beats, exchange places with your partner. Move right into her [or his] spot. 'Trade places, 2, 3, 4; now go back, 2, 3, 4; trade again, 2, 3, 4; and go home, 2, 3, 4.' [Say the task aloud as you tap a steady rhythm on a drum. If using "The Black Nag," this is a repeat of theme A and consists of 16 counts.]

3.1 Remember to move quickly into your partner's spot, staying with the beat, then face your partner immediately to return to your own home. Eye contact is important. [Repeat.] Think of coming back even as you are crossing over.

3.2 It will be much easier to exchange places quickly if your bodies are lifted and alert. Pull in your abdominal muscles and lift the head proudly. Use your arms to help you travel and show me ready feet.

3.3 Join another set of partners so there are now four of you in a group. Make the first crossover with your own partner, then the second time cross over with one of the other people in the set. Decide who to cross with and how to most efficiently and effectively make your crossovers. Some of you may want to just trade places side by side. Let's try this as I tap the drum, then we will play the music. 'Trade with your own, 2, 3, 4; and go home, 2, 3, 4; now with your guest, 2, 3, 4; we are the best, 2, 3, 4.' [Repeat many times to work out problems and refine crossovers. Have students point where they are going. Accompany drum taps and music with verbal counts until all students understand the structure.]

3.4 Let's change this slightly. Circle around your partner for a full eight counts. After one full circle, change directions and circle the other way. Join hands [wrists, elbows] and go. 'Circle, 2, 3, 4 . . . eight; the other way, two . . . eight.' [Accompany with taps on drum.] Keep tension in the arms as you circle.

3.5 See if you can change the body parts to link with your partner in different ways for each eight-count circling action.

3.6 Consider barely touching body parts and circling around each other [shoulders, waist, fingers, and so on]. Remember to select body parts that are safe for you and your partner and that allow for circling action. We have only eight counts to complete each turn, so try to get organized quickly.

4.0 The older person in your partnership is now the first leader. Leaders, travel in a way that your partner can copy and follow. After 16 counts, change leaders. As you travel, I will accompany you with my drum.

4.1 Leaders, you need to make fairly simple, repetitive, traveling movements so your partners can follow exactly what you are doing. Remember also that since we are simply following the leaders, you will be in front of your partner. What happens to the follower's ability to see you if you turn around?

4.2 Challenge your partner by traveling a greater distance in those 16 counts or making a rhythmic sequence with your feet as you travel. [For some students, it may be more important to focus on adjusting to a partner's step size, rather than distance or rhythmic variations.]

4.3 Leaders, try to change levels and add simple gesturing actions as you travel. Remember that gestures done in front of you won't be visible to your follower, who is behind you. Make your gestures large and out to the side so they can be seen.

4.4 [Accompany this task with selected music. If using "The Black Nag," this is a repeat of theme B and consists of 32 counts.] Design a repeatable sequence for performance in which leader #1 leads for 16 counts, then leader #2 immediately takes over the lead for the next 16 counts.

5.0 [Post a large printout of all parts of the dance to help cue students as they move; see 5.4.] In our first theme A, let's meet and part twice. Two meetings and partings in 16 counts. Next, let's mirror your partner as you travel and change directions. This is theme B in the music and takes 32 counts. 'Meet . . . four, and part . . . four; [repeat] meet . . . four, and part . . . four. Now mirror . . . four, change directions . . . four; change again . . . four and *bow* to your partner . . . four.' [Accompany with taps on a drum initially and say counts aloud. Later practice with music.]

5.1 Let's add another A phrase and B phrase. Change places with your partner in four counts and go home in four counts, then repeat. This much takes 16 counts. For the B theme in the music, let's have leader #1 lead for 16 counts, then leader #2 take over for the next 16 counts. 'Change . . . four, and home . . . four; again change . . . four, go home . . . four. Leader #1 lead . . . 16; change leaders . . . 16.'

5.2 [Combine 5.0 and 5.1 together to form an *ABAB* sequence. Accompany with drum and say counts aloud initially.]

5.3 Let's try circling and turning around your partner, with at least one change of direction during the A theme. Remember this musical theme has 16 counts. During our B theme, follow the leader, each partner leading for 16 counts. Decide what body parts to connect or link and who the first leader will be. 'Circle . . . eight; and change . . . eight. Now leader #1 travel and lead . . . 16; and leader #2 take over and lead . . . 16.' [Accompany with drum and say counts aloud. Add music after students demonstrate understanding of sequence.]

5.4 [Combine all movement ideas from 5.0, 5.1, and 5.3.] Let's listen to the music this time with an ear for putting all the parts together. Notice there is an

(A) Meeting and parting for 16 counts

(B) Mirroring while traveling and changing directions for 32 counts

(A) Exchanging places for 16 counts

(B) Leading and following for 32 counts [16 counts for each leader]

(A) Circling with partner for 16 counts

(B) Leading and following for 32 counts [16 counts for each leader]

A theme of 16 counts and a B theme of 32 counts. The themes repeat three times altogether, forming an *ABABAB* structure. Let's design a dance that goes to the music and has these parts: [Post cue words.]

Let's put it all together into one long dance with the music. We have practiced all the separate parts; now we are putting it all together. I'll call it and tap the drum as we practice. [Glance at directions on the board if you need to. Tap the drum and talk through the entire sequence as in 5.0, 5.1, and 5.3 but at a slower tempo. Once the students are familiar with the sequence and format, play and dance to the music.]

6.0 [Fifth and sixth graders enjoy learning Elizabethan country dances as they study Shakespeare and the Elizabethan Period.

7.0 [As further enrichment (or after-school activities), introduce a variety of easy to moderately difficult country dances of Colonial America. Invite a parent or musician from your community to play authentic dance melodies on the violin or flute. (See Millar 1989, for dance instructions and musical arrangements.)]

Appendixes

APPENDIX A: CONTENT STANDARDS IN PHYSICAL EDUCATION

A physically educated person

1. Demonstrates competency in many movement forms and proficiency in a few movement forms.

2. Applies movement concepts and principles to the learning and development of motor skills.

3. Exhibits a physically active lifestyle.

4. Achieves and maintains a health-enhancing level of physical fitness.

5. Demonstrates responsible personal and social behavior in physical activity settings.

6. Demonstrates understanding and respect for differences among people in physical activity settings.

7. Understands that physical activity provides opportunities for enjoyment, challenge, self-expression, and social interaction.

Reprinted from Moving into the future: National standards for physical education, 1995, with permission from the National Association for Sport and Physical Education (NASPE). Requests for permission to reprint can be sent to NASPE, 1900 Association Drive, Reston, VA 20191. [This source provides an introduction to the rationale underlying National Standards, descriptions of content standards, sample benchmarks, and assessment examples for Kindergarten through Grade 12.]

APPENDIX B: CONTENT STANDARDS IN DANCE

The National Standards for Arts Education are a statement of what every young American should know and be able to do in four arts disciplines—dance, music, theatre, and the visual arts (p. 131). Two different types of standards are used to guide assessment of student learning and program goals: (p. 18).

- Content standards specify what students should know and be able to do in the arts disciplines.
- Achievement standards specify understandings and levels of achievement that students are expected to attain in the competencies, for each of the arts, at the completion of grades 4, 8, and 12.

1. Content Standard: Identifying and demonstrating movement elements and skills in performing dance
2. Content Standard: Understanding choreographic principles, processes, and structures
3. Content Standard: Understanding dance as a way to create and communicate meaning
4. Content Standard: Applying and demonstrating critical and creative thinking skills in dance
5. Content Standard: Demonstrating and understanding dance in various cultures and historical periods
6. Content Standard: Making connections between dance and healthful living
7. Content Standard: Making connections between dance and other disciplines

Reprinted with permission of the National Dance Association from: Consortium of National Arts Education Associations (1994). *National Standards for Arts Education: What Every Young American Should Know and Be Able to Do in the Arts. Dance, Music, Theatre, Visual Arts.* Reston, VA: Music Educators National Conference, pp. 39-41. [For a rationale, description, and clarification of the National Standards in Dance, including Achievement Standards "a" through "h," write the National Dance Association, 1900 Association Drive, Reston, Virginia 20191).

References

These references are for the Preface and the Introduction.

Barrett, K. R. (1984a). Educational dance. In B. J. Logsdon, K. R. Barrett, M. Ammons, M. R. Broer, L. E. Halverson, R. McGee & M. A. Roberton, *Physical education for children* (2nd ed., pp. 144-192). Philadelphia, PA: Lea & Febiger.

Barrett, K. R. (1984b). Educational games. In B. J. Logsdon, K. R. Barrett, M. Ammons, M. R. Broer, L. E. Halverson, R. McGee & M. A. Roberton, *Physical education for children* (2nd ed., pp. 193-240). Philadelphia, PA: Lea & Febiger.

Barrett, K. R. (1984c). The teacher as observer, interpreter, and decision-maker. In B. J. Logsdon, K. R. Barrett, M. Ammons, M. R. Broer, L. E. Halverson, R. McGee & M. A. Roberton, *Physical education for children* (2nd ed., pp. 295-355). Philadelphia, PA: Lea & Febiger.

Barrett, K. R., & Collie, S. (1996). Children learning lacrosse from teachers learning to teach it: The discovery of pedagogical content knowledge by observing children's movement. *Research Quarterly for Exercise and Sport, 67* (3), 297-308.

Clark, J. E. (1995). On becoming skillful: Patterns and constraints. *Research Quarterly for Exercise and Sport, 66* (3),173-183.

Consortium of National Arts Education Associations. (1994). *National standards for arts education: What every young american should know and be able to do in the arts (dance, music, theater, visual arts).* Reston, VA: Music Educators National Conference (MENC). (Also see National Dance Association, 1994.)

Danielson, C. (1996). *Enhancing professional practice: A framework for teaching.* Alexandria, VA: Association for Supervision and Curriculum Development (ASCD).

Ennis, C. D. (1996). A model describing the influence of values and context on student learning. In S. J. Silverman & C. D. Ennis, *Student learning in physical education: Applying research to enhance instruction* (pp. 127-147). Champaign, IL: Human Kinetics.

Fernandez-Balboa, J., Barrett, K., Solomon, M., & Silverman, S. (1996). Perspectives on content knowledge in physical education. *JOHPERD, The Journal of Physical Education, Recreation & Dance, 67* (9), 54-57.

Graham, G., Holt/Hale, S., & Parker, M. (1993). *Children moving: A reflective approach to teaching physical education* (3rd ed.). Mountain View, CA: Mayfield.

Herkowitz, J. (1978). Developmental task analysis: The design of movement experiences and evaluation of motor development status. In M. Ridenour (Ed.), *Motor development: Issues and applications* (pp. 139-164). Princeton, NJ: Princeton.

Lee, T., Swinnen, S., & Serrien, D. (1994). Cognitive effort and motor learning. *Quest, 46,* 328-344.

Logsdon, B. J. (1984a). Creating materials for teaching. In B. J. Logsdon, K. R. Barrett, M. Ammons, M.R. Broer, L. E. Halverson, R. McGee & M. A. Roberton, *Physical education for children* (2nd ed., pp. 422-454). Philadelphia, PA: Lea & Febiger.

Logsdon, B. (1984b). *Educational gymnastics.* In B. J. Logsdon, K. R. Barrett, M. Ammons, M. R. Broer, L. E. Halverson, R. McGee & M. A. Roberton, *Physical education for children* (2nd ed., pp. 241-294). Philadelphia, PA: Lea & Febiger.

Logsdon, B. J., & Barrett, K. R. (1984). Movement—the content of physical education. In B. J. Logsdon, K. R. Barrett, M. Ammons, M. R. Broer, L. E. Halverson, R. McGee & M. A. Roberton, *Physical education for children* (2nd ed., pp. 123-143). Philadelphia, PA: Lea & Febiger.

McGee, R. (1984). Evaluation of processes and products. In B. J. Logsdon, K. R. Barrett, M. Ammons, M.R. Broer, L. E. Halverson, R. McGee & M. A. Roberton, *Physical education for children* (2nd ed., pp. 356-421). Philadelphia, PA: Lea & Febiger.

National Association for Sport and Physical Education (NASPE) Standards and Assessment Task Force. (1995). *Moving into the future: National physical education standards: A guide to content and assessment.* St. Louis: Mosby.

National Dance Association (NDA). (1994). *National standards for dance education.* Reston, VA: American Alliance for Health, Physical Education, Recreation & Dance (AAHPERD).

Preston-Dunlop, V. (1980). *A handbook for modern educational dance.* London: Macdonald and Evans. (Original work published 1963) (1990 ed. published, Boston: Plays.)

Rink, J. E. (1993). *Teaching physical education for instruction* (2nd ed.). St. Louis: Mosby Year Book.

Rink, J. E. (1996). Effective instruction in physical education. In S. J. Silverman & C. D. Ennis, *Student learning in physical education: Applying research to enhance instruction* (pp. 171-198). Champaign, IL: Human Kinetics.

Roberton, M. A., & Halverson, L. E. (1984). *Developing children—their changing movement.* Philadelphia, PA: Lea & Febiger.

Roberton, M. A. (1989). Developmental sequence and developmental task analysis. In J. Skinner, et al. (Eds.), *Future directions in exercise and sport science research* (pp. 369-381). Champaign, IL: Human Kinetics.

Russell, J. (1975). *Creative dance in the primary school* (2nd ed.). London: Macdonald & Evans. (Original work published 1965.)

Safrit, M. J., & Wood, T. M. (1995). *Introduction to measurement in physical education and exercise science* (3rd ed.). St. Louis: Mosby.

Siedentop, D. (1996). Physical education and education reform: The case of sport education. In S. J. Silverman & C. D. Ennis, *Student learning in physical education: Applying research to enhance instruction* (pp. 247-267). Champaign, IL: Human Kinetics.

Wahl, J., & Murray, N. (1994a). The games program. In J. Wahl & N. Murray, *Children & movement: Physical education in the elementary school* (2nd ed., pp. 297-298). Madison, WI: Brown & Benchmark.

Wahl, J. & Murray, N. (1994b). The teaching process. In J. Wahl & N. Murray, *Children & movement: Physical education in the elementary school* (2nd ed., pp. 87-91). Madison, WI: Brown & Benchmark.

SUGGESTED READINGS

These sources relate to the book's Introduction.

Graham, G. (1992). *Teaching children physical education: Becoming a master teacher.* Champaign, IL: Human Kinetics.

Hellison, D. R. (1991). *A reflective approach to teaching physical education.* Champaign, IL: Human Kinetics.

Hellison, D. (1995). *Teaching responsibility through physical activity.* Champaign, IL: Human Kinetics.

Laban, R. (1975). *Modern educational dance* (3rd ed., revised by L. Ullman). Great Britain: The Chaucer Press, Ltd. (Original work published 1947, Macdonald & Evans) (1990 ed. published, Plymouth, UK: Northcoate House, distr. in U.S.A. by State Mutual Book and Periodical Service, 5th Ave. 17th Floor, New York, NY 10175 Tel 1-212-682-5844).

Mosston, M., & Ashworth, S. (1994). *Teaching physical education* (4th ed.). New York: Macmillan.

National Association for Sport and Physical Education (NASPE) Motor Development Task Force. (1994). *Looking at physical education from a developmental perspective: A guide to teaching.* [Position paper]. Reston, VA: NASPE & American Alliance for Physical Education, Recreation & Dance (AAHPERD).

Silverman, S. J., & Ennis, C. D. (1996). *Enhancing student leaning in physical education: Applying research to enhance instruction.* Champaign, IL: Human Kinetics.

Sylwester, R. (1995). *A celebration of neurons: An educator's guide to the human brain.* Alexandria, VA: Association for Supervision and Curriculum Development (ASCD).

Young, J., Klesius, S., & Hoffman, H. (1994). *Meaningful movement: a developmental theme approach to physical education for children.* Madison, WI: Brown & Benchmark.

RESOURCES FOR UNIT PLANS

Readings

Armstrong, T. (1994). *Multiple intelligences in the classroom* (pp. 124-125). Alexandria, VA: Association for Supervision and Curriculum Development (ASCD).

Barrett, K. R. (1984a). Educational dance. In B. J. Logsdon, K. R. Barrett, M. Ammons, M. R. Broer, L. E. Halverson, R. McGee & M. A. Roberton, *Physical education for children* (2nd ed., pp. 144-192). Philadelphia, PA: Lea & Febiger.

Barrett, K. R. (1984b). Educational games. In B. J. Logsdon, K. R. Barrett, M. Ammons, M. R. Broer, L. E. Halverson, R. McGee & M. A. Roberton, *Physical education for children* (2nd ed., pp. 193-240). Philadelphia, PA: Lea & Febiger.

Belka, D. (1994). *Teaching children games: Becoming a master teacher.* Champaign, IL: Human Kinetics.

Bennett, J. P., & Riemer, P. C. (1995). *Rhythmic activities and dance.* Champaign, IL: Human Kinetics.

Buschner, C. A. (1994). *Teaching children movement concepts and skills.* Champaign, IL: Human Kinetics.

Flynn, Rosalind. (1995). Developing and using curriculum based creative drama in fifth grade reading—language arts instruction: A drama specialist and a classroom teacher collaborate. *Dissertation Abstracts International, 41* (9A). (University Microfilms No. 9622061).

Grant, J. M. (1995). *Shake, rattle, and learn: Classroom-tested ideas that use movement for active learning.* York, Maine: Stenhouse.

Haywood, K. (1993). *Lifespan motor development* (2nd ed.). Champaign, IL: Human Kinetics.

Hopper, C. Munoz, K., & Fisher, B. (1996). *Health-related fitness for grades 5 and 6.* Champaign, IL: Human Kinetics.

Logsdon, B. (1984b). *Educational gymnastics.* In B. J. Logsdon, K. R. Barrett, M. Ammons, M. R. Broer, L. E. Halverson, R. McGee & M. A. Roberton, *Physical education for children* (2nd ed., pp. 241-294). Philadelphia, PA: Lea & Febiger.

Millar, J. F. (1985). *Elizabethan Country Dances* (authentic dances and melodies, including "The Black Nag," "Greensleeves," "Picking of Sticks," and "Oranges and Lemons"). Williamsburg, VA: Thirteen Colonies Press. (Available from Thirteen Colonies Press, 710 South Henry Street, Williamsburg, VA 23185-4113 Tel 1-757-229-1775). (Also see "The Black Nag" listed below in Recorded Music.)

Millar, J. F. (1990). *Country Dances of Colonial America* (259 dances with instructions and authentic melodies for violin or flute). Williamsburg, VA: Thirteen Colonies Press. (Available from Thirteen Colonies Press, 710 South Henry Street, Williamsburg, Virginia 23185-4113 Tel 757 229 1775.) (Also see recording *The Village Green: Dance Music of Old Sturbridge Village*, 19th century colonial dance music, on [CD] NS0038 from North Star Music, East Greenwich, RI; request catalogue Tel 1-800-346-2706.)

Purcell, T. (1994). *Teaching children dance: Becoming a master teacher*. Champaign, IL: Human Kinetics.

Ratliffe, R. and Ratliffe, L. M. (1994). *Teaching children fitness: Becoming a master teacher*. Champaign, IL: Human Kinetics.

Watkins, A. (1990). *Dancing longer, dancing stronger*. Pennington, NJ: Princeton.

Werner, P. H. (1994). *Teaching children gymnastics: Becoming a master teacher*. Champaign, IL: Human Kinetics.

Recorded Music

Listed by composer, musician or song/album title.

Bach, J. S. "Fugue" in G minor [Recorded by Kevin Bowyer]. On *Organ Works*, Vol. 4 [CD] Nimbus NI 5377 (1994). Charlottesville, VA: Nimbus. (Recorded 1992) (Also on *Adventures in Music*, Grade 6, Vol. 1 [LP]. Available: Folkraft Records, P. O. Box 404, Florham Park, N.J. 07932 Tel 1-201-377-1885.)

Bach, J. S. *Goldberg Variations* [Recorded by Perre Hantai]. On *Goldberg Variations* [CD] Opus 111 0PS 30-84 (1994). Los Angeles, CA: Opus 111, distr. by Harmonia Mundi. (Also [Recorded by Glenn Gould]. On *Goldberg Variations* [CD] Sony Classical Glenn Gould Edition SM 2K 52594 [1993]. New York, NY: Sony Music Distribution.) (Also [Performed by Wanda Landowska]. On Harpischord Works [CD] RCA Victor Red Seal GD 60919 [1993]. London: RCA, distr. in USA by BGM.)

*Bach, J. S. "Jesu, Joy of Man's Desiring." On *Adventures in Music,* Grade 5, Vol. 1 [LP]. Available: Folkraft Records, P. O. Box 404, Florham Park, N.J. 07932 Tel 1-201-377-1885. (Also [Recorded by Bach Ensemble/Joshua Rifkin]. On *Cantata BWV 147* [CD] 417250-2 (1987). London, England: Decca, distr. in U.S.A. by UNI Distribution Corp., Universal City CA.)

Beethoven, L. van "Eroica" Variations [Recorded by Sviatoslav Kichter]. On *15 Variations and a Fugue on an Original Theme in E flat major, Op. 35, "Eroica"* [CD] Olympia OCD 339 (Eurodisc, 1994). Portland, OR: Olympia, distr. by Allegro.

The Black Nag. On [7" 45 rpm record] Catalogue No. 1174. Available: Folkraft Records, P. O. Box 404, Florham Park, N.J. 07932 Tel 1-201-377-1885. (Additional period dances, such as "Greensleeves," "Picking of Sticks," and "Oranges and Lemons," are available on [7" or LP] records from Folkraft [above] or from the Country Dance and Song Society, 17 New South St., Northhampton, MA 01060.)

Brahms, J. Variations on a Theme by Handel [Recorded by Cleveland Orch/Vladimir Ashkenazy]. On *Variations and Fugue on a Theme by Handel, Op 24* [CD] Decca 436 853-2DH (1994). Universal City, CA: Decca, distr. by UNI Distribution Corp.

Chappell, J. Various piano selections. On *Living the Northern Summer* [CD] RM-0133 or [CS] RM-0133 (1992). Sausalito, CA: Real Music.

Classical music selections set to nature sounds. On *Pachelbel with Ocean Sounds* [CD] CHA-22-2 or [CS] CHA-22-4 (1995); *Mozart with Ocean Sounds* CHA-HD-931-2 or [CS] CHA-HD-931-4 (1996); or *Satie with Ocean Sounds* CHA-43-2 or [CS] CHA-43-4 (1995). Portland, OR: Chacra, distr. by Allegro. (Check local record and nature stores for a wide variety of New Age sound recordings.) (Also see "Dinner Classics" on [CD or CS] for unobtrusive background music. New York, NY: CBS Records.)

Copland, A. "Hoe Down" [Recorded by Detroit Symphony Orchestra/Antal Dorati]. On *Rodeo—Four Dance Episodes* [CD] Decca Ovation 430 705-2DM (1991). Universal City, CA: Decca, dist. by UNI Distribution Corp. (Recorded 1982)

Cuckolds All A-row. (See Millar, 1985.)

Cusco. Various selections—soft to strong drum rhythms. On *Apurimac II—Return to Ancient America* [CD] HOMC-7067 or [CS] 7067 (1994). Los Angeles, CA: Higher Octave Music.

Heartsease. (See Millar 1985.)

Kazan, C. Y. Complete instrumental music. On *Tinikling* [CS] KEA 9015C or [LP] 9015 (1972). Available: Kimbo Educational Records, Dept. Y, P.O. Box 477, Long Branch, NJ 07740-0477 Tel 1-800-631-2187. (Also available widely from physical education and dance supply companies) (Also see "Tinikling.")

Kitaro. "Silk Road" [Recorded by Yu-Xiao Guang]. On *World of Music* [CD] 71011-2 9 (1996). Beverely Hills, CA: Domo Records.

*Menotti, G. C. "Shepherd's Dance." On *Amahl and the Night Visitors*, a Christmas Opera, [CD] MHS 51204. Musical Heritage Society.

*Nakai, R. C. Native American flute music. On *Desert Dance* [CD] 13033-2 or [CS] 13033-4 (1990). Tucson, AZ: Celestial Harmonies. (Also see Nakai, C. R., and Eaton, W., with the Black Lodge Singers. Contemporary Native American flute music. On *Ancestral Voices* [CD] CR-7010 (1992). Phenix, AZ: Canyon Records Productions) (Also see "Americana series" [Recorded by various artists, including Nakai]. On *Desert Aire* [CD] Special Music Co. EMD-5805 (1996). Petaluma, CA: Samurai Sound.)

The Prologue [Recorded by Leonard Bernstein]. On *West Side Story* [CD] Columbia CK-32603, [CS] JST-32603, and [CD] Columbia/Legacy CK-64419 (1994). New York, NY: Legacy, distr. by Sony Music Distribution. (Also [Recorded by various artists]. On *West Side Story* [CD] RCA Victor 09026-62707-2 or [CS] 09026-62707 (1996). New York, NY: RCA Victor, distr. by BMG) (Also [Recorded by Oscar Peterson]. On *West Side Story* "24 Karat Gold Compact Disc" series [CD] DCC Compact Classics GZS-1068 (1995). Chatsworth, CA: DCC Compact Classics.)

Respighi, O. Danza [Recorded by Cincinnati Symphony Orch/Jesus Lopez Cobos]. On *Brazilian Impressions* [CD] Telarc 80356 (1994). Cleveland, OH: Telarc Records. (Recorded 1993) (Also [Recorded by Philharmonia Orch/Geoffrey Simon]. On *Brazilian Impressions* [CD] CHAN 8313 (1984). Port Washington, NY: Chandos, distr. by Koch International.)

Schoenberg, A. Variations for Orchestra [Recorded by Chicago Symphony Orch/Pierre Boulez]. On *Variations For Orchestra, Op 31* [CD] CHAN 8619 (1988). Port Washington, NY: Chandos, distr. by Koch International. (Also [Recorded by Berlin Philharmonic Orch/Herbert von Karajan]. On *Variations* for Orchestra, Op 31 [CD]DG 415 326-2GH [1986]. London: Deutsche Grammophon) (Also [Recorded by City of Birmingham Symphony Orch/Sir Simon Rattle]. On [CD] EMI CDC5 55212-2 [1995]. Woodland Hills, CA: EMI, distr. EMD Music Distributors.)

*Sousa, J. P. Semper Fidelis, and The Stars and Stripes Forever [Recorded by Boston Pops Orchestra/Arthur Fiedler]. On This Is My Country [CD] 09026-61545-2. New York, NY: RCA Victor, distr. by BMG. (Also available on Stars and Stripes Forever and the Greatest Marches [CD] Catalogue No.28557 or [CS] Catalogue No. 29509 from Public Radio Music Source, Classics, P.O. Box 64502, St. Paul, Minnesota 55164-0502 Tel 1-800-949-9999) (Also available on Marches [2 LP's] Catalogue No. HYP-R11, and on Patriotic Songs & Marches [Recorded by D. Buck] [LP or CS] from Educational Activities, P. O. Box 87, Baldwin, NY 11510 Tel 1-800-645-3739) (Also see Washington Post, and other marches [Recorded by Goldman Band] on Sousa Marches in Hi-Fi [LP] available from Folkraft Records, P. O. Box 404, Florham Park, N.J. 07932 Tel 1-201-377-1885.)

Tinikling. On Folk Dancing for People Who Love Folk Dancing #7 from Young People's Folk Dance Library series [CS or LP]; also on Tinikling Dances Catalogue No. 9015; and Contemporary Tinikling (4/4 rhythm) Catalogue No. 8095 [CS or LP]. Available: Folkraft Records, P. O. Box 404, Florham Park, N.J. 07932 Tel 1-201-377-1885. (Also available on [CS] Catalogue No. MAV 1047C from Wagon Wheel Records and Books, 17191 Corbina Lane #203, Huntington Beach, CA 92649 Tel 1-714-846-8169.) (Widely available from physical education supply companies.) (Also see Kazan, 1972, above for traditional folk music.)

*Troika. On Rhythmically Moving 2 [Produced by Phyllis Weikart] [CD, CS or LP]. Available: High/Scope Press, 600 North River Street, Yipsilanti, MI 48198 Tel 1-313-485-2000 or from Wagon Wheel Records & Books, 17191 Corbini Lane #203, Huntington Beach, CA 92649 Tel 1-714-846-8169.) (Also available on [7" 45 rpm record] Catalogue No. 1170 from Folkraft Records, P. O. Box 404, Florham Park, N.J. 07932 Tel 1-201-377-1885.)

Windham Hill. New Age music collection [Recorded by various artists]. On Sanctuary: 20 Years of Windham Hill [2 CD's] 1934-11180-2 or [2 CS's] 1934-11180-4 (1996). Stanford, CA: Windham Hill.)

Winston, G. Various solo piano selections. On Forest [CD] 01934-11157-2 or [CS] 01934-11157-4 (1994). Santa Cruz, CA: Dancing Cat Records, dist. by Windham Hill, Stanford, CA.) (Also see Windham Hill above.)

*Winter, P. Ocean Child, and other selections [Recorded by P. Winter]. On Earth: Voices of a Planet [CD] Living Music LD-0019 or [CS] LC-0019 (1990). New York, NY: Living Music.

Weikart, P. S. Teaching movement & dance: A sequential approach, and the Rhythmically moving record series [CD, CS and LP]. Available: High/Scope Press, 600 North River Street, Yipsilanti, MI 48198 Tel 1-313-485-2000.

*Available on compact disk [CD] in Silver Burdett & Ginn's The Music Connection, 1995 series, Morristown, NJ, and from other leading music education resources. [Ask the music teacher in your school for a piano or instrumental version of this music.]

Note: Recorded music may be found in local record stores or via mail-order services, such as Public Radio Music Source at 1-800-75-MUSIC or Tower Records at 1-800-ASK-TOWER. Physical education and dance supply companies and educational catalogue companies are also excellent sources.

EQUIPMENT SUPPLY CATALOGUES

Listed here are a few of the many companies (local, national and international) that carry movement education and educational games, gymnastics, and dance equipment and materials for young children. We encourage you to review this list and the physical education and dance supply companies in your locality; ask your school librarian or administration for additional resource catalogues on elementary childhood movement education.

Chimetime—Division of Sportime
Movement Products
One Sportime Way
Atlanta, GA 30340
1-800-477-5075 or 1-770-449-5700
Fax 1-800-845-1535 or 1-700-263-0897

Flaghouse
150 North MacQuesten Pkwy.
Mount Vernon, NY 10550
1-800-793-7900; outside USA: (914) 699-1900
Fax 1-800-793-7922 or (914) 699-2961

Porter Athletic Equipment
9555 Irving Park Rd.
Schiller Park, IL 60176
(708) 671-0110 (gymnastics apparatus)

Toledo Physical Education Supply
Box 5618
Toledo, OH 43613
(419) 476-6730 or 1-800-225-7749
Fax 1-419-476-1163

UCS
One Olympic Drive
Orangeburg, N.Y. 10962
1-914-365-2333 or 1-800-526-4856
Fax 1-914-365-2589 (gymnastics apparatus)

U.S. Games.
P. O. Box 117028
Carrollton, TX 75011-7028
1-800-327-0484
Fax 1-800-899-0149 or 1-214-243-0149

Wolverine Sports
745 Circle
Box 1941
Ann Arbor, MI 48106
(313) 761-5690

About the Authors

Bette J. Logsdon, PhD, has 37 years of physical education experience—5 years in public schools and 32 years at the university level, preparing teachers with special interest in elementary school physical education. She spent the last 15 years of her career at Bowling Green State University (Ohio). During this time, she taught regularly scheduled elementary physical education classes to learn more about children, test theories, and stay abreast of the challenges facing elementary school teachers. Bette lives in Toledo, Ohio.

Luann M. Alleman, MEd, has 25 years' teaching experience in public and private schools. She has worked with children, including physically challenged students, at the elementary and high school levels, and with college students in university teacher-preparation courses. She was the first intern consultant for physical education in the Toledo School System and provided in-service training for Toledo public school elementary physical education teachers. Retired after 17 years as department chair of elementary school physical education for the Toledo School System, Luann resides in Holland, Ohio.

Sue Ann Straits, PhD, has been a lecturer in the Department of Education at The Catholic University of America (Washington, D.C.) since 1993. Since beginning her career in physical education in 1972, she has gained extensive practical experience teaching physical education and dance in early childhood and elementary education settings both overseas and in the United States. She also has conducted workshops around the world on movement education. Sue Ann makes her home in Reston, Virginia.

David E. Belka, PhD, has taught physical education classes to elementary school students and pedagogy and elementary content courses at the college level. An expert in developing and teaching games, David is the author of *Teaching Children Games*, a practical guide that explains the why and how of teaching children to become skilled games players. For more than two decades, he has analyzed, critiqued, and reviewed elementary physical education texts. David lives in Oxford, Ohio, where he is a professor at Miami University.

Dawn Clark, EdD, is an associate professor and the coordinator of dance education at East Carolina University, where she teaches dance pedagogy. She taught physical education and dance at the elementary level for five years. In 1987 Dawn earned a certificate in Laban studies; this background has been especially helpful for the *Physical Education Unit Plans* books, whose units are organized around Laban's movement themes and movement framework. Dawn is a resident of Greenville, North Carolina.

162